PIMLICO

144

FREEDOM'S BATTLE
III: THE WAR ON LAND
1939–1945

The late Ronald Lewin was a classical scholar at The Queen's College, Oxford, where he obtained a Double First. During the Second World War he served as an officer in the Royal Artillery with the Eighth Army in Africa, and in north-west Europe from Normandy to Germany. From 1946 he worked for the BBC – from 1957 to 1964 as Head of the Home Service. His publications include studies of Rommel and Montgomery, as well as numerous articles on recent military history.

Freedom's Battle

Volume III

THE WAR
ON LAND
1939–1945

An anthology of personal experience selected and
edited by Ronald Lewin

With an introduction by the Viscount
Montgomery of Alamein

'For Freedom's battle once begun,
Bequeathed by bleeding Sire to Son,
Though baffled oft is ever won.'
Lord Byron, *The Giaour*

PIMLICO

PIMLICO
An imprint of Random House
20 Vauxhall Bridge Road, London SWIV 2SA

Random House Australia (Pty) Ltd
20 Alfred Street, Milsons Point Sydney
New South Wales 2061, Australia

Random House New Zealand Ltd
18 Poland Road, Glenfield
Auckland 10, New Zealand

Random House South Africa (Pty) Ltd
PO Box 337, Bergvlei, South Africa

Random House UK Ltd Reg. No. 954009

First published by Hutchinson 1969
Pimlico edition 1994

1 3 5 7 9 10 8 6 4 2

Printed and bound in Great Britain by
Clays Ltd, St Ives plc

ISBN 0–7126–6074–7

Contents

Illustrations

Dunkirk: the beach (*Fox Photos*)
Returned via Dunkirk
North Africa: a typical tank crew
North Africa: sharing a waterhole
North Africa: patrol of the Long Range Desert Group (*Associated Press Ltd*)
North Africa: six-inch gun, Halfaya Pass
Tobruk: at ease
Tobruk: prisoners on lighters in the harbour
Kohima: Garrison Hill
Kohima: Naga village
The Arakan
The Arakan: Hill 1301
Imphal: combing elephant grass
Burma: crossing the Irrawaddy
Burma: 'the road to Mandalay'
Burma: mortaring Fort Dufferin, Mandalay
Burma: by the Shweli river
North Africa: survivors of 'Snipe'
North Africa: the Grants arrive
Normandy: typical *bocage*
Normandy: Shermans and Sannerville château
Normandy: advance to the River Odon
Normandy: Shermans near Caumont
Normandy: the liberators
Normandy: the Falaise road
Normandy: Canadian 'Sextons'
Arnhem: some survivors
Italy: mud by the Rubicon
Italy: mopping up Umbertide
Germany: the road to the Rhine (*editor's collection*)
Italy: Popski's Private Army in Venice

Unless otherwise indicated, all illustrations are reproduced by permission of the Imperial War Museum.

Acknowledgements

Acknowledgements are due to George Allen & Unwin Ltd. for extracts from *The Siege* by Arthur Campbell and for 'The Mahratta Ghats' from *Ha! Ha! Among the Trumpets* by Alun Lewis; to the Australian War Memorial for an extract from *The New Guinea Offensive* by David Dexter; to G. Bell & Sons Ltd. for extracts by Captain R. L. Banks, Lieutenant-Colonel Dobree, Brigadier W. D. Graham, General Sir Cameron Nicholson and Major F. C. M. Reeves from *The Royal Artillery Commemoration Book 1939–1945*; to The Bodley Head Ltd. for extracts from *The Naked Island* (Werner Laurie) by Russell Braddon; to Curtis Brown Ltd. for extracts from *The Eleventh at War* (Michael Joseph) by Brigadier Dudley Clarke, for extracts from *Baker Street Irregular* (Methuen) by Bickham Sweet-Escott and for extracts from *Still Digging* (Michael Joseph) by Sir Mortimer Wheeler; to Jonathan Cape Ltd. for extracts from *Popski's Private Army* by Lieutenant-Colonel Vladimir Peniakoff and for 'Naming of Parts' from *A Map of Verona* by Henry Reed; to Cassell & Co. Ltd, for extracts from *The Second World War* by Sir Winston S. Churchill, for extracts from *The Tanks* by Captain Sir Basil Liddell Hart, for an extract from *Arnhem* by Major-General R. E. Urquhart and for a quotation by Max Hickman in John Laffin, *Digger*; to Chatto & Windus Ltd. for an extract from *The Jungle is Neutral* by Lieutenant-Colonel Spencer Chapman; to Collins Publishers for extracts from *A Full Life* by Lieutenant-General Sir Brian Horrocks, for extracts from *Memoirs* by Field-Marshal Lord Montgomery and for extracts from *Dinner of Herbs* and *Going to the Wars* by John Verney; to Constable & Co. Ltd for extracts from *Take These Men* by Cyril Joly; to René Cutforth for an extract quoted in *The Listener*; to Brigadier J. Durnford-Slater for an extract from *Commando* (William Kimber Ltd.); to Faber & Faber Ltd. for an extract from *Eritrea 1941* by A. J. Barker, for 'One Trumpet Lost' from *Talking Bronco* by Roy Campbell, for an extract from *Dunkirk* by A. D. Divine, for 'Aristocrats' from *Collected Poems* by Keith Douglas, for an extract from *Alamein to Zem Zem* by Keith Douglas and for 'Sentries' from *Springboard* by Louis MacNeice; to John Farquharson Ltd. for an extract from *The Desert and the Jungle* (William Kimber) by Lieutenant-General Sir Geoffrey Evans; to Brigadier Sir Bernard Fergusson for an extract from *Beyond the Chindwin* (Collins); to Gale & Polden Ltd. for extracts from *From the Beaches to the Baltic* by Major Noel Bell, for an extract from *The Path of the 50th* by Major Ewart W. Clay, for extracts from *The Fifth Inniskilling Dragoon Guards* by Major-General Roger Evans and for extracts from *The Rifle Brigade in the Second World War 1939–1945* by Major Robin Hastings; to Granada Publishing Ltd. for an extract from *Mailed Fist* by John Foley; to The Green Howards for a quotation from Captain K. A. Nash in *The Story of the Green Howards 1939–1945*, published by the Regiment; to A. Gwynne-Brown for an extract from 'F.S.P.' (Chatto & Windus); to Hamish Hamilton Ltd. for 'St. Aubin D'Aubigné' from *The Day's Alarm* by Paul Dehn; to George G. Harrap & Co. Ltd. for an extract from *Report My Signals* by Anthony Brett-James; to Rupert Hart-Davis for extracts from *A Very Quiet War* by Ralph Arnold; to A. M. Heath & Co. Ltd. for an extract from *The Military Orchid* (The Bodley Head) by Jocelyn Brooke, for an extract, 'The Kill', from *The Monastery* (The Bodley Head) by Fred Majdalany and for an extract from *The Fortress: A Diary of Anzio and After* (Collins) by Raleigh Trevelyan; to William Heinemann Ltd. for an extract from *Alamein* by Brigadier C. E. Lucas Phillips; to David Higham Associates Ltd. for an extract from *The Desert Generals* (William Kimber) by Corelli Barnett, for an extract from *The Battle of Arnhem* (Batsford) by Christopher Hibbert and for extracts from *Defeat Into Victory* (Cassell) by Field-Marshall Lord Slim; to Hodder & Stoughton for extracts from *Return via Dunkirk* by 'Gun Buster' and an extract from *Grey and Scarlet: Letters from the War Areas by Army Sisters on Active Service* by Ada C. Harrison; to Hutchinson Publishing Group for extracts from *Fighting Mad* (Jarrolds) by Michael Calvert and an extract from *Armoured Crusader* (Hutchinson) by Major K. Macksey; to the Institution of Royal Engineers for an extract from Volume 8 of *History of the Corps of Royal Engineers* by Major-General R. P. Pakenham-Walsh; to William Kimber & Co. Ltd. for an extract by Fusilier D. Needham quoted in *Salerno* by Hugh Pond and an extract from *Flame Thrower* by Andrew Wilson; to E. P. S. Lewin for extracts from *The Happy Hunted* (Cassell) by Brigadier G. Clifton; to Jack Lindsay for 'Squadding' from *Second Front* (Dakers); to Lieutenant-Colonel Sir Martin Lindsay for extracts from *So Few Got Through* (Collins); to Dr. Jan Van Loewen Ltd. for an extract from *Pebbles From My Skull* (Hutchinson) by Stuart Hood; to Longmans, Green & Co. Ltd. for an extract from 'The Monastery' from *Cassino, Portrait of a Battle* by Fred Majdalany; to George Macbeth for 'Remembering the War' quoted in *The Listener*; to MacLaren & Sons Ltd. for an extract from Jemadar Dewan Sing quoted in *Fourth Indian Division* by Lieutenant-Colonel G. R. Stevens; to Macmillan & Co. Ltd. for an extract by

Lieutenant A. Weir quoted in *Imphal* by Geoffrey Evans and Anthony Brett-James; to The Macmillan Company of Canada Ltd. for extracts from *Gauntlet to Overlord* by Ross Munro; to Methuen & Co. Ltd. for an extract from *Vanguard to Victory* by Skene Catling and for 'Midnight: May 7th 1945' from *A Stone in the Midst and Poems* by Patric Dickinson; to Frederick Muller Ltd. for an extract from *The Singapore Story* by Kenneth Attiwill and extracts from *Brazen Chariots* by Robert Crisp; to Oxford University Press Ltd. for extracts from *Infantry Brigadier* by Brigadier Sir Howard Kippenberger; to A. D. Peters & Co. for extracts from *The Fuel of the Fire* by Douglas Grant (Cresset), for an extract from *Through the Dark Night* (Victor Gollancz) by J. H. Hodson, for an extract from *Overture to Overlord* (Hodder & Stoughton) by Sir Frederick Morgan, for an extract from *Orde Wingate* (Collins) by Christopher Sykes, for extracts from *Put Out More Flags* (Chapman & Hall) by Evelyn Waugh and for an extract by Chester Wilmot quoted in *War Report* (O.U.P.); to Laurence Pollinger Ltd. for an extract from *Norway 1940* (Cassell) by Bernard Ash, for extracts from *The Road Past Mandalay* by John Masters and for extracts from *Eclipse* and *African Trilogy* (Hamish Hamilton) by Alan Moorehead; to Purnell for an extract by Peter Elstob quoted in *History of The Second World War*, Vol. 6, No. 4; to Sampson Low, Marston & Co. Ltd. for an extract from *With the Sixth Airborne Division in Normandy* by General Sir Richard Gale; to Martin Secker & Warburg Ltd. for 'The Transparent Prisoner' from *Still and All* by Burns Singer; to Sphere Books for a quotation by Philip Norman in *Alamein and the Desert War*; to Laurens Van Der Post for an extract from 'Another Way Out' (*The Listener*); to Winant-Towers Ltd. for an extract from *Approach to Battle* (Cassell) by Lieutenant-General Sir Francis Tuker.

Every effort has been made to trace the holders of copyright in the quotations included. For any error in establishing the exact source the editor naturally and formally apologises.

Introduction

by

Field-Marshal the Viscount Montgomery of Alamein, KG

This anthology of *The War on Land* is in no sense a history of the 1939–45 war. Rather it is a most interesting collection of statements and opinions of individuals who took part in that war, so presented as to give the reader a vivid impression of the human endeavour which is essential when great armies join in battle.

When a nation goes to war, some fight on land, some in the air, some on and under the seas, and some on the home front. Furthermore, the whole manpower of a nation, and womanpower too, together with its industrial strength, must be mobilised to provide the necessary sinews of war. The conflict is finally won by this great team, integrated and directed by political leaders—in whose hands lies the higher direction of the war. I make this point lest the non-military reader should gain the impression that the world conflict unleashed by Hitler in 1939 was won only by soldiers fighting on land. It was not.

Let me give examples from my own experience.

During the campaign in France and Belgium which ended when the British Army was defeated by the Germans and had to be evacuated from the beaches of Dunkirk, it was brought home to me that you must win the air battle before you can fight successfully on land. This great tactical truth formed the basis of the series of victories which enabled me to lead the Eighth Army from Alamein, through Sicily, and halfway up Italy. The same principle formed the background to the Allied success in Normandy—we owned the sky.

When Allied air supremacy over the area of operations during the 1939–45 war was decisive, the mighty weapon of air power enabled victory on land to be achieved more quickly and with less casualties than would otherwise have been the case. Where mastery in the air over the area of operations was with the enemy, we generally failed.

Now the navies. A study of warfare reveals that from the earliest days of the Greek and Roman empires, that side which had command of the seas in the end prevailed on land—because the enemy was confined to a land strategy. The German war had to be won finally on land by the defeat of Hitler's armies, but the stranglehold of sea power exerted such an influence on the German economy that the end was certain.

And in the case of the Japanese war, it was the defeat of the Japanese fleets in the Pacific by American sea power, with its carrier-borne air power, which led to the collapse of the home front—thus leading to the doom of Japanese armies on land in the Burma campaign and in the Philippines, New Guinea, and other islands.

I have always considered that the main burden in battle is borne by the soldier. He remains in the battle on land day and night, with little rest and without adequate sleep. He faces the almost certainty of wounds and the probability of death. Indeed, during the 1914–18 war the average life of a platoon commander in the infantry in France was only a few weeks. But although the soldier bears a heavy burden in war, he will gladly admit that without the navies and air forces he could hardly achieve any great success on land.

Against the background of what I have written above, I commend this anthology of *The War on Land* to all who are interested in a study of the 1939–45 war.

Montgomery of Alamein
F.M.

Editor's Preface

In putting together this selection from the memoirs of the men who fought on land during the Second World War I have always heard, at the back of my mind, a voice speaking . . . the voice of Wilfred Owen, the poet who died in the last days of the First World War, and who, before he died, found words in which the soldier's suffering, the 'military necessity', became articulate. His message was 'don't glorify'. Owen's famous remark about the poetry being in the pity was only another version of what he said about a man gassed on the Western Front:

> If in some smothering dreams, you too could pace
> Behind the wagon that we flung him in,
> And watch the white eyes writhing in his face,
> His hanging face, like a devil's sick of sin;
> If you could hear, at every jolt, the blood
> Come gargling from the froth-corrupted lungs,
> Bitter as the cud
> Of vile, incurable sores on innocent tongues—
> My friend, you would not tell with such high zest
> To children ardent for some desperate glory
> The old Lie : *Dulce et decorum est*
> *Pro patria mori.*

I've tried, in compiling this anthology, to avoid the 'high zest'. And I've also had in mind the Wilfred Owen of the Second World War, Keith Douglas, gallant in his tank in Africa and dead in his tank in Normandy. He, in his way, also wrote about 'the old Lie'.

> Time's wrong-way telescope will show
> a minute man ten years hence
> and by distance simplified.
>
> Through that lens see if I seem
> substance or nothing; of the world
> deserving mention or charitable oblivion,

>   not by momentary spleen
>   or love into decision hurled,
>   leisurely arrive at an opinion.
>
>   Remember me when I am dead
>   and simplify me when I'm dead.

This anthology is a simplification of the dead—and the living: a distillation of what the fighters put down at the time or in retrospect to tell others (or perhaps convince themselves) what it was all about. Here are the words of the wise, the witty, the nonchalant, the devil-may-care: the poets and the prodigals. I have tried, too, to seek out the incidental poetry of war—the Dutch woman whose house became a hospital for the wounded at Arnhem, and who observed that the glass fragments from her broken windows spread over their shattered bodies like sugar; the artillery officer in his observation post facing the monastery at Cassino who noted that in the silences when the firing stopped you could hear a bird pecking at a snail's shell. Owen and Douglas would, I think, have approved: this was their world, their inhabitable Armageddon.

There is another truth about this world . . . another variant of the poetry in the pity. I would point to the account I quote of a platoon of the superb New Zealand Division finished, but *finished* by their endurance of a bitter winter in the Gustav Line in Italy. Nothing of 'the old Lie' here. Or Colonel Martin Lindsay's account of the damage done to a company of the Highland Division in the fields of Normandy. Or Russell Braddon's description of the ultimate human degradation which was reached by the men who slaved on the Japanese 'railway'.

There is, finally, an important fact which an anthologist must face. Of the 55,000,000 or so numbered in the last Census as inhabitants of the British Isles, just under half had not reached thirty years of age. In other words, one out of two of the people now alive in our islands was either born during the war, or else too young to have any definite memory, or to have participated. For these I feel it to be especially important that 'the old Lie' should not be perpetuated: but equally important that they should be able to learn from first-hand accounts how things really were.

                                                                    R.L.

1939

‘A world that came to its last dated year’
RAYNER HEPPENSTALL

Some of those who were to serve in the British Army had tasted war before 3rd September 1939. There were, for example,

SUMMER MANŒUVRES

The battle had been raging since dawn, Northland chasing Southland over the Quantocks, like the flying cloud shadows which clung to the oak scrub and modelled each subtle combe. With the smell and sound of horses close by my head I had bivouacked the previous night in the heather, the sea breeze off Bridgwater Bay nipping me in my blankets. Now, though dirty and sleep-eyed, I rejoiced to be riding over wild country in early morning sun and wind. There was something, perhaps, to be said for Army life after all. Even my uniform, uncomfortably new, added a pleasure by identifying me, through wearing it, with other cavalry exploits in the past. I thought of Tolstoy's description of the young Nikolai Rostoff riding into his first action. 'There was not only nothing terrible about it, but it seemed ever more and more jolly and lively.'

It was pleasure, too, to escape for a day from the many social and military pitfalls of the camp. The effort of pretending to be someone I was not was proving a strain. I hated the ritualistic dinners and the long hours of horseplay which, by tradition, followed them. My brother officers were squires, farmers, land agents and the like, born and bred in the country and sharing a hundred tastes and acquaintances from childhood. In after years, drawn together by the boredom and the exile of war, I came to love them. But on first acquaintance they struck me as formidably different from myself, a Londoner whose chief interests, priggish though it sounds, were modern Literature and modern Art. None of my brother officers had ever heard of Proust or of Picasso. Nor did this gap in their education trouble them unduly.

As a supernumerary officer with no 'command' of my own, I had been attached for the Battle to a Squadron Leader to be 'shown the form'. He was a fierce Major called Victor Bone and as I jogged along beside him, hoping that I looked more at home on a horse than I felt, he attempted some conversation.

'And what's your line of country in civvy street?'

'Well, um—as a matter of fact, I'm an assistant film director, sir.'

'Oh. What does all that mean?'

'Well, it's a bit difficult to explain really, sir. I have to see that the actors are ready to go on the set when they're wanted and that sort of thing.'

'Good God!' snorted the fierce Major.

After that we rode on in silence and for my part, so far as the Battle went, in mystified ignorance, though I tried to pick up such clues to the confused military situation as Victor Bone let fall. For military tactics, even of the simple Boer War variety used by a Yeomanry Regiment training in 1937, were as yet unintelligible to me. Two rival kingdoms, Northland and Southland, were supposed to be at war. A Squadron, with two troops of C Squadron, represented the aggressor, Northland, and wore distinguishing blue bands on their caps. B Squadron and HQ Squadron represented Southland, with the two remaining troops of C Squadron attached to them in the guise of a Mountain Battery with pack mules. We were now, it was to be assumed, picking up the threads of a battle that had begun the week before and in which, by 0500 hours this very morning, the opposing forces had reached positions —there had followed a fantastically complicated string of map references.

To digest even this initial hypothesis required, I felt, prodigious feats of memory and imagination. I glanced enviously at Victor Bone's red neck, considerably awed that above it should exist a brain capable of performing these feats. He was a soldierly-looking figure whom I rather feared and whom, because he had shown me a gruff kindness, I was prepared to idolise. It was thus a shock to discover later that he had in fact no military qualifications—unless a permanent state of inebriation at the yearly camp for the past ten years could be called a military qualification. In 'civvy street' he himself was an insurance agent with sporting tendencies and he enjoyed these battles in the spirit of a day's foxhunting in midsummer.

For the moment the hounds, so to speak, had lost the scent. The squadron huddled together on horseback under cover of a wood. Tense with the excitement of the chase, Victor Bone sat erect on his horse, his heavy cavalry moustache stirred gently by the morning breeze. He sniffed the air as if to sense from it the whereabouts of the missing enemy. Then, with a few curt orders, he sent a patrol forward to reconnoitre. I wondered whether the time would ever come when I would attain to a comparable grasp of these complex matters.

The patrol assembled itself without seeming haste; and without seeming haste trotted off ahead. Obviously we had some time to wait before fighting could recommence. I took out a packet of cigarettes and offered one to my idol.

'Have a smoke, sir?'

His prominent, rather red-rimmed blue eyes stared at me in outraged astonishment.

'We never smoke during battle,' he said angrily.

Later in the morning, the enemy or some of them having been located on the ridge of one of the Quantock hills, he gave me the chance to redeem this unfortunate lapse by sending me on a desperate mission.

'It is vital, absolutely vital,' said Victor Bone, 'that we should know how many of them are up there. Gallop off, young what's-your-name, and try to work your way up to them from behind. Then report back to me with the names of any officers you can identify. That will tell me all I want to know.'

Horsed cavalry operations, it had been disillusioning to discover, are seldom conducted at more than a trot. The excuse for a legitimate gallop came rarely and though I was not confident of being able to identify any of my brother officers by name, I set off lightheartedly on my mission. For a happy and breathless twenty minutes I galloped across streams, through beech woods, into and out of combes. Then tethering my horse on the edge of a coppice I crept on my stomach through the heather. I could hear the enemy just ahead of me firing blanks, presumably at the squadron I had left. I spotted their blue-banded caps on the skyline and crawled very stealthily forward. It was a situation that I found I enjoyed and the whole episode would hardly be worth mentioning except that it made me aware, for the first time, of a latent and unsuspected Red-Indianism in myself.

Peering round a bush of golden broom I came face to face with another officer of my regiment. He was pale and very tall, and I knew his face though not his name. He was eating his sandwiches and looked rather astonished. I was unknown to him, but he must

have guessed that I was the enemy for he drew his revolver and
snapped it at me.

'Clicketty-click, you're dead,' he said.

'No, I'm not!' I shouted, and dashed away.

JOHN VERNEY

*

*But behind such charades lay a terrible reality. Once again a British
Expeditionary Force was to be despatched to France; but whatever their
elation, its soldiers were in no position to cry*

'READY, AYE, READY'

In September 1939 the British Army was totally unfit to fight a
first class war on the continent of Europe. It had for long been
considered that in the event of another war with Germany the
British contribution to the defence of the West should consist mainly
of naval and air forces. How any politician could imagine that, in a
world war, Britain could avoid sending her Army to fight alongside
the French passes all understanding.

In the years preceding the outbreak of war no large-scale exercises
with troops had been held in England for some time. Indeed, the
Regular Army was unfit to take part in a realistic exercise. The
Field Army had an inadequate signals system, no administrative
backing, and no organisation for high command; all these had to be
improvised on mobilisation. The transport was inadequate and was
completed on mobilisation by vehicles requisitioned from civilian
firms. Much of the transport of my division consisted of civilian
vans and lorries from the towns of England; they were in bad
repair and, when my division moved from the ports up to its concentration area near the French frontier, the countryside of France
was strewn with broken-down vehicles.

The anti-tank equipment of my division consisted of 2-pounder
guns. The infantry equipment against tanks was the ·8-inch rifle.
Some small one-pounder guns on little hand-carts were hurriedly
bought from the French and a few were given to each infantry
battalion. Apart from these, a proportion of the 25-pounders of my

Divisional Artillery was supposed to be used in an anti-tank role, firing solid shot.

There was somewhere in France, under GHQ, one Army Tank Brigade. For myself, I never saw any of its tanks during the winter or during the active operations in May. And we were the nation which had invented the tank and were the first to use it in battle in 1916.

Field-Marshal the VISCOUNT MONTGOMERY OF ALAMEIN,

KG

Techniques for employing modern armoured forces had been evolved by the British before the Germans had even started. But once this development became successful enough to threaten tradition and precedent the Establishment dug in its toes, worshipping, as it did

THAT COMPARATIVELY SWIFT ANIMAL, THE HORSE

Whatever may be the relative mechanical proficiency of converted cavalry regiments and of Tank Corps units, there is another equally important factor to be considered—the tactical handling of these new formations. It is, I think, common knowledge that the natural enthusiasm for machinery, with which the Tank Corps is doubtless endowed, has tended in the past to lead them to concentrate on this side of their duties, to the comparative neglect of those tactical principles, ignorance of which has always invited, and always will invite, disaster . . . the Tank Corps have no tactical tradition on which to build.

In our old cavalry regiments on the other hand, successes and failures in innumerable wars, greatly reinforced by a constant association in peace with *that comparatively swift animal the horse,* have resulted in a quickness of thought and an elasticity of outlook which are almost second nature. I venture to suppose that it is the possession of this attitude of mind, based on tradition rather than on considerations of *esprit de corps,* which have led the Army Council to convert cavalry regiments rather than to replace them by new Tank Units. Major-General R. G. HOWARD-VYSE (late Inspector of Cavalry)

At the battle of Alamein in 1942 a good half of the British armour came from 'the Tank Corps'!

★

As the war clouds gathered, there was an enthusiastic rallying to the colours. One distinguished archaeologist started his war in a hurry.

'ENFIELD'S OWN'

By the middle of August 1939 the international situation had tightened beyond bearing, and one Friday afternoon I suddenly handed the archaeological destinies of Normandy over to my partners, Miss K. M. Richardson and Miss Theodora Newbould, and took the night-boat from Dieppe. I went straight from Victoria Station to the Association's headquarters nearby. The moment was exact; the War Office had just issued executive orders and my arrival was acclaimed. By lunchtime I was in Enfield for the first time in my life, searching for a vacant house from which to recruit 'Enfield's Own'. I found one in the London Road.

Alas, it was a Saturday, and the house-agent had vanished with the keys. I ran him eventually to earth on a golf-links a few miles away. In the King's name I dragged him from the second green, and by the middle of the afternoon I was installed. On a window-sill I drafted a forthright appeal to the patriotic citizens of Enfield, bidding them rally to the colours at No. —, London Road, on the Monday morning. A visit to the local newspaper office—the only printing establishment open at the weekend—speedily produced a liberal edition of the appeal, tricked out prettily in red, white and blue, and ending with a resounding 'God Save the King'. By Sunday morning it adorned the windows of nearly every shop in Enfield. Nor were the local cinemas behindhand; their films were thenceforth punctuated by the new battle-cry hastily scribbled on lantern-slides. Urgent telephone conversations with a variety of military depots produced the necessary recruitment form and a medical officer. By Monday morning at eight o'clock we sat on borrowed chairs behind an improvised counter, and with combined anxiety and curiosity awaited custom.

'We' had now swollen to five. To the medical officer and myself had been added J. B. Ward Perkins (now Director of the British School at Rome), long a friend and colleague of mine, and my son Michael (a youthful barrister), together with a young sergeant of the regular army from headquarters. Michael and Ward Perkins were awaiting their commissions but were meanwhile a tower of strength. With the exception of the sergeant, we were all still in civilian clothes; we were learning our job and improvising as we went along. On that morning we sat awhile and waited.

The start was a slow one, and it must have been after nine o'clock when the doorway was filled by an immense figure. For a moment the newcomer surveyed with mild surprise the threadbare scene in front of him, and then a quiet, pleasant voice mounted up within him, and he announced his name with a suspicion of hesitation, almost apology. 'A. Goodman,[1] solicitor' went down on the form, and thus a Cambridge graduate headed our list of gunners. Unambitious but out to do his bit, Gunner Goodman had become a quarter-master sergeant when I parted from him two years later, and I wish him well. He was followed by a thickening stream of schoolmasters, tradesmen, mechanics, labourers—a mixed lot typical of those fine early days of the war, when the spirit of service was universal and unabated. By the end of the week our number was full to overflowing. In the absence of uniforms, the new unit was arrayed in brown overalls and was thus reviewed, at my request, by the brigadier in a carefully chosen cul-de-sac where the most inquisitorial of inspecting officers could not expect manœuvre.

SIR MORTIMER WHEELER (who in a letter to a friend written in the Egyptian desert, at Alamein in October 1942, was able to say: 'I boast that I've been able to lead this gang from the suburbs of northern London right into the very middle of the picture. The rest doesn't matter now.')

★

A FORM OF TRAINING

Another great bugbear of the Territorial Army was the question of drill. There are, of course, very great merits in the correct performance of barrack-square drill. The more terrifying and destructive

[1] Now Lord Goodman, Chairman of the Art Council.

war becomes the more essential it is that the standard of discipline should be raised so that the natural instincts of every man to hide and remain under cover in the face of danger may be overcome. It has been found from experience that units which are good at drill and which are well turned out rarely fail in battle. At the head of the Army at that time were men like Lord Gort, a Guardsman, and General Dill, who were both great believers in drill, and many of the senior officers of the Army in 1939 were apt to judge a unit entirely by its appearance on parade. Now drill is a form of training which must be learnt and performed correctly from the very start. The Territorial soldier had, in peacetime, only a limited number of hours a month to give to military training. It was rightly regarded as absurd that he should give up all these precious hours to learning drill. But when the Territorial battalion became embodied it was constantly inspected and every inspecting officer commented adversely on its drill. Great efforts were made to improve in this particular, but without great result, for having always performed his drill in a slipshod manner, it was extremely difficult for the Territorial to get out of the bad habit.

This question of drill, unimportant as it may sound, had a considerable effect on the efficiency of the Territorial Army. The men became depressed at the constant adverse criticism on their drill and either concentrated far too much upon trying to remedy matters or else gave up the unequal struggle and resigned themselves to being considered no good, which was extremely bad for their morale and self-respect. There was no one senior enough in the Territorials—or big enough—to realise that a very much more simplified form of drill was required for the Territorial soldier.

Brigadier SIR JOHN SMYTH, BT, VC, MC, MP

SQUADDING

The sergeant's roar, interpreted aright
by instinct of fear, dies bouncing on the asphalt.
The squad, grey-denimed in the distinct light
stand-easy, adjust a cap or finger a belt.

Shedding its shell, a crab must feel like this,
lost between two worlds, not so much scared as wary.

They consider the sergeant without prejudice
and accept the insulting candour of his stare.

Why is it then that with arms and legs loosened
out of a random rhythm they are forced to move
in a strange unison? Apart from the nuisance,
there is a buoyancy, even a kind of love.

Yet still, as the clue's emerging, they feel again
that pull of difference splitting each life in two.
More than the sergeant, each stands apart. The brain
is numbed with a semi-defiance. It isn't true.

It isn't true, each insists. It isn't happening.
This is not me. But it is. And you grin to find
the will re-welded, richer. You lose your cap,
feel foolish; and an urgency raps your mind—

tightened, look, in the buckle of belt and sling,
jestingly sealed in each momentous trifle,
stamped now, clamped in the bolt and the bayonet-ring,
fondled and final in the uplifted rifle.

> JACK LINDSAY (the Australian poet and
> novelist, who served in the Royal Signals)

Some of those who thought they had joined up to fight 'for King and Country' discovered that they lacked other qualifications besides a capacity to march like a Guardsman.

OFFICER UNDER INSTRUCTION

I arrived at the racecourse grandstand, which was then serving the Infantry Training Centre as its officers' mess, at about eight o'clock in the evening.

The Adjutant, summoned from his dinner by the mess corporal, was young, a regular soldier, and properly proud of his regiment and its traditions.

'Those trousers,' he muttered, averting his eyes.

I apologised, explaining the circumstances.

'You can't,' he kept on repeating, 'come into the mess in those God-awful trousers.'

I had been travelling all day. I was tired, hungry and rather frightened. Visions of a drink, followed by dinner, began to fade.

Taking me out into the decent obscurity of the platform at the top of a long flight of concrete steps, the Adjutant asked if I had brought a civilian suit. I told him I had.

'In that case,' he said with evident relief, 'you must go and change into it at once. *At once.*'

He organised transport to take me to my billet, an opulent villa, full of pink lampshades, situated about a mile and a half from the mess. The driver waited while I changed out of the faulty uniform which I had put on so proudly. I was driven back to the mess, where a late supper had been laid on. The Adjutant darted in and out like a flustered mother-bird. He did his best to dispel an unfortunate first impression, but I was painfully aware that whenever he set eyes on me during my sojourn at the ITC the recollection of those khaki slacks came between him and a proper appreciation of my military potentialities.

He had, poor chap, plenty of other troubles in connection with the newly joined wartime officers, of whom I was only one among many.

Three days after we had reported for duty he announced that a special parade had been laid on for us in the dining-room. When we assembled we observed that one place, and one place only, had been laid on the long mahogany dining-table which had been transported to the grandstand from the regimental mess. There was a lavish display of knives, forks, spoons and wine-glasses. Had we, the Adjutant inquired, brought our notebooks? Some of us had; others, imagining perhaps that we were to receive encouragement in the shape of a buckshee and supplementary meal, had not. While the ill-equipped retired to make good their deficiencies, the rest of us regarded the dining-room table with puzzled concern. When we were all in a state of readiness the object of the exercise was explained.

The Colonel, the Adjutant told us, had been concerned and shocked on the previous evening—a guest night—to observe that some of the newly joined officers had been in doubt about the correct implements and glasses to employ for the successive courses.

If we would be kind enough to pay attention and take notes, he would give us a practical demonstration. Without batting an eyelid this impeccable young man then sat down at the table and an equally solemn mess waiter served him first with token soup, then with token fish, then with token meat, then with a token pudding and finally with a token savoury. The wine waiter went through the motions of pouring out sherry, burgundy, port and brandy. Somewhere I still possess the valuable notes I made.

RALPH ARNOLD (who shortly afterwards became ADC to
Lord Ironside, Chief of the Imperial General Staff)

*

At 11.15 am on 3rd September the British Prime Minister, Neville Chamberlain, informed by a broadcast the people he governed that they were already at war. 'Immediately upon the outbreak,' Winston Churchill recalled, 'our Expeditionary Army began to move to France.' Advance parties proceeded across the Channel on the 4th and by mid-October four divisions had arrived.

FAIR STOOD THE WIND FOR FRANCE

The ss *Fenella* slipped gently down-stream from Bristol in the golden glow of a perfect autumn day, the soft rays of the sun touching with glowing silver the barrage balloons overhead and warming the cold grey sides of the escorting destroyers. The gentle promise of fair sailing was all too soon belied; as the afternoon drew on and Land's End came in sight, the breeze began to freshen ominously: the little lapping waves gave way to a sullen heaving roll which even the most optimistic stomach found it difficult to ignore. An atmosphere of uneasy introspection spread abroad as in the gathering dusk the destroyers began to pitch and heel in great clouds of spray. Darkness fell with the *Fenella* labouring in a twisting, tossing stagger as she met the fierce gusts which blew thick wafts of that indescribable steamship smell—a nauseating compound of warm castor-oil, mouldy upholstery, and stale cooking—down upon her queasy travellers. Even the most stalwart, and of these there were but few, could scarcely keep a foothold on the drenched and slippery decks as they heaved and swung to the grey-green seas; as for the others, most of them were long past caring what might befall them, and it was only the special Providence which watches over the helpless that kept some from washing overboard. All through that interminable night the storm raged—the soaring, long-drawn rise and sickening drop, the dizzy corkscrew roll from side to side. As the heaving darkness began to give way to the cold grey light of a rough and stormy dawn the decks and cabins of the *Fenella* yielded a spectacle calculated to provoke a long-drawn shudder from the most hardened beholder.

But every nightmare has its merciful awakening. Gradually the horrors of the night began to die as a watery sun broke through the scurrying clouds and the day began to warm; the angry seas subsided. A few wan, yellowish faces were even raised to catch a longed-for glimpse of *terra firma*, the coast of Brittany, and here and there were men of iron who could even weakly nibble a biscuit.

By early afternoon, when the *Fenella* was entering the port of St Nazaire, the remarkable recuperative powers of the British soldier were at work and by the time the ship was docked the sufferings of the voyage were all forgotten. Men thronged the ship's rails in highest spirits—eager for the first sight of France, the first picture of war. Soon they were in full voice. On 29th September 1939 the 5th Royal Inniskilling Dragoon Guards landed on the continent of Europe singing 'South of the Border Down Mexico Way' and 'Roll out the Barrel' just as their forebears had landed in 1914 to the strains of 'Tipperary'.

Major-General ROGER EVANS, CB, MC

I'm afraid we all found it something in the nature of an anti-climax. Undoubtedly we had expected a welcome. We had expected cheers, and smiles, and perhaps kisses. We had read that such things happened to the first British soldiers to land in France in 1914. And we were not far behind the very first in 1939. We expected we would be going into battle almost immediately. We were sure the French would be overjoyed to see our faces and our new battle-dress.

Perhaps we were foolish to expect all this. Perhaps times have changed. Perhaps this is a war in which nobody feels inclined to cheer. Or perhaps we were just unlucky.

Still, the fact remains that when we landed at Cherbourg at 8 am on a dreary and depressing morning the crowds assembled to welcome us consisted of a French naval sentry, some old market women, a fisherman and two or three gendarmes. As a reception committee they were a decided failure. They vouchsafed us a disinterested glance or two, and then went about their business.

And some of us had actually expected kisses!

GUN BUSTER

UP THE LINE

In the forward areas, save for wire entanglements visible here and there in front of hidden trenches, there were few signs of war. Farmhands worked unhindered in the fields; the placid cattle grazed their fill; villages and farms lay inviolate. In the west, the forts of the Maginot Line, the great system on which France implicitly relied for her security against the aggressor, crouched silent and concealed. By day, the watchers cowered from sight, hidden; by night, patrols skulked stealthily from bush to bush, their hands and faces darkened.

This furtive, creeping warfare in the West, this imperceptible oozing forward from a zone of supine fortresses formed ignoble contrast to the great battle on the Eastern front. Here the last desperate resistance of Poland was beaten down by the mighty torrent of German arms. Soon Germany had achieved strategic freedom to concentrate her every effort on her main object—the defeat of France.

For the British, digging was the order of the day—digging in cold, wet soil behind the Franco-Belgian frontier. Day after day and week after week the trenches slowly grew.

Major-General ROGER EVANS

The production of large numbers of concrete pillboxes and many miles of anti-tank obstacles threw a heavy extra load on the RE units of formations already fully employed on the normal duties of engineers of a force undertaking the preparation of a strong defensive position, and the many duties which fall to the Corps with a force settling down in an area which it expects to occupy for a considerable time. It was, therefore, necessary to simplify as far as possible the construction of these works. With this end in view the C-in-C agreed that, except in special circumstances, the types of pillboxes should be limited to about half a dozen. This decision had advantages beyond those immediately obvious. From the operational point of view similarity in design made relief by garrisons easier, and, further, as it could never be certain which allied force would in operations occupy a particular sector, it was necessary that each work should be suited to the weapons of both armies. . . .

These designs were issued to the RE of formations and used almost exclusively. The composition and organisation of 'X' Force made it ideal for the mass production of pillboxes. Its field park companies formed a central workshop in which standard shuttering was produced until specially designed steel shuttering could be obtained from England, and reinforcement bars could be cut and bent *en masse*. Its efforts were chiefly directed to the construction of works in the rear portions of the position. In this way a rapidly increasing speed of erection was attained, so that, when the German offensive started and the Allies moved forward from the prepared position, over 400 pillboxes had been completed and another 100 were in various stages of construction. This number of 400 was well in excess of the standard of six works per kilometre set by the Supreme Commander.

The other major task in connection with the development of the position was the construction of a network of anti-tank obstacles. These were, for the most part, excavated and revetted ditches, though existing streams and rivers were improved, and sites for minefields selected. Various forms of anti-tank road blocks were also constructed. As some of the ditches were excavated by hand this proved a slow and difficult job in Flanders mud. Using all available means some forty miles of ditch had been dug when active operations started in May 1940.

Though sites for minefields were selected and mines stored in the neighbourhood, no actual mines were laid. To have done so would not have been possible at this juncture. The 'War' at this time was most unrealistic. The BEF was sitting down more than a hundred miles from any enemy forces and these were also quiescent.

Major-General R. P. PAKENHAM-WALSH, CB, MC

SOMETHING ACCOMPLISHED,
SOMETHING DONE

I got into serious trouble during that first winter of the war. It happened in this way. After a few months in France the incidence of venereal disease in the 3rd Division gave me cause for alarm. To stop it I enlisted the aid of the doctors and even the padres; but all efforts were unsuccessful and the figures increased. Finally I decided to write a confidential letter to all subordinate commanders in which I analysed the problem very frankly and gave my ideas about how to solve it. Unfortunately a copy of the letter got into the hands of the senior chaplains at GHQ and the Commander-in-Chief (Gort) was told of my action. My views on how to tackle the problem were not considered right and proper and there was a father-and-mother of a row. They were all after my blood at GHQ. But my Corps Commander (Brooke) saved me by insisting on being allowed to handle the matter himself. This he did in no uncertain manner and I received from him a proper backhander. He said, amongst other things, that he didn't think much of my literary effort. Anyhow it achieved what I wanted, since the venereal disease ceased.

Field-Marshal LORD MONTGOMERY

THE CHIEF

Unfortunately (Gort's) brain was geared to details the whole time. He wandered about scratching the barks of the trees and you could never get him to come out and look at the wood as a whole. The important points such as the system of defence to be adopted, lines of advance into Belgium, relative advantages of remaining on the frontier as opposed to advancing to meet the Germans, all such and many others he left to his staff, whilst he dealt with such details as platoon log-books, carrying of sandbags, booby-traps. Repeatedly Dill and I called for conferences to discuss specific points. He would agree to hold the conferences, but when we met all these points were handed over to Pownall or Neame to deal with. He took practically no part in the discussion and was eager to get on to some minor points which he had brought with him. As time passed, these failings became more and more disconcerting.

Field-Marshal the VISCOUNT ALANBROOKE, KG

*

On 30th November the invasion of Finland by Russia caused a flurry in Whitehall. 'Nothing in fact of any use was done,' says Churchill: but troops were prepared to move

TO THE FINLAND STATION

Suddenly into the room strode the gigantic and dramatic figure of General 'Tiny' Ironside, Chief of the Imperial General Staff. He had on an enormous pair of black rubbery-looking boots which seemed to reek of winter snows and, having seated himself at the end of the table, he proceeded to tell us that we were to be sent to Finland to fight the Russians. As he went on to talk of fighting in the snow and the midnight sun I thought I was living in a dream. We were to be equipped with shorts and topees—the very idea made me shiver—and clad thus, we were to embark. Then, when all the world thought we were going East, we were to change into special arctic costumes and fall upon the Russians.

After this truly stunning pronouncement the General asked if there were any questions. There was only one and that one seriously endangered my gravity and my reputation. One of the COs asked if we could have an issue of boots which were properly soled and which did not let the wet in. This question bounced off Tiny like water off a duck's back as he rose and made for the door. Seeing me —I had been one of his pupils at the Staff College—he came over and kindly wished me luck, which I felt I should most certainly need! While he was having a few last words with the divisional commander I took his staff officer aside and said 'But how the hell will we get there? Neither Norway nor Sweden will let us pass through.' To which he replied somewhat vaguely that 'it would be quite all right on the night'.

GUN BUSTER

*

MUTILÉ DE LA GUERRE

I have seen the first man wounded by a British bullet on the Western Front.

He is a Frenchman.

I saw him in a French military hospital. He was lying on a hospital trolley on his way from the X-ray theatre to the operating table. His left arm had been ripped open by a shot from a rifle. Four doctors and three nurses were in attendance.

A simple peasant, he had been pushing a barrow across a field after dark and approached a position guarded by a British sentry.

The sentry challenged him. He made no reply; but went slowly on his way.

The sentry fired. The countryman dropped.

Later, the sentry discovered the cause of the man's failure to answer his challenge.

The peasant is stone deaf.

SKENE CATLING

*

INSTEAD OF A CAROL

The winter hardens. Every night, I hear
The patient, khaki beast grieve in his stall,
His eyes behind the harsh fingers soft as wool.
His cheerful morning face puts me in mind
Of certain things were rumoured far and near
To hearts wherein there fretted and repined
A world that came to its last dated year.

RAYNER HEPPENSTALL

1940

'I wonder what the New Year will bring for us? Bad times, I fear.'
DIARY OF FIELD-MARSHAL LORD IRONSIDE

Now the moment approached when the British Army would again be fighting with the German. The setting—the steep defiles and mountain wasteland of central Norway—was one which no observer could have foreseen six months before. Patient, khaki beasts still continued their training.

NAMING OF PARTS

Today we have naming of parts. Yesterday,
We had daily cleaning. And tomorrow morning,
We shall have what to do after firing. But today,
Today we have naming of parts. Japonica
Glistens like a coral in all the neighbouring gardens,
   And today we have naming of parts.

This is the lower sling swivel. And this
Is the upper sling swivel, whose use you will see,
When you are given your slings. And this is the piling swivel,
Which in your case you have not got. The branches
Hold in the gardens their silent, eloquent gestures,
   Which in our case we have not got.

This is the safety-catch, which is always released
With an easy flick of the thumb. And please do not let me
See anyone using his finger. You can do it quite easy
If you have any strength in your thumb. The blossoms
Are fragile and motionless, never letting anyone see
   Any of them using their finger.

And this you can see is the bolt. The purpose of this
Is to open the breech, as you see. We can slide it
Rapidly backwards and forwards: we call this
Easing the spring. And rapidly backwards and forwards
The early bees are assaulting and fumbling the flowers:
   They call it easing the Spring.

They call it easing the Spring: it is perfectly easy
If you have any strength in your thumb: like the bolt,
And the breech, and the cocking-piece, and the point of balance,
Which in our case we have not got; and the almond blossom
Silent in all of the gardens and the bees going backwards and
                                                    forwards,
    For today we have naming of parts.

                                        HENRY REED

                            *

TO NORWAY

Cedric plunged down again into the darkness and found the ESO.
They studied the embarkation orders with the aid of a dimmed
torch. There was no doubt about it; the Highlanders were in the
wrong ship. This was the *Duchess of Cumberland*; they should be in
the *Duchess of Clarence*. 'But the *Clarence* isn't here,' said the ESO.
'I daresay they were told to go to the *Cumberland* by someone.'
    'By whom?'
    'Not by me, old man,' said the ESO.
    Cedric went on board and looked for the CO of the Highlanders
and found him at length in his cabin asleep in his battledress.
    'These are my orders,' said the Highland Colonel, taking a sheaf
of typewritten sheets from the pocket on his thigh. They were
already tattered and smeared by constant reference. '*Duchess of
Cumberland*. Embark 2300 hrs. with full 1098 stores. That's plain
enough.'
    'But our men come on board in an hour.'
    'Can't help you, I'm afraid. These are my orders.'
    He was not going to discuss the matter with a subaltern. Cedric
fetched his CO. Colonel to Colonel they talked the thing out and
decided to clear the after troop decks. Cedric was sent to wake the
Highland duty officer. He found the duty sergeant. Together they
went aft to the troop decks.
    There were dim lights along the ceiling—electric bulbs recently
daubed with blue paint, not yet scratched clear by the troops.
Equipment and kit-bags lay about the deck in heaps; there were
Bren gun boxes and ammunition and the huge coffin-shaped chests
of the anti-tank rifles.

'Oughtn't that to be stored in the armoury?' asked Cedric.

'Not unless you want to get it pinched.'

Amid the heaps of stores half a battalion lay huddled in blankets. Very few of them, on this first night, had slung hammocks. These lay, with the other gear, adding to the piles.

'We'll never get them moved tonight.'

'We've got to try,' said Cedric.

Very slowly the inert mass was got into movement. They began collecting their own gear and swearing monotonously. Working parties began man-handling the stores. They had to go up the ladders on to the main deck, forward through the darkness and down the forward hatches. Presently a voice from the top of the ladder said, 'Is Lyne down there?'

'Yes.'

'I've been told to bring my company to this troop deck.'

'They'll have to wait.'

'They're coming on board now.'

'Well for God's sake stop them.'

'But isn't this D deck?'

'Yes.'

'Then this is where we are to come to. Who the hell are all these men?'

Cedric went up the ladder and to the head of the gangway. A stream of heavily-laden men of his regiment were toiling up. 'Go back,' ordered Cedric.

'Who the hell's that?' asked a voice from the darkness.

'Lyne. Take your men back to the quay. They can't come on board yet.'

'Oh, but they've got to. D'you realise half of them've had nothing to eat since midday.'

'There's nothing to eat here till breakfast.'

'Oh, but I say, what rot. The RTO at Euston said he'd telegraph through and have a hot meal ready on arrival. Where's the Colonel?'

The line of soldiers on the gangway turned about and began a slow descent. When the last of them was on the quay invisible in the darkness, their officer came on board.

'You seem to have made a pretty good muck-up,' he said.

The deck was full of the other regiment carrying stores.

'There's a man there smoking,' shouted a ship's officer from above. 'Put that cigarette out.'

Matches began to spurt up on the quay. 'Put those cigarettes out, down there.'

'——y well travelling all the ——ing day. No ——ing supper. ——ed about on the ——ing quay. Now a —— won't let me have a ——ing smoke. I'm ——ing ——ed with being ——ed about by these ——ers.'

A dark figure passed Cedric muttering desperately.

'Nominal rolls in triplicate. Nominal rolls in triplicate. Why the devil can't they tell us beforehand they want nominal rolls in triplicate?'

Another dark figure whom Cedric recognised as the ESO.

'I say, the men are supposed to strip down their equipment and pack it in green sea bags before embarking.'

'Oh,' said Cedric.

'They don't seem to have done it.'

'Oh.'

'It upsets all the storage arrangements if they don't.'

'Oh.'

An orderly came up. 'Mr Lyne, sir, will you go and see the CO.' Cedric went.

'Look here, Lyne, aren't those infernal Scotsmen out of our troop decks yet? I ordered that deck to be clear two hours ago. I thought you were looking after that.'

'I'm sorry, Colonel. They're getting a move on now.'

'I should bloody well hope so. And look here, half our men have had nothing to eat all day. Go up to the purser and see what you can rout out for them. And find out on the bridge exactly what the sailing orders are. When the troops come on board see that everyone knows where everything is. We don't want anything lost. We may be in action before the end of the week. I hear these Highlanders lost a lot of kit on the way up. We don't want them making up deficiencies at our expense.'

'Very good, sir.'

As he went out on deck the ghostly figure brushed past him in the darkness muttering in tones that seemed to echo from another and even worse world, 'Nominal rolls in triplicate. Nominal rolls in triplicate.'

At seven o'clock the Colonel said, 'For God's sake someone take over from Lyne. He seems to have lain down on the job.'

EVELYN WAUGH

REARGUARD

King-Salter busied himself helping to recover transport from which the Norwegian civilian drivers had fled. Then he went in search of Hvinden Haug once more, to see what more could be done, and found him waiting for the German aircraft to go home for the night before moving his headquarters back. He repeated that the British troops, whatever state they were in, must stand that night and the following day, so that their companies to the west of the river and the Norwegians beyond them could get across the bridge at Tretten. Here is his own account of the hours that followed—a rare, eye-witness description of 148 Brigade's last lonely action in Tretten Gorge. A forgotten action in a forgotten campaign, fought by troops whose plight and whose condition was an indictment of the nation that had sent them there, wishfully magnifying them into a fully equipped and conquering army:

'. . . I went back to Tretten—at perhaps about 1000 hours—intending to send forward the other company to Major Roberts, to inform General Ruge that the position was occupied, and to try and arrange for protection of the left, or east, flank from the Tretten side of the high spur; because I was still not satisfied that that flank was adequately protected and an approach through the deep snow over the plateau was more direct than the line of the road which went round two sides of a triangle. I sent forward Major Roberts' spare company, telling them, as Major Roberts had asked me to do, to drop one platoon to give depth to the defences on the road itself. While looking for a telephone I met a Norwegian staff officer (Colonel Beichmann) who promised to pass my message to General Ruge; and then I motored up a mountain road above Tretten to reconnoitre; but found that owing to the forest it was very difficult to do anything to protect that flank adequately. Eventually I decided to post a small party of troops on the eastern outskirts of

Tretten where they could oppose, across some open snow-covered fields, any attempt to attack Tretten from over the mountains. While this party was being organised from some of the HQ company troops still in Tretten, I had some dinner which they offered me.

'Shortly afterwards I again happened to meet the Norwegian staff officer and with him the OC Norwegian motor machine-gun unit. They were both extremely anxious lest the enemy should be working up the west bank of the valley, on the other side of the river or lake, and asked me if I could send some troops southwards on that side. I was surprised, as I had assumed the forces on the west bank were responsible on that side. The river was in many places so wide as to resemble a lake. When receiving this request from the Norwegians, I was uncertain whether to take action, not knowing if Lieutenant-Colonel German was back yet or if Brigadier Morgan had resumed control now that his units were together again; I felt that I had accomplished the special task which I had been given. But the Norwegians were very insistent and I agreed to act. They sent a Norwegian officer with me to find a local guide and I motored to the west side of the Tretten bridge where I found Major Kirkland, at perhaps 1400 hours, holding a bridgehead with his company (one of the two which had been under Major Roberts on the west of the lake). I explained to him what was required and he agreed to take his company one or two miles south down the west side of the valley. Dinners were to be served soon and I told him to wait until the men were fed; a difficult decision because it seemed of great urgency for him to move without any delay.

'I then decided to revisit the defensive position. I had heard no firing whatsoever and as it was by now about three o'clock I was feeling very hopeful; and the shock was very great when about half a mile south of Tretten at the entrance to the forest I met some stragglers, utterly exhausted, who told me that German tanks had just broken through their position. An RE officer, Major M. R. Jefferies, was with me, who had earlier been carrying out demolitions on his own. I sent him back in my car to warn the troops at Tretten of what had happened.

'More men appeared, all with the same story. There were some felled trees at that point and some of the men helped me to make an improvised tank obstacle. All this time—about fifteen minutes—I felt that I ought perhaps to go forward to see what the situation was and to help if I could. I always remembered that it was vitally important to hold the position all day if the forces on the west bank were to be saved. Then an officer, I think an IO called Barratt, arrived with a message for the commander of the forward troops, to hold their position until 2000 hours. I felt that he must go on with his message and decided to go with him. An officer called Bradley who came up at that moment volunteered to come with us. We three then walked up the road, each carrying a rifle. We had gone about three-quarters of a mile through the forest when, on approaching a bend, we heard shots round it, some of which passed over us. As we had been prepared to meet tanks at any moment we immediately ran into the forest and lay down in a slight depression about twenty yards from the road, but in full view of it. The snow had melted here and we were not conspicuous. A few seconds later we could hear tanks; and we then lay motionless, and momentarily expecting to be discovered, as we watched the German tanks and infantry go by.

'From now until the 27th I was behind the German lines, but before describing what happened to me during that time, I will give a short account, as I know it, of the general events that followed that afternoon of 23rd April. When I sent Major Jefferies back to Tretten, I told him to try and get hold of Major Kirkland's company if it had not already started off. I have subsequently met Major Kirkland who tells me that he did receive fresh orders and that these orders were to take one and a half platoons to the east bank and go forward and "deal with a German tank which has broken through and broken down!" He came up the road with his one and a half platoons shortly after us and encountered the German advance just inside the forest. The Germans were halted and Major Kirkland saw them first and deployed an anti-tank rifle and a Bren gun, to engage the leading German tank and the infantry section immediately behind it. He opened surprise fire but the German tank came on notwithstanding and Major Kirkland's troops were overrun. He himself was wounded and captured, and lost a leg. The Germans then proceeded to bombard Tretten heavily both with 6-inch infantry guns and from the air, and with machine-guns which had worked forward on the other side of the water. Eventually they advanced on Tretten and captured it. The garrison of Tretten can only have consisted of those men who had been too exhausted to be put into the defensive position earlier in the day, and of the remainder of Major Kirkland's company, and of various HQ details. After capturing Tretten the Germans pushed on some miles, before being checked by Norwegian troops at Faavang.

'As a result of the failure to hold the forest position the whole of the Norwegian force on the west bank was cut off.'

BERNARD ASH

DEATH IN THE AFTERNOON

It was now mid-day. Battalion headquarters ate some luncheon—biscuits and chocolate; the adjutant had a flask of whisky. No one was hungry but they drank their bottles empty and sent the orderlies to refill them at the spring B Company had found. When the men came back the Colonel said, 'I'm not happy about the left flank. Lyne, go across and see where those bloody Loamshires are.'

It was two miles along a side track to the mouth of the next pass, where the Loamshires should be in defence. Cedric left his servant behind at battalion headquarters. It was against the rules, but he was weary of the weight of dependent soldiery which throughout the operations encumbered him and depressed his spirits. As he walked alone he was exhilarated with the sense of being one man, one pair of legs, one pair of eyes, one brain, sent on a single, intelligible task; one man alone could go freely anywhere on the earth's surface; multiply him, put him in a drove and by each addition of his fellows you subtract something that is of value, make him so much less a man; this was the crazy mathematics of war. A reconnaissance plane came overhead. Cedric moved off the path but did not take cover, did not lie on his face or gaze into the earth and wonder if there was a rear gunner, as he would have done if he had been with head-quarters. . . .

He came to the place where the Loamshires should have been. There was no sign of them. There was no sign of any life, only rock and ice and beyond, in the hills, snow. The valley ran clear into the hills, parallel with the main road he had left. They may be holding it higher up, he thought, where it narrows, and he set off up the stony track towards the mountains.

And there he found them; twenty of them under the command of a subaltern. They had mounted their guns to cover the track at its narrowest point and were lying, waiting for what the evening would bring. It was a ragged and weary party.

'I'm sorry I didn't send across to you,' said the subaltern. 'We were all in. I didn't know where you were exactly and I hadn't a man to spare.'

'What happened?'

'It was all rather a nonsense,' said the subaltern, in the classic phraseology of his trade which comprehends all human tragedy. 'They bombed us all day yesterday and we had to go to ground. We made a mile or two between raids but it was sticky going. Then at just before sunset they came clean through us in armoured cars. I managed to get this party away. There may be a few others wandering about, but I rather doubt it. Luckily the Jerries decided to call it a day and settled down for a night's rest. We marched all night and all today. We only arrived an hour ago.'

'Can you stop them here?'

'What d'you think?'

'No.'

'No, we can't stop them. We may hold them up half an hour. They may think we're the forward part of a battalion and decide to wait till tomorrow before they attack. It all depends what time they arrive. Is there any chance of your being able to relieve us?'

'Yes. I'll get back right away.'

'We could do with a break,' said the subaltern.

Cedric ran most of the way to the cave. The Colonel heard his story grimly.

'Armoured cars or tanks?'

'Armoured cars.'

'Well, there's a chance. Tell D Company to get on the move,' he said to the adjutant. Then he reported to brigade headquarters on the wireless what he had heard and what he was doing. It was half an hour before D Company was on its way. From the cave they could see them marching along the track where Cedric had walked

so exuberantly. As they watched they saw the column a mile away
halt, break up and deploy.

'We're too late,' said the Colonel. 'Here come the armoured cars.'

They had overrun the party of Loamshires and were spreading
fanwise across the low plain. Cedric counted twenty of them;
behind them an endless stream of lorries full of troops. At the first
shot the lorries stopped and under cover of the armoured cars the
infantry fell in on the ground, broke into open order and began their
advance with parade-ground deliberation. With the cars came a
squadron of bombers, flying low along the line of the track. Soon
the whole battalion area was full of bursting bombs.

The Colonel was giving orders for the immediate withdrawal of
the forward companies.

Cedric stood in the cave. It was curious, he thought, that he
should have devoted so much of his life to caves.

'Lyne,' said the Colonel. 'Go up to A Company and explain
what's happening. If they come in now from the rear the cars may
jink round and give the other companies a chance to get out.'

Cedric set out across the little battlefield. All seemed quite unreal
to him still.

The bombers were not aiming at any particular target; they were
plastering the ground in front of their cars, between battalion headquarters and the mouth of the valley where A Company were dug
in. The noise was incessant and shattering. Still it did not seem real
to Cedric. It was part of a crazy world where he was an interloper.
It was nothing to do with him. A bomb came whistling down, it
seemed from directly over his head. He fell on his face and it burst
fifty yards away, bruising him with a shower of small stones.

'Thought they'd got him,' said the Colonel. 'He's up again.'

'He's doing all right,' said the adjutant.

The armoured cars were shooting it out with D Company. The
infantry spread out in a long line from hillside to hillside and were
moving steadily up. They were not firing yet; just tramping along
behind the armoured cars, abreast, at arm's length apart. Behind
them another wave was forming up. Cedric had to go across this
front. The enemy were still out of effective rifle range from him, but
spent bullets were singing round him among the rocks.

'He'll never make it,' said the Colonel.

I suppose, thought Cedric, I'm being rather brave. How very peculiar. I'm not the least brave, really; it's simply that the whole thing is so damned silly.

A Company were on the move now. As soon as they heard firing, without waiting for orders, they were doing what the Colonel intended, edging up the opposing hillside among the boulders, getting into position where they could outflank the party. It did not matter now whether Cedric reached them. He never did; a bullet got him, killing him instantly while he was a quarter of a mile away.

EVELYN WAUGH

*

In France, even before the German attack, there wild rumours of spies behind the Allied lines. There was also the question of

LIGHTS

There were various sorts of lights. There was a perfectly dreadful one I think it was in Hyland's area, everyone had a perfectly dreadful light sooner or later but this one was in Hyland's area and it took him several reports to get worked out the accuracy of it. I forget all the details but the chief ingredients were a French count his German mistress and a sinister visitor to their house of shame, anyway it was all very Oppenheim and Boris Karloff and there was a marsh with a mist on it. Hyland turned on the accuracy and there emerged into the hard drab light of truth an eminently respectable French bachelor, a Polish maidservant and her Polish lover. While the bachelor dozed in his carpet slippers the little Greta would show a lighted candle from an upper chamber and by the time Boris Karloff had traversed the mist and marsh she had slipped the well oiled bolt in the scullery door and met her lover there. Then up the stairs they crept, snuffed out the candle and well there they were, two Poles on a perch. After what we must suppose to have been a sufficient if not a very decent interval, the little Greta would relight the candle, descend the stairs, slip the well oiled scullery bolt, and send off Boris Karloff into the murky morn. Unfortunately for them their performance was observed by a passing poacher, at least not all of it but quite enough to start a pretty story.

As Ashby said, it was a pleasing report but GHQ would never in the circumstances accept the accuracy of the French man's being a bachelor. Well anyway that was lights.

A. GWYNN-BROWNE

*

The War Office barely had time to collect its breath after the Norwegian débâcle when the Western Front burst into flame. 'Plan D' dictated that the British and French armies should leave their prepared defences along the Belgian frontier and march north-east, aiming at a head-on collision with the most powerful and mobile army in the world, on ground of the German's own choosing.

TO THE TATTOO

Yesterday, so overjoyed were the Belgian people to see our troops that the BBC car was partly filled with tulips and narcissi, our drivers were taken to lunch and loaded with cigarettes. A Lancashire lad said, 'Ee, I'm havin' a terrible time'—he'd been kissed by half-a-dozen girls.

The bombing, so far as my colleagues have been able to judge at the moment, appears to be directed for the most part at military objectives—aerodromes, railway stations, level crossings and so forth. But on this, indeed, it is extremely difficult to form an opinion. The pilot tries to bomb a level crossing—he misses the crossing and demolishes a couple of villas two hundred yards away. Or a pilot is attacked by a fighter and, in making his escape, lightens his machine by dropping his bombs indiscriminately. That action kills half-a-dozen civilians. It seems to their friends deliberate murder; to the pilot no more than the chance of war.

I'm told four British airmen interned in Belgium through a forced landing have now been able to go to England, that they were not on parole, but found the life lonely because few besides members of the British Embassy could visit them.

This is a day of great beauty, and if the occasion were not so grave one could enjoy it thoroughly. Even so, it is difficult not to enjoy it. The sun is always the sun, and flowers are no less lovely because bombers zoom overhead. Indeed, war puts an edge on beauty—it is as though beauty said, 'Take a long look at me, enjoy me while you may. Who knows for how long it will be?' It may seem incongruous that spring's foliage should be used to camouflage motorcycles and that steel helmets should be adorned with green leaves, but so it is.

The procession on the roads has drawn villagers to their doors. They sit on chairs on the pavement watching the cavalcade go by: British guns (medium and light) draped in dust-sheets, Bren carriers, motor lorries—all the impedimenta of war; and on the other side of the road, speeding towards us, those fleeing from war as from the plague—thousands upon thousands of refugees. I don't know how many passed this way yesterday but the numbers today are colossal. Somebody said last night to me, 'It is Poland over again'. But, I thought, hardly that, for these can, at least, put British troops between themselves and German horde. These seem to be the richer folk with cars—some are large cars, and they go by at a great pace; others are ramshackle affairs—one with two people clinging to the running-board. A host of them carry a mattress on top, partly to guard against machine-gun bullets, partly because this is the most convenient way of carrying it.

And yet even this pitiful sight—and you cannot see it unmoved— bears from time to time, and for a swift instant or two, an air of holiday, a touch of Derby Day. For a lorry will come along holding a large family—grandfather driving the old horse, mother and grandmother sitting aloft surrounded by young children, and all of them raising a hand or waving a greeting. A moment later that impression is blotted out by the sight of a sick woman lying back on her pillows open to the sky.

The route by which we go is marked by sticks on which is painted a black upright arrow rather resembling a plane in flight. Within two or three hours of our entry into Belgium, roads were marked as clearly and traffic guided as efficiently as to the Aldershot Tattoo.

J. H. HODSON

The Germans struck on 10th May: and as they rolled forward others retreated.

The stream of refugees which had begun to flow thinly on 10th May had by the 11th swelled into a turgid flood. During that day all roads leading westwards became choked with a slowly moving mass of traffic which seemed to grow more dense every hour. High farm-wagons drawn by teams of great Flemish horses, their harness gay with brass and ribbons, creaked along laden with a pathetic burden of personal possessions and small children still clinging to the toys that they had been playing with when panic struck their homes. Motors crammed with suitcases and strange, shapeless bundles, and almost invariably topped by a canopy of striped mattresses tied on with scraps of rope, chugged slowly along with frequent checks and halts. Scores of cyclists, their cycles hung from handle-bars to mud-guard with packages, wound their way along wearily pushing their overloaded machines in front of them. Aged peasants trudged on foot, silent, uncomplaining, perhaps uncomprehending. Over all the sweating, toiling column brooded an atmosphere of latent terror—a terror rooted in history, nourished by remembrance of that other exodus that so short a time ago had been overtaken by murder, rape and torture. Here and there in the shifting pattern of the column a thin thread of Belgian soldiery showed plain . . . moving *westwards*. To the British soldier, scion of an island race inviolate for a thousand years, it was a strange and moving spectacle. All that night and next day, the 12th, the endless stream flowed on, while overhead the enemy's bombers droned over Louvain and its neighbouring villages.

Major-General ROGER EVANS

THE BOMBERS

Next second they broke into view—nine twin-engined Stukas, flying over ten thousand feet up, bunched close together in the shape of an arrow-head.

Hardly had they topped the Ridge when the point of the arrow-head seemed to wobble violently. The Troop Commander understood the grim significance of that wobble. At the leader's signal the Stukas circled round the battery area, taking up positions behind one another.

'It's for us this time,' the Troop Commander said softly to the

GPO. Then at the top of his voice, he roared:

'Take cover . . .'

Out of the gun-pit that the GPO had just quitted fifty yards away, the crew of six, still clutching their half-empty mess-tins, bolted like rabbits and disappeared into a slit trench by the side of the pit. The sergeant spat out the mouthful of food he was about to swallow, as being the quickest way to get rid of it.

'Cover . . .' he echoed at the top of *his* voice, but it was drowned immediately by the sudden barking of all the Bofors in the area.

Crouched in their narrow ditch, tingling with expectation of their first dive-bombing ordeal, the six men all peered upwards, curiosity stronger than any other emotion, tense and breathing heavily.

Above the blue sky was alive with the white tufts of the bursting Bofors shells. Thousands of feet beyond the dotted screen the watchers in the trench saw the leading plane do a half-roll and dive (so it seemed) straight for them. Down it came at a terrific speed, at the same time piercing the air with a maniacal high-pitched scream that froze their blood, and for the moment bound them petrified, staring upwards. Then, as if on a common impulse, the six men hurled themselves down, down, as flat as they possibly could wedge themselves into the bottom of the trench, seized with a double fear that for the instant deprived them of all rational thought. Nothing mattered but to hide from this fearful nerve-shattering scream, this demon laugh, that grew louder and louder as it came nearer and nearer, searching them out, each of them individually, louder and louder, high above the bark of the Bofors, unearthly, diabolical.

'Gawd! . . . What's happening to us?' said the gun-layer with unsteady lips. He found it difficult to speak, and the words sounded like an inward prayer forced to the surface under torture.

No one else spoke. Words were beyond their power. The only sounds they could have uttered were inarticulate sounds of their gripping fears, and these they were choking back, still ashamed to show the terror that had momentarily overtaken them. They were suffering under the illusion that afflicts all men, however brave, when subjected to their first dive-bombing attack—the terrible, ineradicable belief that you yourself have been singled out specially for destruction, that the diving plane has seen you personally, and is coming straight for you, and that nothing on God's earth can stop it.

On top of this, the fearful long-drawn shriek, as if of triumph over *you*, the destined and inescapable victim. A man must have more than nerves of iron to remain unaffected by such an experience. He must be utterly devoid of the slightest spark of imagination. In fact, not a man at all. Something of a lower species.

Only brief seconds had elapsed since the six men first cowered in the trench—no longer than the time taken for the leading Stuka to half complete its headlong three-hundred miles an hour dive from a height of ten thousand feet. But with that harrowing scream filling their ears, unnerving them, and gripped with the agony of that wait for the thunderbolt to strike them, Time, for every man in the trench, lost all values. It might have been years.

Not far away the Troop Commander and the GPO crouched in an angle of the wall of the farmhouse. They also, to begin with, had been impelled by an overpowering curiosity to watch proceedings. Spellbound, they saw the leading Stuka dive, straight for *them* so they thought. If they could have spoken each would have uttered the same words: 'He's coming to bomb *me*'. They, too, found themselves petrified by the unhuman scream. They saw the dive continue. The plane was now only four hundred feet from the ground. Nothing surely could stop it from crashing—into *them*. Suddenly they saw three bombs released. As they dropped the machine instantaneously stopped falling, and shot up into the sky again at an incredibly steep angle. And at the same moment they became aware of the crescendo scream of the second plane making, in turn, its dive.

The first group of bombs landed amid the Bofors emplacements. One of the second salvo made a direct hit in the Bofors gun-pit that was nearest to B Troop position. A second before the GPO had been staring very fixedly at that Bofors, repeating to himself:

'Damn good . . . damn good . . .'

Like the six men in the trench, the GPO had been considerably shaken up. He was now making a powerful effort to recover himself by concentrating his attention on the Bofors gun crew, which in the midst of this terrifying, screaming hell, continued coolly firing. The sight braced him up like a tonic. It was something to take his mind off these infernal, nerve-shattering screams.

'Damn good . . . damn good . . .'

He was quite unconscious of paying tribute to the gallant Bofors gunners. He just continued to repeat the words automatically, even desperately, for his own salvation.

Then, as the bomb burst in the pit, he saw the wreck of the brave little gun hurled bodily into the air. The gunners staggered blindly for a moment or two in all directions, dropped to the ground, and moved no more.

GUN BUSTER

ANTIDOTE

All experienced soldiers know that troops may lose all power of self-control for a short time when they are heavily bombarded for the first time in their lives.

Every effort was made in the 50th Division to safeguard against this danger. The point was stressed that whenever the enemy concentrated a very heavy bombardment on any part of the front, a senior commander or staff officer should be ready behind that portion of the front and waiting for the inevitable reaction. Sometimes brigade commanders went there, sometimes the GOC himself was there. After about an hour a few men would start to trickle back in a completely dazed condition. The senior officer dealing with the situation would go and talk to them. He would ask:'Do you mean that you—men of the 50th Division—are leaving your posts because of shell fire?'

Dazed as such men usually were, when they realised what they had done they were heartily ashamed of themselves. They were then taken back to the line. Neighbouring posts had often seen such men trickling back. They wondered whether a withdrawal had been ordered. Sometimes they had joined the trickle, but when they saw the men brought back with senior officers present confidence was at once restored.

The 50th Division took endless trouble to carry out this process of implanting confidence in the men for the first three or four days under heavy fire. The result was splendid. After that period there was never any necessity to take these precautions, for the men had gained their confidence in themselves and their comrades.

The effect on the Division was striking. Many divisions which had certainly had no more serious fighting than the 50th were down to half strength or less as they were withdrawing into the bridgehead. A considerable proportion of the missing had trickled back into the rear areas and did not join up again until their units entered the bridgehead. The 50th Division kept up their strength with practically no men missing right up to the last day.

Major EWART W. CLAY, MBE

*

Within forty-eight hours the BEF made contact with the main mass of German infantry, which had already forced its way across the Maastricht appendix of Holland and deep into Belgium. But co-operation with the Belgians, notwithstanding the precipitate rush which had been made to their assistance, was at a low ebb:

OH! DO YOU SPEAK FRENCH?

The interview (with the King of the Belgians, the Commander-in-Chief) was fixed up . . . the Admiral (Keyes) took me into the King's room and introduced me to him in English. I found no one else in the room, and Roger Keyes withdrew and left me alone with the King. I explained to him my difficulties . . . in English. I found him charming to talk to, and felt that I was making progress . . . when I suddenly heard a voice speaking French from behind my right. On turning round I found an officer there who did not introduce himself to me but went on speaking in French to the King. His contention was that the Belgian Division could not be moved, that the whole of the BEF should be stepped farther south and be entirely clear of Brussels. I then turned on him in French and told him that he was not putting the full case before the King, since he had not mentioned that the 10th Belgian Division was on the wrong side of the Gamelin Line. He then turned to me, and said: 'Oh! do you speak French?' I assured him that I did, and that I happened to have been born in France. By that time he had interposed himself between me and the King. I therefore walked round him and resumed my conversation with the King in English.

This individual then came round again and placed himself

between me and the King, and the King then withdrew to the
window. I could not very well force my presence a third time on the
King, and I therefore discussed the matter with this individual whom
I assumed must be the Chief of Staff. I found that arguing with him
was sheer waste of time; he was not familiar with the dispositions of
the BEF and seemed to care little about them. Most of his suggestions
were fantastic. I finally withdrew, and on going out I met the
French general, Champon, who was the appointed Liaison Officer
between the French and Belgian forces. I told him about my interview and asked him who it was I had met with the King. He told
me his name was van Overstraeten and that he was the ADC to the
King with the rank of Major-General. I asked him where the Chief
of Staff was. . . . He then told me that it was quite useless my
bothering to see him, as van Overstraeten had taken all control
in his hands and that he could get the King to do just what he
wanted.

Champon told me, however, that he could get the matter put
right for me, as the King had to attend a conference of General
Georges's that afternoon at Mons. He told me that he would inform
General Georges that the 10th Belgian Division was in its wrong
place and ask him to issue orders to the King for the withdrawal of
this division. He kept his word and within twenty-four hours orders
were issued and the matter was put right. . . .

I left the Belgian GHQ with many misgivings in my heart. As I
motored back to Brussels I wondered whether the Belgians would
turn out to be no better than the French. My left flank was to rest on
the Belgian Army; these thoughts were consequently most disconcerting. . . .

Field-Marshal LORD ALANBROOKE

*

IN REVERSE

Mile after mile down the road the column grew and grew, and
crawled and crawled. Everyone was worn out for want of sleep.
Drivers kept going mechanically, the movement just sufficient to
keep them awake and no more. If an enforced halt occurred, how-

ever brief, they dropped sound asleep in their seats instantly. When we moved on a bit, many of the drivers remained asleep. The column proceeded, leaving them behind, blocking the road. Traffic Control of the Divisional Staff, and the CMP (Military Police) then chased up and down the road in the darkness waking up the delinquents in no gentle fashion.

'Wake up, blast you. . . .'

'Get moving, you bastard. . . .'

'You're holding the whole bloody column up, curse you. . . .'

Officers and men, they all got it alike. A blinding torch flashed in the sleeper's face, then—salvo.

On through what had been Henin-Lietard. The bombers had left little of it standing. Piles of broken masonry and rubble choked the roads. The main avenue was impassable, so the column wriggled through the side-streets so narrow that the guns were forced on to the pavements. A sort of dry rasping noise kept us company; the hard crunch of wheels on the carpet of broken glass.

On to Carvin. And here another petrifying horror. One of those appalling spectacles that, like the shambles in our Vimy gun-pits, strike the heart cold. Something transcending even the normal imagined horrors of War.

Behind some railings in the main street stood a redbrick convent school that had been badly bombed. And spread out on the wide white pavement in front were the bodies of sixty victims, all girls between the ages of fifteen and seventeen. The corpses had been arranged in four regular rows, one behind the other on the broad flags. There they lay, rigid and motionless in the moonlight, staring up at the sky, exactly like a Company that had formed fours and then fallen down flat on their backs. The mathematical precision of the arrangement added to the terror of the scene. You could fancy yourself looking upon the devilish finale of some marionette show— 'Death's Drill', or 'Death by Numbers'. To heighten the horrible, unhuman aspect of this pavement mortuary, the faces, bare arms, and legs were discoloured by a ghastly mauve tint, the result, probably, of shock or blast from the bomb. Perhaps the bodies had been laid-out in this pattern for identification and collection by relatives. But there was little chance of this. All the living inhabitants of the village had fled. Not a soul dared remain to watch over and guard the mauve-faced dead. Alone, deserted, there they lay on their backs. Alone, with their wide-eyed appeal to the Heavens.

GUN BUSTER

NOTHING LEFT

The Commander-in-Chief briefly explained what had happened. North and South of Sedan, on a front of fifty miles, the Germans had broken through. The French army in front of them was destroyed and scattered. A heavy onrush of armoured vehicles was advancing with unheard-of speed towards Amiens and Arras with the intention, apparently, of reaching the coast at Abbeville or thereabouts. Alternatively they might make for Paris. Behind the armour, he said, eight or ten German divisions, all motorised, were driving onwards, making flanks for themselves as they advanced against the two disconnected French armies on either side.

The General talked for perhaps five minutes without anyone saying a word. When he stopped there was a considerable silence. I then asked: 'Where is the Strategic Reserve?' and breaking into French, which I used indifferently (in every sense): '*Où est la masse de manœuvre?*' General Gamelin turned to me, and with a shake of the head and a shrug, said: '*Aucune.*'

There was another long pause. Outside in the garden of the Quai d'Orsay clouds of smoke arose from large bonfires, and I saw from the window venerable officials pushing wheelbarrows of archives onto them. Already, therefore, the evacuation of Paris was being prepared.

'*Aucune.*' I was dumbfounded. What were we to think of the great French Army and its highest chiefs? It had never occurred to me that any commanders having to defend five hundred miles of engaged front would have left themselves unprovided with a mass of manœuvre. No-one can defend with certainty so wide a front; but when the enemy has committed himself to a major thrust which breaks the line one can always have, one *must* always have, a mass of divisions which marches up in vehement counter-attack at the moment when the first fury of the offensive has spent its force.

What was the Maginot Line for? It should have economised troops upon a large sector of the frontier, not only offering sally-ports for local counter-strokes, but also enabling large forces to be held in reserve; and this is the only way these things can be done. But now there was no reserve. I admit this was one of the greatest surprises I have had in my life. Why had I not known more about it, even though I had been so busy at the Admiralty? Why had the British Government, and the War Office above all, not known more about it? It was no excuse that the French High Command would not impart their dispositions to us . . . except in vague outline. We had a right to know. We ought to have insisted. Both armies were fighting in the line together. I went back again to the window and the curling wreaths of smoke from the bonfires of the State documents of the French Republic. Still the old gentlemen were bringing up their wheelbarrows, and industriously casting their contents into the flames.

WINSTON CHURCHILL

Sunday, 19th May 1940

In the morning, refugees, driven to desperation, stampeded the train demanding food, but we had to refuse their requests. Two MOs from No. 10 CCS at Lille came over to visit us and informed us that we were to take on patients at 1430 hours in the afternoon. They were to be brought by ambulance, as the line had been bombed. At 1430 hours a long line of ambulances began to arrive. Each stretcher had to be carried over two railway tracks and along a long platform—a tedious performance. The first patients had been evacuated from hospital and were fairly convalescent, but amongst them were several Belgians, who had come down the line from Ghent and who were very ill. The loading was uneventful and the patients all seemed very pleased and relieved to be in bed and going back to base. They numbered about 170 in all and we gave them hot tea, bread and butter, and, later on, supper. At 1900 hours we heard we were to go into Lille. We moved off slowly and arrived in the station in brilliant moonlight, to see a long line of ambulances awaiting us. We were able to load without artificial light and this time it was the real thing—patients straight from CCS, many of them with nothing but a first field dressing. Overhead there was a terrific bombardment, but we were too busy to take a great deal of notice. We saw a long line of troops marching out of the town, the moonlight glinting on their steel helmets, and heard the low sinister sound of troops on the march, making us wonder all the more where they were going and exactly what their errand was. We finished loading at about 0100 hours on Monday morning, with about 350 patients on board, some very badly wounded. Amongst the patients we had five German officers and two German troops, several French troops, one Spahi and one very severely hurt Belgian civilian. As soon as the patients had all been fed and were all reasonably comfortable, we took turns on duty throughout the night. During the early hours of the morning the train moved off.

Tuesday, 21st May 1940

At 0600 hours in the morning, we reached St Omer, where the station was entirely blocked with traffic. While our water tanks were being re-filled, we saw poor helpless refugees begging to be taken on board trains, and noticed English nuns amongst the mass of humanity being loaded into the cattle trucks. At 0700 hours, our train moved on, this time with Calais as the objective, and spirits ran high. About three hours' journey saw us three miles outside Calais, where we saw streams of traffic moving out of the town along the roads. We got the patients ready to disembark, and at midday, with water becoming very scarce, everybody was given dinner. Immediately after dinner one of the MOs borrowed a bicycle belonging to a refugee and cycled to Calais. We waited patiently for news and at about 1530 hours he returned to say that he had seen the docks heavily bombed and many railway lines broken. At 1730 hours the OC set out for Calais, this time in a car in which he had begged a lift, and about an hour and a half later the train at last moved on to Calais. The congestion on the line was terrific, continuous dog-fights were going on overhead and bombs were bursting close by. We gave a second shot of morphia to all our seriously wounded and bad fracture cases. Our train then moved out of Calais again to Etaples, passing a large but completely deserted camp hospital on the way. On arrival we were met by very harassed French railway officials who informed us that the Germans were only eight miles away and that the railway station was to be blown up! The place was very empty and we saw a motor convoy moving out. There were a few wounded refugees to be seen, one of whom—a boy with a thigh wound, who had been left lying on the platform—we took aboard. At about 1930 hours we moved slowly along to Boulogne, which was being very heavily attacked from the air. We waited outside the town and had a magnificent view of the town and of the harbour. The roar of planes overhead was terrific and we saw British Blenheims fly over the town. Bombs began to fall. The train shook and rocked violently, but we came through quite undamaged, without even a broken window, though the patients, in the confined space of a railway carriage, were badly frightened. We then moved back to Dannes-Camiers, near Le Touquet, only to hear that our wounded could not be taken off the train, as the hospital was evacuating, but that the German wounded were to be unloaded. At 0100 hours the next morning, Wednesday, we unloaded the German wounded and took on twenty walking cases, together with more Nursing Orderlies and dispensary stores. The despatch riders brought quantities of cigarettes and chocolate which they had got from the NAAFI, which was very greatly appreciated by everyone. By 0200 hours all was quiet on the train, though heavy bombing was to be heard at Boulogne through the night; the patients were for the most part asleep, and the MOs having volunteered to stay up all night, we went to bed fully dressed and fell very readily to sleep.

ADA HARRISON

THE 3-INCH LIMIT

Armentières has been very heavily bombed; half the town is demolished, including the madhouse, and its inmates are wandering about the country. These lunatics let loose were the last straw. With catastrophe on all sides, bombarded by rumours of every description, flooded by refugees and a demoralised French army, bombed from a low altitude, and now on top of it all lunatics in brown corduroy suits standing at the side of the road grinning at one with an inane smile, a flow of saliva running from the corner of their mouths, and dripping noses! Had it not been that by then one's senses were numbed with the magnitude of the catastrophe that surrounded one, the situation would have been unbearable.

Several years later, whilst dining at Chequers one weekend,

Churchill said to me the receptive capacity of a man's brain to register disaster is like a 3-inch pipe under a culvert. The 3-inch pipe will go on passing the water through under pressure, but when a flood comes the water flows over the culvert whilst the pipe goes on handling its three inches. Similarly the human brain will register emotions up to its '3-inch limit' and subsequently additional emotions flow past unregistered. This simile of his reminded me of my feelings during those last momentous days in France before Dunkirk. I had reached a stage when the receptive capacity of my brain to register disasters and calamities had become numbed by successive blows. It is a providence of nature that it should be so, otherwise there would be more mad people in this world.

Field-Marshal LORD ALANBROOKE

*

Looking back after the war, Field-Marshal von Rundstedt said:
'A critical moment in the drive came just as my forces had reached the Channel. It was caused by a British counter-stroke southward from Arras on 21st May. For a short time it was feared that the panzer divisions would be cut off before the infantry divisions could come up to support them.'

COUNTER-STROKE

In the valley between the wood and ourselves is a potato clamp and, extraordinary though it may seem, that clamp was there in 1940, and I suppose that each year the farmer stores his potatoes in the same place. Now, swinging round to the left, you can see in the open ground there a wire fence with a sort of chicken house in the middle of it—a square—probably a chicken run. Well now, you will remember how I told you that we crossed the start line and we ran into that Rifle Regiment and we dealt with them, and then we spent I suppose three or four hours moving on from there up to the line of the Arras–Bapaume road, and the whole of the way through there we were dealing with German lorries, infantry and anti-tank guns— and these anti-tank guns which were 37 mm were quite unable to penetrate our tanks, and we really had a highly successful battle. I don't know how many Germans we killed and I don't know how many lorries and other vehicles we set on fire—it was really most successful and we really didn't see why we shouldn't go all the way to Berlin at the rate we were going. Well, we came up this hill, and as we came across the top, I remember, down where the chicken house is there was a very large German tank with a big gun and we had nothing that would deal with that, and so the Colonel called across to me and said, 'Go back to the cemetery where that French tank is and ask him to come up and deal with this German.' Because as we had passed we had seen a French tank sitting outside the cemetery firing into it. Well, I went back there and I drew alongside the Frenchman and he opened the door in the side of his tank and said, 'What do you want?' and I told him, and he said, 'Oh, I can't come, I am very busy, I am shooting into this cemetery.' Why he was shooting into it I don't know, because I couldn't see anybody to provide a target. However, while I was arguing with him there was a sudden burst of firing and some shells fell around us and he shouted, 'Attention! Attention!' and he slammed the door and motored off—and that was the last I saw of him. So I got back into my tank, turned round and went back the way I had come. Well, when I got back I found in fact that the German tank had disappeared —which was very convenient of him—and I looked down the valley and the sight I saw was this.

I could see what I suppose was A Squadron—Oh—more than A Squadron, there must have been some of B Squadron there too because there were upwards of twenty tanks, down in the valley just short of the potato clamp. The Colonel's tank was down there, a little in front of them—I could see it quite clearly, it was stationary and I could see the flag flying from it. The Adjutant's tank was quite close to the Colonel's, but from where I was I wasn't quite sure what to do, so I called up the Colonel to tell him about the French tank and it wouldn't come. I called and I called and I called, but I got no answer, and then the Adjutant came on the air and he just said, 'Come over and join me.' So I motored down to the valley and as I did so I saw the Adjutant drive forward to the area of the potato clamp and start shooting, and as I got closer I saw that there were a whole number of German anti-tank guns in the area of the potato clamp and crews were running about. At that time, a good deal of fire was coming from the area of the wood, and also from the crest lines both to the right and the left of the wood—and it was very heavy fire. It was field-gun fire—much heavier than anything we had encountered so far. At any rate, I went forward through those tanks of A Squadron and I thought it very odd that they weren't moving and they weren't shooting, and then I noticed that there was something even odder about them—because their guns were pointing at all angles; a lot of them had their turret hatches open and some of the crews were half in and half out of the tanks, lying wounded and dead—and I realised then, suddenly, with a shock, that all these twenty tanks had been knocked out, and they had been knocked out by these big guns and they were, in fact, all dead—all these tanks. In the grass I could see a number of black berets as the crews were crawling through the grass which, as you can see, is quite long, and getting away—those who were not dead. At any rate, I went forward as I had been told to do, and joined the Adjutant among those German anti-tank guns. And we began shooting at them, and I remember that I owe my life to the quick-wittedness of Captain Cracroft, the Adjutant, because when we got to the potato clamp I found that on the other side of it were half a dozen Germans and so I drove up to them from my side of the potato clamp and I gave fire orders to my gunner and he was firing down into the thing but he couldn't depress the gun enough, and I was standing on the seat of my tank shouting at the gunner and calling to the driver to reverse a bit so that we could get the bullets down low enough, and I little thought that behind me there was a German lying on the ground and his rifle resting on a kit bag, drawing a very careful bead on the back of my neck. Well, the Adjutant, I heard later—not till I got back to England—pulled out his revolver and, quick as a flash, he shot the chap in the throat. It must have been a jolly good revolver shot, and it saved my life.

Well, I think we killed all those chaps. We then turned our machine-guns on the woods, and we just sprayed the trees. To our astonishment all sorts of Germans and bits of equipment and things fell down out of the trees, where I suppose they had taken refuge. But none the less the fire became heavier and heavier and there were shells falling all round us and striking the tanks, including the tanks already knocked out, and it was high time for us to go, and the Adjutant signalled to me to turn round and drive back. As we did so, I saw the Colonel's tank had had its side blown in, and although I didn't know it the Colonel and Corporal Moorhouse his operator were dead inside. The driver, extraordinarily enough, escaped, and walked back and rejoined us at the final rally. As we drove back through the Matildas my heart sank because I realised what had happened: there were all those tanks that I knew so well—the familiar names—Dreadnought, Dauntless, Demon, Devil; there were the faces of these men with whom I had played games, swum, lived with for years—lying there dead; and there were these tanks—useless— very few of them burning but most of them smashed up in one way or another. And as the Adjutant and I drove back up to the top of the hill, one realised that this really was it. This—this was tragedy— this was the end of the 4th Tanks as we knew it. In that valley, the best of crews, our tanks, our soldiers, our officers were left behind.

Brigadier P. A. L. VAUX, OBE (who was Second Lieutenant
Vaux during this action at Arras on 21st May 1940)

Some small units roamed at will, 'raising hell'. For example, Major John King, of the 7th RTR, drove deeply into the enemy's position, accompanied by another 'Matilda' tank commanded by Sergeant Doyle.

First, they overran an anti-tank battery, and in this fight the forward tool-box of King's tank was set on fire, so that smoke and fumes thenceforth poured back into the tank, and the top-cover had to be repeatedly opened to save the crew from suffocation. Next, four enemy tanks were met and put out of action, two of them burning fiercely—their shells did not penetrate the armour of the Matilda, whereas her 2-pounders 'went right through them'. Then she crashed through a road-block of farm-carts, but her engine temporarily 'conked', and while stationary she was hit by a heavier shell, which jammed the turret and broke the left arm of the gunner, Corporal E. F. Holland—who nevertheless carried on at his post until the end. By this time almost all the 2-pounder ammunition had been fired and only six rounds were left. Driving on, another anti-tank battery was met and knocked out, mainly by Sergeant Doyle's tank, which charged straight at one gun under intense fire and ran over it. On emerging, his forward tool-box also was on fire, his turret jammed, and his periscopes shattered. Shortly after this, King came upon a

German 88-mm gun, but before it could open fire he speeded up to
gain a sunken stretch of track where the high banks provided cover.
On reaching the end of this, he swung the tank so that its jammed
gun-turret should bear on the target, and put in a burst of machine-
gun fire to disturb the Germans' aim. Almost simultaneously, the
other tank came on the scene and decisively relieved the critical
situation by knocking out the 88. But just after this King's tank
caught fire inside, and had to be evacuated at last, while Doyle's was
knocked out by a field-gun when trying to push on.

Captain SIR BASIL LIDDELL HART

*

*All possibility of severing the German corridor had now gone, and the
extrication of the BEF—by sea—became a matter of desperate urgency. To
this end, at least, the Arras counter-attack made a vital contribution. All
the evidence shows that it was a factor in influencing the decision of the
German Command to halt the Panzers' advance outside the perimeter of
Dunkirk.*

THE LITTLE SHIPS

The picture will always remain sharp-etched in my memory—the
lines of men wearily and sleepily staggering across the beach from
the dunes to the shallows, falling into little boats; great columns of
men thrust out into the water among bomb and shell splashes. The
foremost ranks were shoulder deep, moving forward under the
command of young subalterns, themselves with their heads just
above the little waves that rode in to the sand. As the front ranks
were dragged aboard the boats, the rear ranks moved up, from
ankle deep to knee deep, from knee deep to waist deep, until they,
too, came to shoulder depth and their turn.

Some of the big boats pushed in until they were almost aground,
taking appalling risks with the falling tide. The men thankfully
scrambled up the sides on rope nets, or climbed the hundreds of
ladders, made God knows where out of new, raw wood and hurried
aboard the ships in England.

The little boats that ferried from the beach to the big ships in deep water listed drunkenly with the weight of men. The big ships slowly took on lists of their own with the enormous numbers crowded aboard. And always down the dunes and across the beach came new hordes of men, new columns, new lines.

On the beach was the skeleton of a destroyer, bombed and burnt. At the water's edge were ambulances, abandoned when their last load had been discharged.

There was always the red background, the red of Dunkirk burning. There was no water to check the fires and there were no men to be spared to fight them. Red, too, were the shell bursts, the flash of guns, the fountains of tracer bullets.

The din was infernal. The batteries shelled ceaselessly and brilliantly. To the whistle of shells overhead was added the scream of falling bombs. Even the sky was full of noise—anti-aircraft shells, machine-gun fire, the snarl of falling planes, the angry hornet noise of dive bombers. One could not speak normally at any time against the roar of it and the noise of our own engines. We all developed 'Dunkirk throat', a sore hoarseness that was the hallmark of those who had been there.

Yet through all the noise I will always remember the voices of the young subalterns as they sent their men aboard, and I will remember, too, the astonishing discipline of the men. They had fought through three weeks of retreat, always falling back, often without orders, often without support. Transport had failed. They had gone sleepless. They had been without food and water. Yet they kept ranks as they came down the beaches, and they obeyed commands.

While they were still filing back to the beach and the dawn was breaking with uncomfortable brilliance, we found one of our stragglers—a navy whaler. We told her people to come aboard, but they said that there was a motor-boat aground and they would have to fetch off her crew. They went in, and we waited. It was my longest wait, ever. For various reasons they were terribly slow. When they found the captain of the motor-boat, they stood and argued with him and he wouldn't come off anyway. Damned plucky chap. He and his men lay quiet until the tide floated them later in the day. Then they made a dash for it, and got away.

We waited for them until the sun was up before we got clear of the mole. By then, the fighting was heavy in-shore, on the outskirts of the town, and actually in some of the streets.

Going home, the dive bombers came over us five times, but somehow left us alone though three times they took up an attacking position. A little down the coast, towards Gravelines, we picked up a boatload of Frenchmen rowing off. We took them aboard. They were very much bothered as to where our 'ship' was, and said quite flatly that it was impossible to go to England in a thing like ours. Too, too horribly dangerous!

One of the rare touches of comedy at Dunkirk was the fear of the sea among French *poilus* from inland towns. They were desperately afraid to forfeit solid land for the unknown perils of a little boat. When, on the last nights of the evacuation, the little boats got to the mole many refused to jump in, despite the hell of exploding shells and bombs behind them.

A. D. DIVINE

*

Even before the Army was finally expelled from France the Prime Minister had begun to turn his mind to the problems of attacking the enemy coastline.

Prime Minister to General Ismay
The completely defensive habit of mind which has ruined the French must not be allowed to ruin all our initiative. It is of the highest consequence to keep the largest numbers of German forces all along the coasts of the countries they have conquered, and we should immediately set to work to organise raiding forces on these coasts where the populations are friendly. Such forces might be composed of self-contained, thoroughly-equipped units of say one thousand up to not more than ten thousand when combined. Surprise would be ensured by the fact that the destination would be concealed until the last moment. What we have seen at Dunkirk shows how quickly troops can be moved off (and I suppose on to) selected points if need be. How wonderful it would be if the Germans could be made to wonder where they were going to be struck next, instead of forcing us to try to wall in the Island and roof it

over! An effort must be made to shake off the mental and moral prostrations to the will and initiative of the enemy from which we suffer.

WINSTON CHURCHILL

BIRTH OF THE COMMANDOS

When the letter came, in mid-June 1940, Dunkirk was past and the last of the BEF had been evacuated from France. The letter called for volunteers to raid the enemy coast. I liked that. 'Men of good physique', 'able to swim and navigate boats', 'initiative and leadership', 'hazardous work'. Those were the phrases in it.

I was tired of training men for action: I wanted action myself.

I tore upstairs and burst in to see my Commanding Officer, Colonel J. V. Naisby, a tall, competent artillery officer of about forty. I waved the letter before him.

'Here's exactly the thing I want to do,' I said. 'Will you release me?'

I was Adjutant of his unit, the 23rd Medium and Heavy Training Regiment, Royal Artillery. We were stationed at Plymouth.

'Calm yourself, John,' the Colonel said, eyeing me with mild disapproval; and he reached for the letter. He read it and put it down with a sigh. 'But we've plenty of work here. Who's going to do your job?'

It took fifteen minutes to win him round.

'I can see you've made up your mind,' he said finally.

'Thank you, sir. I'll need a recommendation from you, of course.'

He looked up at me, rubbing his chin. Suddenly he grinned.

'You're an old soldier, John: write your own recommendation. I'll sign it.' Which he did.

There was a War Office interview, of course. Then I was back in Plymouth, and almost before I had time to settle back into my old routine, Colonel Naisby walked into my room. He seemed pleased.

'That must have been a good recommendation I signed,' he remarked, and dropped a signal on my desk. It read:

CAPT. J. F. DURNFORD-SLATER ADJUTANT 23rd MEDIUM AND HEAVY TRAINING REGT. R.A. IS APPOINTED TO RAISE AND COMMAND NUMBER 3

COMMANDO IN THE RANK OF LIEUT. COLONEL. GIVE EVERY ASSISTANCE AND RELEASE FROM PRESENT APPOINTMENT FORTHWITH AS OPERATIONAL ROLE IMMINENT.

At that time No. 1 Commando and No. 2 Commando did not exist: it had originally been intended to form them as airborne units, a policy which was subsequently abandoned. This made me the first Commando soldier of the war. I had wanted action: I was going to get it. I should have been delighted to join in any rank, but was naturally pleased to get command. I was confident I could do the work and made up my mind to produce a really great unit. I owed it to my mother.

I travelled and interviewed, interviewed and travelled nonstop: until, finally, I had the officers I needed. Then I sent them out in teams of three to comb the command for other ranks. Each team of three officers was given a selection of units from which to choose men to form their troop. I gave them four days to select their men and to get them to Plymouth.

My appointment had come through on the 28th June. By the 5th July No. 3 Commando was in existence.

Brigadier JOHN DURNFORD-SLATER, DSO

*

Operations such as those of the Commandos must necessarily be on the tiniest scale. The Germans now deployed 190 divisions; in the United Kingdom there were 27, of which only three were substantially ready; none had complete equipment.

This disparity of numbers was echoed in the Middle East, where 36,000 British and Empire troops faced some quarter of a million Italians. The British, however, were a hard, highly trained professional force; the Italians were jittery and cumbersome.

General Wavell, the British Commander-in-Chief, expected reinforcement from both Australia and the United Kingdom, and while he waited he slowly withdrew from the Egyptian frontier to the railhead at Mersa Matruh, rotating his forward units so that each in turn could perfect its tactics and take the measure of its ponderous enemy, in

THE ARENA

Yellow rocks, saltbush, grey earth and this perfect beach was the eternal background wherever you looked in the north of the Western Desert. Except at spots along the coast and far inland it never even achieved those picturesque rolling sandhills which Europeans seem always to associate with deserts. It had fresh colours in the morning, and immense sunsets. One clear hot cloudless day followed another in endless progression. A breeze stirred sometimes in the early morning, and again at night when one lay on a camp bed in the open, gazing up into a vaster and more brilliant sky than one could ever have conceived in Europe. I found no subtle fascination there nor any mystery, unless it was the Bedouin who appeared suddenly and unexpectedly out of the empty desert as soon as one stopped one's car. But there was a sense of rest and relaxation in the tremendous silence, especially at night, and now the silence is still the best thing I remember of the desert, the silence, the cool nights, the clear hot days and the eternal flatness of everything.

The morning I drove towards Mersa Matruh, however, looking for Force quarters, a khamseen was blowing, and that of course changed everything. The khamseen sandstorm, which blows more or less throughout the year, is in my experience the most hellish wind on earth. It picks up the surface dust as fine as baking powder and blows it thickly into the air across hundreds of square miles of desert. All the way through Daba's tent-hospital base and past Fuka it gathered force along the road until at Bagush it blocked visibility down to half a dozen yards. In front of the car little crazy lines of yellow dust snaked across the road. The dust came up through the engine, through the chinks of the car-body and round the corners of the closed windows. Soon everything in the car was powdered with grit and sand. It crept up your nose and down your throat, itching unbearably and making it difficult to breathe. It got in your ears, matted your hair and from behind sandgoggles your eyes kept weeping and smarting. An unreal yellow light suffused everything. Just for a moment the billows of blown sand would open, allowing you to see a little farther into the hot solid fog ahead, and then it would close in again. Bedouin, their heads muffled in dirty rags,

lunged weirdly across the track. You sweated, returned again and
again to your water-bottle for a swig of warm sandy water, and lay
back gasping. Sometimes a khamseen may blow for days, making
you feel that you will never see light and air and feel coolness
again. . . .

More and more I began to see that desert warfare resembled war
at sea. Men moved by compass. No position was static. There were
few if any forts to be held. Each truck or tank was as individual as a
destroyer, and each squadron of tanks or guns made great sweeps
across the desert as a battle-squadron at sea will vanish over the
horizon. One did not occupy the desert any more than one occupied
the sea. One simply took up position for a day or a week, and
patrolled about it with Bren-gun carriers and light armoured
vehicles. When you made contact with the enemy you manœuvred
about him for a place to strike, much as two fleets will steam into
position for action. There were no trenches. There was no front line.
We might patrol five hundred miles into Libya and call the country
ours. The Italians might as easily have patrolled as far into the
Egyptian desert without being seen. Always the essential governing
principle was that desert forces must be mobile: they were seeking
not the conquest of territory or position but combat with the enemy.
We hunted men, not land, as a warship will hunt another warship,
and care nothing for the sea on which the action is fought. And as a
ship submits to the sea by the nature of its design and the way it sails,
so these new mechanised soldiers were submitting to the desert.
They found weaknesses in the ruthless hostility of the desert and
ways to circumvent its worst moods. They used the desert. They
never sought to control it. Always the desert set the pace, made the
direction and planned the design. The desert offered colours in
browns, yellows and greys. The army accordingly took these
colours for its camouflage. There were practically no roads. The
army shod its vehicles with huge balloon tyres and did without
roads. Nothing except an occasional bird moved quickly in the
desert. The army for ordinary purposes accepted a pace of five or six
miles an hour. The desert gave water reluctantly, and often then it
was brackish. The army cut its men—generals and privates—down
to a gallon of water a day when they were in forward positions.
There was no food in the desert. The soldier learned to exist almost

entirely on tinned foods, and contrary to popular belief remained healthy on it. Mirages came that confused the gunner, and the gunner developed precision-firing to a finer art and learned new methods of establishing observation-posts close to targets. The sand-storm blew, and the tanks, profiting by it, went into action under the cover of the storm. We made no new roads. We built no houses. We did not try to make the desert livable, nor did we seek to sub-due it. We found the life of the desert primitive and nomadic, and primitively and nomadically the army lived and went to war.

The Italians failed to accept these principles, and when the big fighting began in the winter it was their undoing. They wanted to be masters of the desert. They made their lives comfortable and static. They built roads and stone houses and the officers strode around in brilliant scented uniforms. They tried to subdue the desert. And in the end the desert beat them.

ALAN MOOREHEAD

THE UNCONQUERED

We were astir early the following morning. By first light we were mounted in our vehicles and ready to move. Preceded by the ar-moured cars, we advanced in the same formation as that of the previous evening. We were soon on to the objective. The infantry quickly began digging what pits and trenches they could in the hard ground and the guns got into position. While this went on we and the armoured cars moved farther west to make contact with the Italians.

About two miles west of the main position Kinnaird found an ideal ridge which flanked, on the south, the direct route which the Italians were expected to take. Here we disposed ourselves in 'turret-down' positions, so that to anyone on the other side of the ridge only the barest minimum of the turret was visible, but we were still able to see the ground before us.

Meanwhile the armoured cars moved a further three miles west before making their first contact. The Italians were preceded as usual by a thin screen of motor-cyclists, spectacular but useless advance-guards. These the armoured cars allowed to within 250 yards of their positions before they moved up on to the ridge behind which they had been hiding. The first thin chatter of their machine-guns told us that the battle had begun.

A moment or two later Bolton, the squadron second-in-command, reported:

'Hello, COMO; COMO Ack calling. Friends in front say that they are engaging about three zero motor-cyclists and that they have destroyed six. The remainder have now withdrawn to the main body. Off.'

Bolton's job was to act as a link between Kinnaird and the force commander, on whose control net the armoured cars were reporting. To do this Bolton, who was in one of the squadron headquarter tanks, placed it next to the one of which the set was on the force-control net. He was then able to pass our news back and transmit to Kinnaird on the squadron net any orders or information, such as that from the armoured cars.

At intervals he continued his commentary:

'. . . The cyclists have now joined the main body of the enemy, which has halted. Off.'

'. . . Still no move by the enemy. There is a lot of to-ing and fro-ing by staff cars, but nothing else is moving. Off.'

'. . . Friends now say that some figures fifteen to twenty tanks have moved forward, very slowly and very cautiously. They say they will have to pull back soon to the next position. Off.'

We knew that there was little that the armoured cars could do against tanks, since they were armed only with a machine-gun. Bolton's next report confirmed this.

'. . . Enemy tanks are now pushing forward quite fast. They seem to have realised that they are only faced by armoured cars. Off.'

Kinnaird now took a hand.

'Hello, COMO ack; COMO calling. That's good. Make sure that friends know exactly where we are. I want them to delay turning south over our ridge until as late as they possibly can, so that the enemy tanks will be drawn on to us face to face. Over.'

'Hello, COMO: COMO Ack answering,' Bolton replied. 'Friends say they know exactly where we are and will try to do as you say. They are finding things a bit tricky at present. They want to with-draw fast enough to get the tanks away from the rest who are now moving again, but if they go too fast they think the tanks will lose heart and give up the chase. Off.'

Soon, in the distance, we could see through our binoculars the small shapes of the armoured cars and beyond them, in a wide fan, those of the pursuing tanks. When the armoured cars were almost due north of us they changed the line of their withdrawal so as to come through our positions. The tanks on the Italian right flank immediately increased speed in an attempt to cut off the armoured cars. This uncharacteristically offensive manœuvre had not been foreseen by Kinnaird, who at once ordered Egerton: 'Hello, COMO Two; COMO calling. Withdraw immediately from your position and face west to take on those enemy tanks when they appear round the end of the ridge. Over.'

'Hello, COMO Two; COMO Two answering. O.K., but the end of the ridge will be a bit bare. Over.'

'COMO Two,' Kinnaird replied, 'you get on with what you have been told to do. I want someone below the ridge as soon as possible—those tanks are coming fast. Off to you.' And since the remainder of the Italian tanks had now conformed to the move of those of their right flank, and were moving to the end of the ridge which Egerton had just vacated, he ordered: 'Hello, COMO Ack. Go to the position which Two had just left. I do not want to move any of the others, and I think you can get there as soon as anybody. Off.'

Bolton immediately moved with all three of the headquarter tanks which had been in the low ground behind us, where Kinnaird had left them when he himself moved up to the ridge into a position where he could see the whole battle.

Though Bolton only just got into position in time, this unplanned manœuvre could not have worked out better as far as we were concerned. Since he was moving, he was the first to be seen by the enemy. Before they could warn the remainder, however, those which had moved round the ridge came face to face with Egerton at short range.

We heard the crack of his first shot, and then in a breathless rush of words:

'COMO Two calling. Three enemy tanks now five hundred yards...' Then in an aside to his gunner he said, 'Down two hundred and fire again,' and continued, '... to my front. Missed first shot. Off.'

Before me now on the other flank the enemy had closed to about 700 yards, and I gave my fire order. 'Holton—traverse right—take the outside tank—seven hundred—fire.'

As I watched the tracer of the shot flying towards the enemy tank I saw, out of the corner of my eye, the flash of Sergeant Wharton's gun and beyond him those of Ryan's troop.

As yet the Italians had not fired. They were handicapped by having to shoot uphill, and moreover had the sun in their eyes.

Ryan was the first to get a kill. He hit an enemy tank which was turning on the slope before him fairly and squarely in the engine, shattering the petrol tanks and starting a fire which spread rapidly. Mixed with the flame, clouds of billowing black smoke rolled across the desert, blocking my view of the enemy entirely. With a dull roar the ammunition then exploded, throwing a mass of debris into the air. A moment later we were horrified to see a figure with face blackened and clothes alight stumbling through the smoke. He staggered for some yards, then fell and in a frenzy of agony rolled frantically in the hard sand in a desperate effort to put out the flames. But to no avail. Gradually his flailing arms and legs moved more slowly, until at last, with a convulsive heave of his body, he lay still.

While my view was blocked, the battle still raged on the other flank. Egerton announced triumphantly:

'COMO Two calling. We have hit this tank three times now, but he won't brew. Hello! Wait a moment; there goes the crew—they're bailing out. I'll let 'em go—doesn't seem right to shoot a sitting bird. That's one, anyway. Off.'

Before anyone else could get a word in he was on the air again, 'COMO Two calling. We've knocked a track off another tank, and the third one has turned and is tearing away flat out. Off.'

Ryan then reported, 'COMO Four calling. We've knocked out another tank—at least, the crew's leaving it now. I can't see anything to my right, as the smoke is blocking the view. Over. . . .'

There was now a pause for some time. The black smoke from the burning tank gradually died away, and I could see that the Italian tanks had withdrawn out of range and were lying about half-way between us and the main Italian column, which had now caught up and was halted immediately to our north, where it had come under shell-fire from our main position to the east.

To break this deadlock and to further his later plans, Kinnaird ordered Egerton:

'COMO Two—we can do little more on this flank. I want to be able to move unobserved via our main position to the other flank. We can't do so while those enemy tanks are so close. I do not want to leave these positions either. So I want you to work your way round the end of the ridge and attack the enemy right flank. Do not get carried way—I just want you to look as aggressive as you can. We may be able to convince them that they must move back a bit for the good of their health. Is this all clear? Over.'

Egerton's enthusiastic reply was, 'COMO Two answering. Quite clear. I don't think they can see me at present, but they may hear me when I move. Can you all do some shooting to drown the noise? Over.'

'COMO Two—good idea. Yes, we will do that. Off to you,' Kinnaird answered. Then, 'Hello, COMO; COMO calling. Start shooting now, Do not waste ammo, but make enough noise. Off.'

Some ten minutes later we saw Egerton's troop emerge round the western end of the ridge, firing on the move as they closed the range to the nearest enemy tank. It must have been by sheer chance—since even on the relatively flat surface of the desert shooting on the move was never very accurate—that this flank tank was hit, and we saw the crew leap out. They tried to run away, but a warning burst of machine-gun fire from Egerton's tank stopped them and we saw them walk towards him with their hands raised.

Egerton reported, 'COMO Two calling. I hope you enjoyed that. Can I send these four prisoners back, as they are rather in the way here? Over.'

By now the remaining Italian tanks had withdrawn well out of range on to the fringe of their main body, so Kinnaird answered, 'COMO Two. Jolly good! The result has been just what we wanted. Stay where you are though until I relieve you. Off.'

During the ensuing lull we withdrew, a troop at a time, to a position some 1,000 yards south of the ridge, where we refilled the tanks with petrol and ammunition. Ryan went first, and then relieved Egerton.

At this first relaxation of tension I found, to my surprise, that it was already eight o'clock and that the battle, which had seemed to take so short a time, had in fact been waging for close on three hours.

CYRIL JOLY

*

Wavell's Western Desert Force contained only two divisions—7th Armoured and 4th Indian—but with these he decided to attack the Italian colossus before the end of 1940. The assault began on 7th–8th December with a bold move forward, by day and night, into the rear of the Italian positions. This was the start of a ten weeks' advance over a thousand miles of desert which ended at Beda Fomm and totally destroyed an Italian army of ten divisions.

FIRST SUCCESS

The 7th RTR began the approach march before the main force, taking two days on the journey, and then lay up for a night and a day—for final adjustments—within twelve miles of Nibeiwa camp, its first objective. The final stage of the approach, through the gap between Nibeiwa and Rabia, was done by night—with screened lights marking the route. The regiment passed about three and a half miles south of Nibeiwa, while aircraft flew continuously over the area to drown the noise. On reaching the line-up area they had about four hours' rest, but the coldness of the night and the tensity of the occasion made sleep difficult.

Soon after first light on 9th December, they set off to deliver the attack, along with the leading brigade of the 4th Indian Division. After advancing due north for four miles, under cover of a low spur, they made a south-easterly turn to the start-line, about 1,500 yards from the chosen sector of entry into the camp. As the sector was narrow, the regiment's attack went in 'one-up' with A Squadron leading, followed by B, while D was kept in reserve. After a short artillery bombardment at 7 am, A Squadron crossed the start-line at 7.25 am, in 'three-up' formation. It covered more than half the distance before the Italian artillery opened fire, and even then with little effect because of the thickness of the Matildas' armour. As the squadron advanced it saw a group of twenty-three Italian M.11 tanks huddled just outside the perimeter of the camp. 'Their crews were in all states of dress and were darting about attempting to start their engines.' Before they could do so their tanks were penetrated, and many set on fire, by a rain of shells from the Matildas' guns. All were knocked out within ten minutes. Meanwhile two of the leading troops of A Squadron drove into the camp, with the squadron-commander, and there tackled the enemy artillery and infantry at close quarters, spreading confusion and panic. The demoralising effect was increased when B Squadron followed up the penetration. The opposing artillerymen continued to fire until they were mowed down, but most of the infantry lost heart on seeing that the on-coming tanks were not stopped even by close-range fire. General Maletti, the divisional commander, was killed by a burst from a Besa gun as he emerged from his dug-out.

The decisive thrust came from C Squadron, 2nd RTR—now commanded by Pat Hobart, since John Brown's death when leading it in the Sidi Barrani battle. The first part of the story of what Birks has called this 'glorious gallop' is vividly told in Hobart's account:

'We drove around to avoid the enemy shelling while the 25-pounders did their bombardment, then formed up in line and advanced at full speed on the fort in what I imagined to be the best traditions of the *arme blanche*. The enemy must have suffered pretty severely from the attentions of the RHA, for in we went unscathed, with every gun and machine-gun firing. My orders to the squadron were to drive straight through the perimeter, doing as much destruction as possible, out the other side, and then to return again and rally back on the near side. I was in the centre of the squadron line, and in an excess of zeal and enthusiasm charged the fort itself. The outer wall was built of solid blocks of stone, and in breaking it I knocked off my nearside idler, so that I found myself inside the courtyard of the two-storey fort, with an immobilised tank. . . . There were some hectic minutes, particularly as my second-in-command, David Wilkie, was shelling the fort from outside with his close-support tank. During this time I had inadvertently left my No. 9 set switched to "send", so that all my frenzied orders and exhortations to my crew were going over the regimental net—which caused considerable pleasure to my brother officers and later embarrassment to me!'

The second part of the story may be given in the words of Sergeant Bermingham, who was driving Wilkie's tank:

'After circling the fort once, my commander gave the urgent order "sharp left". This turn placed the tank facing a large breach in the fort. I sailed across it, with all machine-guns blazing, and came to rest beside the squadron commander's tank. . . . Looking through the visor, I could see Captain Hobart, with steel helmet on, shooting away over the top of his cupola with a pistol. The sight of a second tank inside the fort must have been too much for the Italians and very soon they were appearing from nooks and crannies everywhere to give themselves up.'

Captain SIR BASIL LIDDELL HART

The scale of the total victory was vividly depicted in the reply given to a radio inquiry as to the number of prisoners likely to be sent back.

'So far as I can see there are twenty acres of officers and a hundred acres of men.'

In this classic advance Wavell and O'Connor achieved more than the rout of the Italians and the salvation of Egypt. They renewed the confidence of the Army and revived the morale of the country. The Old Year, in defiance of all prediction, went out in a feeling that the darkest hour was passing.

1941

The year of the Mediterranean

'We who pursue
Our business with unslackening stride,
Traverse in troops, with care-fill'd breast,
The soft Mediterranean side,
The Nile, the East . . .'

MATTHEW ARNOLD

For the Imperial armies 1941 might indeed have been described as 'the year of the Mediterranean'. British, Australian, Indian, New Zealand and South African forces were engaged in almost continuous conflict around its shores. Rommel's first offensive with the Afrika Korps opened at the end of March and drove the Western Desert Force far eastwards, isolating at Tobruk a garrison which would remain besieged throughout the year. The Desert Army had been perilously weakened, by the detachment of many of its best troops to face first the threat and then the reality of a German invasion of Greece. By the end of April Greece had been evacuated, and there followed another threat and then another reality—the German airborne assault on Crete. Crete too was evacuated, by the beginning of June. In the meantime a pro-Axis coup had occurred in Iraq at the beginning of April: this had to be dealt with, while in June the increasingly pro-German proclivities of the French in Syria forced Wavell, against his will, to intervene. It was also against his will and under Churchill's spur that in mid-June Wavell attacked the Afrika Korps in the region of Halfaya Pass—a premature and abortive operation. Then in November the desert fighting rose to a crescendo, when the newly christened Eighth Army, in the great battle called Crusader, attempted and finally achieved the relief of Tobruk—a battle which, at Sidi Rezegh, produced some of the fiercest tank actions of the North African campaign.

Only the most clear-sighted of prophets could have perceived that, nevertheless, 1941 was the year in which perhaps the two most crucial events of the world war occurred—the invasion of Russia by Germany in June and the Japanese attack on Pearl Harbour in December.

*

The turbulent year started auspiciously. On 7th February O'Connor's frail spearhead cut through the escape route of the Italian horde hurrying south from Benghazi. 'I think this may be termed a complete victory,' O'Connor wrote, 'as none of the enemy escaped.' This was a fair comment on the battle of

BEDA FOMM

For all the efforts of the previous day, the Italian column still looked huge and threatening. I watched with apprehension the movements of the mass of vehicles before me. On either side of me, hidden behind the crests of other dunes and ridges, I knew that there were other eyes just as anxious as mine, surveying the scene before them. In the mind of each one of us was the sure knowledge that we were well outnumbered. Each of us knew by what slim margin we still held dominance over the battlefield. Our threat was but a façade— behind us there were no more reserves of further troops. Even the supplies of the very sinews which could keep us going had almost run out. If we lost now we were faced with capture or a hopeless retreat into the empty distances of the inner desert. It was a sobering thought. I felt that the day, with all its black, wet dullness, was heavy with ominous foreboding. The scene before me was made gloomy enough to match my mood by the black clouds of acrid smoke which shrouded the battle-field like a brooding pall.

Gradually I became aware of a startling change. First one and then another white flag appeared in the host of vehicles. More and more became visible, until the whole column was a forest of waving white banners. Small groups of Italians started to move out hesitantly towards where they knew we lay watching them. Larger groups appeared, some on foot, some in vehicles.

Still not able to believe the evidence of his own eyes, the Colonel warned, '. . . Don't make a move. This may be a trap. Wait and see what happens. Off.'

But it was no trap. Italians of all shapes and sizes, all ranks, all regiments and all services swarmed out to be taken prisoner. I felt that nothing would ever surprise me again after my loader suddenly shouted: 'Look, sir, there's a couple of bints there coming towards us. Can I go an' grab 'em, sir? I could do with a bit of home comforts.' We took the two girls captive, installed them in a vehicle of their own and kept them for a few days to do our cooking and washing. I refrained from asking what other duties were required of the women, but noted that they remained contented and cheerful.

CYRIL JOLY

*

*The strategic emphasis now shifted, temporarily and disastrously, from
North Africa to Europe. In his telegram of congratulations the Prime
Minister indicated a new enthusiasm:*

We are delighted that you got this prize three weeks ahead of
expectation, but this does not alter, indeed it rather confirms, our
previous directive, namely that your major efforts must now be to
aid Greece and Turkey. This rules out any serious effort against
Tripoli. You should therefore make yourself secure in Benghazi and
concentrate all available forces in the Delta in preparation for a move
to Europe. . . .

*O'Connor's force was disbanded for the succour of Greece, and its place
taken by inexperienced units. Nemesis followed, in the shape of*

THE AFRIKA KORPS

On March 31st the enemy advanced to the attack. They included
the German 5th Light Armoured Division and two Italian divisions,
all under the command of a distinguished newcomer to Africa,
General Erwin Rommel. Although supported by a considerable air
force, the Axis armour at first came forward with surprising caution,
enabling the light British forces opposing it to withdraw in good
order to Agedabya. General Philip Neame, vc, who had just
assumed the command in Cyrenaica, was warned by General Wavell
that he could not expect any armoured reinforcements, and if
necessary would have to continue to fall back in the face of the
superior forces brought against him.

From that time onwards things went from bad to worse. A series
of misfortunes beset the unlucky 2nd Armoured Division, and by
April 3rd the Australians had been ordered to evacuate Benghazi.
General Neame made one attempt to establish a defensive line
between Derna and Mechili, but on April 8th a final disaster over-
took the 2nd Armoured Division at the latter place. After that only
the Australians remained to hold the enemy advance, the 9th
Division manning the western defences of Tobruk, and a single
brigade of the 7th Australian Division which had arrived the day
before from Palestine to reinforce them.

The impact of these desperate happenings first struck the 11th Hussars about midnight on April 2nd. That evening John Combe sought out Jack Leetham in the Gezireh Sporting Club to tell him that he himself had been promoted to command the 6th Cavalry Brigade in Palestine, and that Leetham was to take over the Regiment next morning. Soon afterwards, however, there came a telephone call from General Arthur Smith, the Chief of Staff at GHQ. Brigadier Combe was wanted instead for temporary duty in the desert, and was to be on the Almaza aerodrome at 7 am. The withdrawal from Benghazi had just been ordered, and the Commander-in-Chief was anxious that General Neame should have the advice of an experienced desert commander in carrying out this tricky operation. Accordingly Sir Richard O'Connor was to fly out there early in the morning, and he had asked specially for the help of John Combe, whose knowledge of the area in question was unrivalled. General Smith's message ended with the words: 'You will only be away for two or three days'.

Three days later Combe and the two generals were in the neighbourhood of Barce, where they were directing the retreat from Derna towards Tobruk. Simultaneously the 2nd Armoured Division was falling back upon Mechili, and a dangerous gap was opening along the southern flank. Unknown to Force Headquarters a fast mobile column of German troops broke through it in the course of the afternoon, and after nightfall they reached the neighbourhood of Derna.

By the very worst of bad luck the generals' car was blocked on the outskirts of Derna behind a long convoy of British transport just as the Germans arrived. A moment before John Combe had dismounted to find out what was happening ahead, and suddenly he heard un-English voices shouting instructions in the darkness. He turned uneasily to General Neame's driver. 'What the devil's that?' he asked, and the soldier with philosophical resignation replied, 'I expect it's some of them Cypriot drivers, sir.' But unhappily it was something very different, for scarcely were the words out of his mouth before the car was surrounded by Germans pointing sub-machine-guns.

Brigadier DUDLEY CLARKE, CB, CBE

*

*The military effort of the Empire now radiated from Cairo. The Expedi-
tionary Force to Greece, the need to consolidate the island of Crete, a
German presence in Cyrenaica, the threats from Vichy, Syria, and Rashid
Ali in Iraq all added to Wavell's burden.*

*In East Africa even the Italians were putting up a bloody fight, at, for
example,*

DOLOGORODOC

By now the West Yorkshires were beginning to assemble on the
saddle just below the Pimple. It had been a long sweat and for speed
they had climbed the hill in single file, dumping their cumbersome
anti-tank rifles *en route*; when the capture of Pimple was assured they
were ready to go. Meanwhile Italian reinforcements had been
scrambling up the ridge on the other side of the hill. Two companies
of the 107th Colonial Battalion, which had been sent up to Corso
Corsi on Sanchil for an attempt to recover Brig's Peak, had been
switched to Dologorodoc and soon after midnight these two fresh
companies with two other companies of Grenadiers charged down
on the features so recently occupied by the Indians. As they came on,
a steady fire from the rifles and machine-guns of the Mahrattas,
Sikhs and Dogras tore great holes in their rank, but in spite of this
the Italians pressed on with considerable determination and for a
short time it was a very close thing as to whether or not the Indians
would be overwhelmed. Suddenly, however, the attackers melted
away, leaving swathes of dead behind them, and as they ran back
the West Yorkshires were stumbling along the knife-edge ridge
towards the fort. It was tough going up the rough precipitous slopes
covered with low thorn bushes and the Yorkshiremen's progress
towards their objective was necessarily slow. Slipping and falling,
they swore profusely—making abundant use of that standard copu-
lative British Army adjective which earlier one had suggested might
well form the basis of their own battle cry. Above them loomed
their objective, looking, in the words of one reminiscence, 'like a
castle in one of Grimm's fairy tales'.

The attack was timed to take place in the half-light of dawn. After
a five-minute concentration of artillery fire on the forward slopes,
the guns were supposed to lift, then fire over the crest to bombard the

reverse slopes; when this happened it was hoped that the Yorkshire-men would be in and amongst the Italian positions and reinforce-ments rushing to the assistance of the defenders would be deterred by the wall of fire behind the ridge. Everything went more or less according to plan until the first assault wave arrived at a point about three hundred feet below the ramparts of the fort. Then, as dawn broke, the Yorkshiremen found themselves on a bare slope in full view of the enemy who could be seen hastily mounting a machine-gun less than two hundred yards away. Worse was in store. Like the Camerons, the men were wearing yellow patches on the back but from the valley below these could not be seen, and in the last few hundred feet of their climb there was the familiar whine of approach-ing shells. This was followed by a rapid succession of crashes as a salvo of shells from their own medium guns burst amongst them; the forward observation officers had taken them to be a party of Italians. Maybe this barrage provided a rearward incentive.

The steep slope which had to be climbed, and the deep ravine separating the Pimple from the fort which also had to be negotiated, had meant that the Yorkshiremen had had to advance on a one-man, one-section, one-platoon, one-company front. They were lucky in a single respect: the route they had chosen avoided and outflanked the Italian defence line which ran along the spur from the fort. In less than five minutes the West Yorkshires were through the rubble and dust of the recent bombardment, over the top of the fort's parapet and in amongst its defenders. By half past six the fort was theirs; inside it the Italians were much too shaken to put up any effective resistance. Yet there were few prisoners, only forty Eritreans and a medical officer were captured and the remainder of the garrison got away down the far side of the hill, the last of them being hotly pursued by the triumphant Yorkshiremen. The objective had been taken; success or failure now depended on whether it was possible to hold on to it. Clearly this was not going to be any sinecure and even as the West Yorkshires started to consolidate their positions, mortar bombs began to rain down on them. Their dull crumps signalled the start of an intense barrage which heralded the first taste of what it was going to be like to hold a position exposed to obser-vation from three sides and which the Italians knew was vital ground.

Contrary to what its name suggests, there was nothing significantly

'Beau Geste' about 'Fort' Dologorodoc; all it comprised was a trench circling the top of the hill enclosing an area of about an acre. The sides and redoubts of the trench had been concreted; the entrances to the few shelters which were of any use all faced in the wrong direction now and, like everywhere else, the rocky surface of the plateau permitted no digging. For its occupants under fire, the noise of exploding shells reverberating amongst the horseshoe of rock-covered hills was deafening, from which there was no respite. If this were not enough to send men crazy, there were the machine-guns which raked the top of the hill from a ridge below Mount Zeban; whilst from Sanchil and Falestoh watchful snipers waited for opportunities to pick off any luckless individual rash enough to raise his head above the parapet of the trenches. But this was only the background scene. With his line seriously dented, it was only to be expected that Carnimeo would react violently and try to recapture Dologorodoc without delay; and he did. Attack after attack was launched from Zeban. Some, which were caught by the British artillery as they formed up, never really got under way; others which did were rolled back and mowed down at point-blank range before they got up to the fort. All of them resulted in frightful losses to the Italians. Casualties amongst the West Yorkshires were also heavy, though small when compared with those of the Grenadiers and Eritreans, whose corpses piling up below the fort bore testimony to the violence and determination of the attacks. On top of the hill there was no way of disposing of the British dead other than to wait for darkness and then toss the bodies over the parapet where they joined those of their former enemies. As the days passed a sickly stench and hordes of sleek, black flies hung with ever-increasing intensity over the region and for weeks afterwards it was said that to drive past Dologorodoc was to be reminded of the approach to the tanneries outside Alexandria.

A. J. BARKER

*

The Germans attacked Greece on 8th April. Within a week Middle East HQ was drawing up plans for its evacuation. Three weeks to the day, and the German victory was complete.

GRECIAN BLITZ

For two days I have been bombed, machine-gunned, and shot at by all and sundry. German Stukas have blown two cars from under me and strafed a third . . . all day and all night there have been waves of Germans in the skies. Eighteen Messerschmidts strafed us on the road last evening. Bullets ripped the trucks and one was destroyed, but nothing was lost except the truck. Before that, the convoy I was in was attacked seven times in two hours, but not once was the convoy disorganised or broken up. The Germans are using a fantastic amount of aircraft, more than I ever saw in Norway under similar conditions of terrain. Goering must have a third of his air force operating here and it is bombing every nook and cranny, hamlet, village and town in its path. . . .

An Australian correspondent in *The Times*, 19th April 1914

During the retreat the Engineers had a desperate task, blocking roads, blowing bridges, improvising all the time. A New Zealander describes a remarkable piece of ingenuity—a road destroyed by

DEPTH-CHARGE

General Freyberg told me it was essential to blow the road somehow, because the Germans had landed light tanks by sea or air, and we had no guns left to take them on. My immediate resources for the job consisted of ten plugs of gelly, a tin of detonators, and a few feet of safety-fuze, which always travelled in the Humber mixed up with tools, loot, and sometimes beer. Engineers there were none, other than my car crew. However, a small party of Div. Cav. reinforcements produced six amateur explosive 'experts' headed by two fellow Hawkes Bay pirates—Sergeant Donnelly and Mike Murphy. Piled into a fifteen-hundredweight truck, they joined me in the search for the wherewithal to blow. When in doubt look for the Navy—and depth charges. I located an Admiral walking round an olive tree, carefully keeping it between him and a rather inquisitive Hun bomber; he agreed that if a destroyer came in that night, it would gladly give me a brace of charges. He 'made a signal', and that was that.

He also told me that the rear party of Force Headquarters, including General Maitland Wilson, would be leaving after dark in a Sunderland, abandoning most of their kit and their cars. Scenting loot, I pushed Doc Macfarlane off hot-foot for the beach at Monemvasia, another hundred miles on, and took my gang down to Miloi pier, where an RAF tender waited for the flying-boat. That tender carried two items of precious cargo; first and most valuable from my angle, a nice depth charge; second and very easy to the eye, two British nursing sisters, salvaged off a beach near Athens and nattily dressed in RAF shirts and shorts. These two stout lasses—the adjective refers to their spirit—manned the two forward twin-Lewis guns against at least one Stuka raid.

Keeping our minds and activities strictly to duty, we extracted the depth charge, rolled it up planks into the truck, then sat back to see Force Headquarters evacuated—a most interesting spectacle. As the light went, the Sunderland crept round the far headland at nought feet to make a perfect landing, perfectly timed. Then a motley collection from Generals to batmen spilled out of various vehicles on to the jetty and prepared to depart. Limited to one suitcase each, great men, accustomed to settle the lives and destinies of thousands by quick snappy decisions, rummaged over masses of kit, trying to decide what should be jettisoned. Having already taken similar action back at Thermopylae, we stood round sardonic-like and vulturish, waiting for the pickings. A pathetic sight. They took so long and fussed so much that finally the skipper of the Sunderland climbed on to a bollard and roared out, 'Gentlemen! If you don't make up your bloody minds and get aboard the tender, I'm leaving in ten minutes' time, otherwise we'll be shot down in daylight tomorrow morning. For God's sake, make it snappy.' Nobody arrested him and they made it snappy. Within five minutes sixty of them were aboard and away. Not many minutes later we had transferred our gear into a sleek Humber-Pullman and gladly jettisoned an historic, battered Utility, veteran of two campaigns. The transfer included four tins of an excellent brand of smoking mixture and two boxes of good cigars which the late, unknown owner had left behind, doubtless with regret. Lounging back puffing easily at our newest acquisitions, we thoroughly enjoyed life as Mac swung us round the winding hill road, which seemed fairly clear of traffic except for waifs and strays from various oddments. We were still using the Greek Automobile Association red-and-yellow map which had guided us up Greece seven eventful weeks earlier.

Brigadier GEORGE CLIFTON, DSO, MC

*

But no amount of nonchalance could now save the Expeditionary Force. It suffered a decisive defeat. Clifton got more depth-charges from his destroyer and neatly blew his road: but the next stop for the New Zealanders was

CRETE

The morning of 20 May was calm and cloudless, as was every day during the battle. Before the sunlight had reached the valleys the German reconnaissance plane appeared. Shortly afterwards a fighter arrived and started to roar up and down the main street of Galatos firing bursts at anything it could see. This struck me as a bit unusual so I hurriedly finished shaving and looked with some caution out of my first-floor window. Other fighters were swooping over the Canea road and there was a great deal of noise from aeroplane engines. Nothing appeared imminent, however, so I finished dressing and went down for breakfast under the trees outside. The plane was still tearing up and down the street and maybe the cooks were bustled, for the porridge was mere oatmeal and water. I was grumbling about this when someone gave an exclamation that might have been an oath or a prayer or both. Almost over our heads were four gliders, the first we had ever seen, in their silence inexpressibly menacing and frightening. Northwards was a growing thunder. I shouted: 'Stand to your arms!', and ran upstairs for my rifle and binoculars. I noticed my diary lying open on the table. Four years later it was returned to me, having meanwhile been concealed by some Cretan girl.

When I reached the courtyard again the thunder had become deafening, the troop-carriers were passing low overhead in every direction one looked, not more than 400 feet up, in scores. As I ran down the Prison road to my battle headquarters the parachutists were dropping out over the valley, hundreds of them, and floating quietly down. Some were spilling out over our positions and there was a growing crackle of rifle-fire. I pelted down the road, outpacing the two signallers who had started with me, and scrambled up the steep track to the battle post, a pink house on a little knoll east of the road. As I panted through the gap in the cactus hedge there was a startling burst of fire fairly in my face, cutting the cactus on either side of me. I jumped sideways, twisting my ankle, and rolled down the bank. After whimpering a little, I crawled up the track and into the house, and saw my man through the window. Then I hopped out again, hopped around the back and, in what seemed to me a nice bit of minor tactics, stalked him round the side of the house and shot him cleanly through the head at ten yards.

Major-General SIR HOWARD KIPPENBERGER, KBE, CB, DSO, ED

During the early stages the Germans by no means had it all their own way. Many of their gliders and transport planes (with contents) were destroyed, and their parachutists were shot in the air or as soon as they reached the ground. At Heraklion, for example, Bofors anti-aircraft guns had a good bag.

If ever there was a fillip to morale, this was it. These guns which we had seen battered twice a day for the past two days were not out of action but merely waited patiently for their target, and there it was sitting on the end of their barrel. The sound of these guns put life into us and we cheered. We had only to wait a short time before one Junkers was hit just as it was about to disgorge its load. It crashed. Perhaps the death of those parachutists was preferable to the death suffered by those who came down with their parachutes on fire, going faster and faster as they neared the earth, only to be followed up by our platoons as they landed. One had the misfortune to land on top of company headquarters as we lay concealed within some standing corn. He drifted slowly to earth as I watched. When he was about ten feet from the ground seven or eight Tigers, each with a bayonet fixed, rose and approached him. That was the first time that I heard a man scream with fear.

Major A. W. D. NICHOLLS

The village from which Kippenberger watched the Germans' arrival was
captured in due course, and he had to put in an urgent counter-attack with
whatever lay to hand on

GALATOS

Two ancient Mark VI tanks of the 3rd Hussars came up the road.
Farran stopped and spoke to me and I told him to go into the village
and see what was there. He clattered off and we could hear him
firing briskly, when two more companies of the Twenty-third
arrived, C and D, under Harvey and Manson, each about eighty
strong. They halted on the road near me. The men looked tired, but
fit to fight and resolute. It was no use trying to patch the line any
more; obviously we must hit or everything would crumble away.
I told the two company commanders that they would have to retake
Galatos with the help of the two tanks. No, there was no time for
reconnaissance; they must move straight in up the road, one company either side in single file behind the tanks, and take everything
with them. Stragglers and walking wounded were still streaming
past. Some stopped to join in as did Carson and the last four of his
party. The men fixed bayonets, and waited grimly. One of the
platoon commanders, Connolly, came up and gave me a photograph
of my wife and family which he had brought from New Zealand.

Farran came back with his two tanks and put his head out of the
turret. 'The place is stiff with Jerries,' he said. I told him that I had
two companies of infantry; would he go in again with them?
Certainly he would, but he had a driver and a gunner wounded;
could they be replaced? I turned to a party of Sappers who had just
arrived and asked for volunteers. Two men, one named Lewis,
immediately volunteered, the wounded men were dragged out, and
they clambered aboard. I told Farran to take them down the road to
give them a ten minutes' course of instruction and that we would
attack as soon as he came back. My batman went off to John Gray
with a message that we were counter-attacking and an order to
join in.

We waited another ten minutes, the air filled with noise and
tracer crackling incessantly overhead—and then Farran came
rattling back. He stopped and we spoke for a moment. I said the

infantry would follow him, and he was not to go farther than the village square: 'Now get going.' He yelled to the second tank to follow him, pulled the turret lid down, and set off. The infantry followed at a walk, then broke into a run, started shouting—and running and shouting disappeared into the village. Instantly there was the most startling clamour, audible all over the field. Scores of automatics and rifles being fired at once, the crunch of grenades, screams and yells—the uproar swelled and sank, swelled again to a terrifying crescendo. Some women and children came scurrying down the road; one old woman frantic with fear clung desperately to me. The firing slackened, became a brisk clatter, steadily became more distant, and stopped. The counter-attack had succeeded, it was nearly dark, and the battlefield suddenly became silent.

Major-General SIR HOWARD KIPPENBERGER

As in Greece, sheer gallantry was not enough; all too soon the dismal retreat to the southern shore of the island began, over cruel mountains by rough paths to the little beaches from which the evacuation was effected. A medical officer describes the last stages of the journey, through

SPHAKIA

It was an eerie experience as we groped our way along the streets of that murdered and deserted village, skirting huge bomb craters or clambering over masses of rubble and smashed brick-work. Every now and then the men in front would come to a sudden halt, and then the whole column would stand stock-still for several long minutes before moving on again. Now that deliverance seemed so near, everybody's nerves were on edge; people were cursing and swearing at each other at the slightest provocation in venomous whispers. I wondered—and others, no doubt, were thinking along the same lines—if something would not happen at the very last moment to prevent us getting away. I wondered too if enemy planes might not suddenly pounce down on us and start their usual bombing and machine-gunning. Each time the column stopped, I wondered if some hitch had occurred, and if we were going to be told that the ships would not come for us after all. Yet, in a way, I did not feel things anywhere near as keenly as I would have done normally; I was so exhausted that I lived in a kind of daze, rather as if I were following the doings of someone else in a cinema film. As a matter of fact, to me the one concrete and all-pervading reality was the pain in my feet. . . . At last after many delays, we neared the beach, and I could make out the shadowy outlines of several ships looming faintly through the night some distance from the land. Smaller craft flitted about in the darkness, and crowds of soldiers and sailors jostled each other on the shore. From time to time a pale light flashed out at sea and was answered by another light from the water's edge. Finally we were on the beach and moving along a rough jetty with sailors all around us; the next moment, though I cannot remember how, we were filing aboard an iron self-propelled invasion-barge manned by several officers and ratings. What struck me most when we set foot on the barge was the efficiency of everything. We seemed to have been translated to another world where everything was more civilised, trimmer, cleaner, better run—even the officers' uniforms were neat. Orders were given in a calm, matter-of-fact manner, there was brightly polished machinery around us and a bell which clanged to the engine-room with a very reassuring sound. Everyone relaxed almost instantaneously. . . . Once more the unanimous refrain was on everybody's lips, 'Thank God for the Navy'.

CAPTAIN STEPHANIDES

*

During the week in which Rommel attacked in the desert, and the Germans invaded Greece, Rashid Ali in Baghdad made a coup. The Axis was pressing him for co-operation. Imperial troops acted with vigour, and at the end of May Rashid fled and a pro-British Prime Minister was installed. In Syria the Vichy French were also aiding the enemy: during the last three weeks of May some hundred German and twenty Italian planes had the use of Syrian aerodromes. This was intolerable. The British reacted— successfully in the end—but the French fought back.

STRAFED

The next morning, just after stand-down, idly glancing up from some paper work, I saw a Hurricane approaching low across the desert—another, another. . . . There weren't that many Hurricanes east of Suez! I leaped for a trench, blowing my whistle.

They were French Morane fighters, tearing in at 300 miles an hour, twenty feet above the desert, six of them in line ahead. All round the whistle went, men dived for cover. The lead plane opened fire when almost directly over me and I heard a multi-gun fighter, close to, for the first time. It is not a long-drawn sound, like a machine-gun's, which can at a pinch be represented by ratatatatatatat. The guns have a rate of fire of 1,300 rounds a minute each, as against 650 for the ground gun, and there are six or eight of them. The sound of this weapon firing at you is a single enormously loud CRRRRRRUMP, and in those two seconds three hundred bullets have crashed by. The sound hangs in the air behind the plane, and if you are watching it closely as it fires you can see it check momentarily in mid-air, while grey smoke flickers along the leading edge of the wing. Then, as it pulls up its nose to climb away the hail of empty cases and brass links falls out of the wings, but are only seen if the light is at the right angle. CRRRRRRUMP.

By now two Bren guns were at them—four, five, six—twenty. The racket grew to formidable dimensions. The Moranes went for the armoured cars dispersed along the river and in the orchards the other side of the town. The armoured cars fired back with their turret machine-guns. Everyone fired. As each Morane finished his first attack it turned its nose straight to the sky and climbed away under full power. At about fifteen hundred feet they fanned out right, left, right, left alternately, and swooped down in six different, lovely parabolas to attack again. It was beautiful, and a good target, so it deserved the attention it got. Converging streams of tracer from all over Raqqa formed a tent over my head, the apex around the plane that was nearing the top of its power climb. CRRRRRRUMP! The ground a hundred yards from me boiled momentarily and was still. CRRRRRRUMP! 'Shirley' Temple was bathing in the river, his revolver strapped round his naked body. He danced about in the shallows, firing at them, but they ignored him.

They vanished. We listened cautiously, the sentries scanning the air, everyone else busy refilling magazines. Time for breakfast.

JOHN MASTERS

FRATERNISATION

The day after the signing of the Armistice we were at an outpost. Everything beyond the occupied area was out of bounds. However, someone said there was a river on the other side of the mountain, and we were badly in need of a wash, so Pete McGowan and I decided to take a risk. In case there were any fish we took a couple of hand grenades.

About two hours' mountaineering brought us into a little township. On the corner as we entered was a chemist's shop, and as we passed the chemist greeted us with 'Bonjour, Messieurs!' We shook hands, Pete keeping one hand on his grenade (just in case) and by signs the chemist indicated that he wanted us to have a cup of coffee. Meanwhile, he sent a number of men out on messages, and in a few seconds the shop was full, and two or three hundred people had gathered outside. Pete was quite sure we were in a trap, when the crowd parted and a number of fellows whose deportment marked them as notable came in.

The foremost spoke in English, and told us that although Syrian by birth, he was an American citizen. He also told us that Machgarah was a Syrian township, and that eighty per cent of the people were British sympathisers. He assumed that we were Australian officers (as we were the first British troops to enter the town) and had come to see the place before occupying it.

Our Yankee friend introduced us to the Mayor, the town councillors, the priest, and two doctors. They then hurried us away to the police station. Here fourteen gendarmes formed a guard of honour. At the door we were welcomed by the Commissioner or Chief of Police. Presently, accompanied by the Commissioner and the Mayor, we toured the town. The streets were lined with people, who cheered and waved. Then we inspected a number of houses damaged by our artillery, and assured the owners that they'd get a good hearing when the place had been occupied.

During our tour quite a number of them asked us for permits to visit other towns in the war zone, and we told them it was not safe just then, but arrangements would be made as soon as possible. In the afternoon we were invited to a function welcoming home a prominent citizen, who had been imprisoned for British sympathies at the outbreak of the show.

As we entered the door someone said, '*Les Capitaines,*' and everyone stood up until we had taken the seats of honour. We listened to numerous speeches, drank arak and more coffee,—and through the interpreter made our good-byes, the Mayor asking that we bring our troops as soon as possible.

It would have been just too bad if an officer had arrived while we were there. As it was, we got our ears chewed a bit when we got back.

MAX HICKMAN

*

While the Australians helped to subdue the French in Syria their compatriots were bearing the lion's share of the defence of Tobruk, and adding to army lore:

TOBRUK

This bloody town's a bloody cuss,
No bloody trams, no bloody bus,
And no one cares for bloody us.
Oh bloody! Bloody! Bloody!
No bloody sports, no bloody games,
No bloody fun with bloody dames,
This place gives me a bloody pain,
Oh bloody! Bloody! Bloody!
All bloody fleas, no bloody beer,
No bloody booze since we've been here,
And will it come? No bloody fear,
Oh bloody! Bloody! Bloody!
The bloody rumours make me smile,
The bloody wogs are bloody vile,
The bloody Tommies cramp your style,
Oh bloody! Bloody! Bloody!
All bloody dust, no bloody rain,
All bloody fighting since we came,

This army's just a bloody shame.
Oh bloody! Bloody! Bloody!
The bully makes me bloody wild,
I'd nearly eat a bloody child,
The salty water makes me riled.
Oh bloody! Bloody! Bloody!
Air raids all day and bloody night,
Huns striving with all bloody might,
They give us all a bloody fright.
Oh bloody! Bloody! Bloody!
Best bloody place is bloody bed,
With blanket over bloody head.
And then they think you're bloody dead.
Oh bloody! Bloody! Bloody!

HUGH PATTERSON

*

The four months' campaign which destroyed the Italian colonial empire in East Africa eliminated a quarter of a million men and freed a million square miles. One casualty was Orde Wingate, to become famous later for his Chindit operations behind the Japanese lines in Burma. In Ethiopia he had also performed brilliantly behind the enemy lines. Now he was back in Cairo, ignored, over-wrought, ill, and suffering from fantasies induced by the over-large doses of drugs he was mistakenly taking. A devastating despair led him to attempt

SUICIDE

At three o'clock in the afternoon of July 4th he took his temperature and read that it was standing at 104 degrees. He had no more atabrin left. He got out of bed, made his way downstairs and out into the street, and tried to walk to the doctor's house. He could not find it although he had been there more than once. He became terrified. He now believed that his loss of memory was the beginning of madness. In his weakness he had to hold on to the walls as he made his way back to the hotel. In his confusion and despair he had now made up his mind.

In the bedroom corridor he found the floor-waiter who used to bring him meals. He said something to him, thanking him for his services. The waiter noticed something odd in his behaviour, followed him to the door and waited outside it. Wingate wanted to lock the door, but feared to increase the waiter's suspicions, so he half-locked it and waited till the man had gone. Then he took out his pistol and saw that it had not been cleaned for a long time and was still choked with Ethiopian sand. It was empty and he could not find the ammunition. (In fact Akavia had forgotten to pack it when Wingate left Addis Ababa.) He put the pistol away and took out a hunting-knife which a friend had given him. He went to the mirror above the wash-basin. He held the knife in his right hand and thrust into the left side of his neck. He found the effort of cutting through greater than he had guessed. He saw he must try again and suddenly remembered that the door was not locked. With the knife still in his neck, and drenching blood from the wound he went to the door and locked it, went back to the mirror, plucked out the knife, and taking it in his left hand, thrust with all his force at the jugular vein on the right, then fell unconscious on the floor.

He would have died within the hour, but rescue came quickly. In the next room Colonel Thornhill was enjoying a siesta. He heard unusual sounds through the wall. They gave him an idea (though there was no shout or cry) that something untoward was happening. He decided he had better look into it. He gave his reasons afterwards. He said: 'When I hear a feller lock a door, I don't think anything about it, and if I hear a feller fall down, that's his affair, but when I hear a feller lock his door and then fall down—it's time for action.' He pulled on his clothes quickly, went out into the corridor and knocked on the door. There was no sound that he could hear. He shook the handle and pushed. He ran to the lift, went down, rushed to the manager's office for the master key. He and the manager and others ran back, swept up the corridor, and forced the door because the key was in. As they burst in, Wingate came back to partial consciousness. He remembered after that it seemed to him that he was dead and in hell.

CHRISTOPHER SYKES

*

*Throughout these months convoys sailed continuously, across the Atlantic,
round the Cape, and even, daringly, down the Mediterranean to bring
troops, equipment and supplies to the Egyptian base. There were the
inevitable sinkings.*

ONE TRANSPORT LOST

Where, packed as tight as space can fit them
The soldiers retch, and snore, and stink,
It was no bunch of flowers that hit them
And woke them up, that night, to drink.
Dashing the bulkheads red with slaughter,
In the steep wash that swept the hold,
Men, corpses, kitbags, blood, and water,
Colliding and commingling rolled.
Some clung, like flies, in fear and wonder,
Clutched to the cross-beams, out of reach,
Till sprayed from thence by jets of thunder
That spouted rumbling from the breach.
In this new world of blast and suction,
The bulkhead tilted to a roof;
Friend aided friend—but to destruction,
And valour seemed its own reproof.
Forced by the pent explosive airs
In the huge death-grasp of its shell,
Or sucked, like Jonah, by their prayers
From forth that spiracle of Hell—
The ones that catapulted from it
Saw the whole hull reverse its dome,
Then ram the depths, like some huge comet,
Flood-lit with phosphorus and foam.
The shark and grampus might reprieve,
After their jaunt upon a raft,
The few that got Survivors' Leave—
But those who perished would have laughed! . . .

ROY CAMPBELL (who served in the ranks in East
and North Africa until he was disabled and took
his discharge with the rank of sergeant)

IT'S A HONEY, SIR

We regarded the advent of our new tanks with a good deal more vital interest than a newly-married couple inspecting their first home. We were also fascinated by the group of American Army technicians who came with them.

The Stuart was a strange-looking contraption, straight from Texas, tall in the saddle and with the Western flavour accentuated by a couple of Browning machine-guns and the rangy Texans. The main armament was similar to the pea-shooter that all British tanks carried at this time, but the frontal armour was much thicker than in our own light tanks and cruisers. The really intriguing things about the M3 were its engine and the tracks. Drivers gasped in astonishment when the back covers were lifted off . . . it was simply an aeroplane engine stuck in a tank, with radial cylinders and a fan that looked like a propeller. Fuel was to present a new problem to the supply services, as the engine ran efficiently only on high octane aviation spirit. But this was not our problem, and the consensus of opinion was that anything that was likely to assist in a fast take-off was probably a good thing.

After the engines had received their share of comment, we gave our undivided attention to the tracks. There had never been anything like them in the British Army. Each track link was mounted in solid rubber blocks on which the vehicles moved. After one look we wondered why the hell British tank designers had never thought of it.

As soon as I could, I got my crew into one of the Stuarts and headed out of Heliopolis for the first patch of open, sandy desert— not always as easy to find as you might think. We tested her for speed first, and found that on good going we could get up to 40 mph. It was a comforting thought, in the circumstances, to know that the German Marks III and IV could manage only 20 or so.

Then I told my driver, Whaley, to make a few fast turns, and waited with some foreboding for the inevitable bang-clatter and swerving halt that meant a broken track. Nothing happened. It was wonderful. That tank handled like a well-trained cow-pony.

'Let's see just what it will take,' I said down the intercom. 'Try and shed one of these tracks.'

Whaley put her through a variety of turns and manœuvres that made the sandy floor of the desert look like an ice-rink after a hockey match, spurting up great fountains of sand and dust behind the tracks.

'That'll do,' I shouted to the driver at last. 'We're beginning to wear out the desert.'

Back at the camp the CO and a small crowd were waiting for us. We climbed out, all grinning happily.

'Well, Whaley,' I asked my driver, 'what do you think of it?'

He, plainly under the influence of the nearby Texan, beamed and said simply: 'It's a honey, sir.'

From that moment they were never known as anything else.

ROBERT CRISP, DSO, MC

*

Me—no likee English sold-ier,
Yank-ee soldier come ashore;
Yank-ee soldier plenty mon-ey,
Me—no jigajig for you no more.

Song of the girls of Lagos

*

While the convoys flowed, training proceeded unremittingly in the Home Forces, and throughout the Empire, as more men were enrolled and more divisions formed. Strange new 'irregular' units were also burgeoning. Michael Calvert (later to lead with distinction one of Wingate's columns in Burma) was sent from England to a wild spot on the southern tip of Australia to set up a school for commando-type training. Then he was posted to Burma.

What we were doing in Maymyo was, of course, very unneutral. The name Bush Warfare School was in itself a deception. We were not preparing people to fight in the Burma jungle; our task was to train officers and NCOs to lead guerillas in the plains of China, a very different type of warfare. But, in view of our on-the-surface impartiality in the Japanese-Chinese conflict, we could hardly give the mission its proper title, which would have been something like China Gucrilla Training School.

The school was split for training purposes into cadres known as 'commandos', to confuse the situation even more. This deception was also part of the deliberate policy, but unfortunately it ultimately deceived many of our own people as well as the Japs. When the Jap war finally began the school was criticised—by General Alexander, among others, who took over as C-in-C Burma at the time of the retreat—for not having done its job of training commando troops to fight in the Burma jungle! As we had never set out to do this the criticisms made us extremely angry, but events were moving so rapidly that there was no time to explain the position and we just had to accept it philosophically.

MICHAEL CALVERT, DSO, MC

In North Africa, too, a special body had been formed—the Long Range Desert Group—to penetrate in small units deep into enemy territory and radio back information about troop movements, Axis tank strengths and so on; to explore possible routes for a British advance; and to deliver intelligence agents and saboteurs to their appointed places. When disaster struck, it was no easy matter for survivors of a LRDG patrol to return home. A corporal of the Wilts Yeomanry was captured at Mechili in Rommel's first attack, escaped with three Australians, and trudged cautiously eastwards:

By midday on the 25th we were halted by another camp, right on the coast, but could not pass it till late afternoon when the men had finished swimming. After we had got by and walked on for a bit we decided to find some cover and try to sleep for the rest of the night. We made an early start next morning, passing several German camps in the semi-darkness, but once again we were halted by another camp at midday. These continual halts had been a great strain on our water and that afternoon I shared my last drop with Alfred, although at first he refused to take any, saying that he ought to have been more careful with his own. We decided that as soon as it was dark one of us would have to try and get water from the camp. The lot fell to me, so taking off what remained of my boots, I wrapped my feet in rags so as to make no noise on the rocky ground. Leaving the other three on the shore I managed to reach one of the trucks without being seen, and had just spotted a couple of likely tins when a German popped his head round the corner and no doubt said in his own language, 'What the hell are you doing?' I did not wait to tell him but beat it for the shore as fast as I could with the German in full cry after me. In the dark I missed the others so could only make my way along the beach and hope that they would catch me up later on. Meanwhile the German's yells had roused the whole camp. Men were shouting and dogs barking and rifles being let off. Gradually the whole noise died away as I got further off, and when I was out of earshot I flopped down on the sand, absolutely dead beat. I stayed here some time, hoping the others would catch me up, but at last I gave it up and staggered off along the coast. The rags had fallen off in the mad rush and my feet were cut to ribbons on the sharp stones. To keep myself going I had to roll constantly in the sea which made me cold and wet and forced me to keep walking to get warm again. Later on I was lucky to run into an Arab camp. I woke up an Arab who gave me a piece of stale bread and filled my water bottle. Again I made the mistake of drinking too much and was doubled up with pains in the stomach for the rest of the night. . . .

Sometimes I wandered up and down the *wadi* beds with the crazy idea that I might find water. I found a cactus and breaking off one of the leaves pulped it between two stones and sucked it. It tasted bitter and made my mouth and throat terribly sore, but it did ease my thirst a bit. I crawled out of this *wadi* only to find myself on top of another one. Slowly I crawled to the bottom and began to walk across the beach. Suddenly I dropped flat by sheer instinct; in front of me were rows of barbed wire. I lay still but nothing happened, so I slowly crawled up to it and still there was nothing to be seen or heard. It did not penetrate my muddled brain that I had reached the British front line.

Corporal A. H. CAVE, MM

Back in England the Special Operations Executive, or SOE, had by now set up a network of communications with Resistance movements in the occupied territories of Europe, and was expanding its secret activities to other parts of the world. A senior officer returned from a trip to Tehran to obtain from the Persians a powerful radio transmitter for SOE purposes. When he got back to London he found that

Astonishing progress had been made since I had left for the Middle East in the summer. We were now in close and constant touch by wireless with the nucleus of resistance organisations in Norway, Holland, Belgium and France, as well as in Poland and Czechoslovakia. There was a number of sections, each dealing with activities in these and other countries in the west such as Denmark and Germany, where it had not yet been possible to create anything on the ground. Each of them now had its own schools for physical toughening, sabotage and para-military training, designed so far as possible to prevent potential saboteurs destined for one country from meeting their colleagues destined for another. This they occasionally did when the time came for them to learn how to operate a wireless set, if this was to be their job. They could not be prevented from seeing one another either at the parachute school at Ringway or at the school for agents' work at Beaulieu in Hampshire. Here they learnt about secret inks, ciphering, lock-picking, underground propaganda, and similar requirements of our work.

BICKHAM SWEET-ESCOTT

*

During October the New Zealand Division was back in the Nile Delta. One day the following message was received by Kippenberger:

Headquarters,
Southern Inf. Trg. Depot,
18th October 1941

Memorandum for:
Headquarters,
20th Battalion,
2nd NZEF

HONOURS & AWARDS

Reference our communication 11/1/4630 dated 15th October 1941, for 2nd Lieut. Upham read 2nd Lieut. Upham and Sergeant J. D. Hinton. It would be a convenience to this Headquarters if in future the names of members of the Twentieth Battalion who win Victoria

Crosses were published in one list and not on different days as appears to be the present practice.

Sgd. J. T. BURROWS
Lieut.-Colonel

*

THE DJEBEL STAKES

Yearly we've ridden the Djebel Stakes,
Yearly fought back on our course,
Yearly we've made the same silly mistakes,
Over-ridden a failing horse,
At a fence too stiff for his strength to leap,
With a rotten take-off, unfirm, too steep,
Heavily breasted the top of the bank,
Pawed, gasped and struggled, then hopelessly sank,
Shocked, hurt and surprised at the toss we took—
Rolling back adown the ditch at Tobruk.

The Djebel Stakes were now on again, and this time the horse would not fail. General Auchinleck, who had relieved Wavell, sent General Cunningham and the newly named Eighth Army on their way to the west, with 'the ditch at Tobruk' and its beleaguered garrison for a target, in Operation Crusader, as it was called. The first moves were made on 18th November, nicely anticipating the offensive which Rommel had been planning. The battle was prolonged and infinitely complicated: the most violent fighting occurred south of Tobruk on and around the airfield at Sidi Rezegh. Kippenberger describes an episode during the earlier stages of the advance:

I returned to find the battalion formed up and the tanks passing through. They did not check, charged on at about fifteen miles an hour on a bearing more like seventy degrees than the prescribed forty, spotted our carriers moving out of the way to the right flank, opened fire and knocked out two of them, one bursting into flames, and carried madly on. Things happened very quickly. Through the control tank I yelled to the tanks to get on the right bearing but without result. The infantry trucks leapt forward, keeping stubbornly to the correct bearing and steadily increasing speed. The guns opened, unluckily on the wrong target, a newly appeared mass of transport miles farther away. The machine-gun platoon had got well forward and came briskly into action, as did the carriers. So did the enemy, with guns, mortars and automatics. The tanks saw the enemy and swung into their correct course, slackened speed, and opened fire. Several were hit and blazed up, others stopped. Rhodes and I had followed up in a carrier and we stopped to speak to the control tank, sheltering in its lee from a hail of bullets. The tank commander called me and said: 'I've had seven tanks hit; I'll have to stop.' I had just seen the leading companies debus and advance, one steadily and nicely spaced, the other in rushes and evidently under fire. I replied: 'The infantry are attacking; go on or I'll court-martial you.' This was unfair to a very gallant officer, killed a few days later, but it was no time for politeness. The tanks went on slowly, firing fast, but the infantry passed through them and closed swiftly and savagely. I passed through the empty trucks coming back to get out of range and found that the fight was over. Most of the enemy transport had got away but about a dozen trucks were abandoned and we had captured three 88s with their crews all dead, except one slightly wounded man whom we picked up.

Major-General SIR HOWARD KIPPENBERGER

ARISTOCRATS

'I think I am becoming a God'

The noble horse with courage in his eye
clean in the bone, looks up at a shellburst:
away fly the images of the shires
and he puts the pipe back in his mouth.
Peter was unfortunately killed by an 88:
it took his leg away, he died in the ambulance.
I saw him crawling on the sand; he said:
It's most unfair, they've shot my foot off.
How can I live among this gentle
obsolescent breed of heroes, and not weep?
Unicorns, almost,
for they are falling into two legends

in which their stupidity and chivalry
are celebrated. Each, fool and hero, will be an immortal.
These plains were their cricket pitch
and in the mountains the tremendous drop fences
brought down some of the runners. Here then
under the stones and earth they dispose themselves,
I think with their famous unconcern.
It is not gunfire I hear but a hunting horn.

(Keith Douglas composed this poem in Tunisia in 1943; but it is a universal epitaph for the many gallant follies of the British armour—and the gallant victories. Douglas served in North Africa from 1941 to 1943. He was killed on his third day in Normandy, at the age of twenty-four.)

For bravery during Crusader—and specially at Sidi Rezegh—many men were awarded decorations and many earned decorations not awarded. Let two actions stand for them all: first, the one in which Ward Gunn of the Royal Horse Artillery earned a posthumous VC. The scene is Sidi Rezegh and the German armour is thrusting.

Five Crusader tanks were sent over. These were set on fire before they could get near enough to engage the enemy with their 2-pounders. Two of the vehicles of battalion headquarters—and the Adjutant's best hat—were soon in flames. Corporal Warner of the signal section jumped into the third, started it up and drove it to safety without being put out of action—one of the unaccountable miracles of this desperate battle. The enemy tanks were now being engaged by the 25-pounders of 60th Field Regiment and some guns of 4th RHA which had come into action behind them. Apart from these, unsuitable but brilliantly fought, there were three weapons capable of taking on the enemy tanks—two 2-pounders under Ward Gunn (3rd RHA) and one Bofors anti-aircraft gun commanded by Pat McSwiney. These three engaged the enemy as best they could, outranged and unarmoured as they were. The Bofors fired self-destroying 40-mm anti-aircraft ammunition and, though it had the range, its effect on the Mark III and IV tanks was not decisive.

The small party round the blazing pick-ups watched these three guns firing away at the enemy, watched the crews, completely composed, completely undaunted, picked off one by one. The enemy gave everything they had: machine-gun fire from the tanks and the supporting infantry, mortars, shells from the Mark IVs and the field guns. One 2-pounder was destroyed; the Bofors was set on fire. All the crew of the remaining gun were either killed or wounded, and the driver not unnaturally began to drive it out of the battle. Ward Gunn, at battalion headquarters, was joined at that moment by Bernard Pinney, the commander of 'M' Battery 3rd RHA. He said to Ward: 'Go and stop that blighter!' and even then it seemed hard to be so described for driving a useless gun and a dead crew out of action. Ward immediately ran out and stopped him and, together, they dragged the bodies off the portée and got the gun into action, Bernard Pinney joining in. No one could gauge the effect of his fire, because to look over the edge of a slit trench was suicidal. Dick Basset had already been wounded in the head and Tom Bird in the heel. A little dog was running round from trench to trench, trying hard to find its master and being distressingly friendly to each person in turn—distressingly because its movements attracted a hail of machine-gun fire. The Germans concentrated their fire on the burning vehicles of battalion headquarters and the one remaining gun. But at least the two nearest enemy tanks were blazing.

In a matter of seconds the portée was on fire, the offside front wheel had been hit, and the tyre was blazing; two boxes of ammunition held in brackets behind the passenger seat were also in flames. Pinney took the Pyrene fire extinguisher and got the fire in the tyre under control; but the ammunition boxes continued to burn. Ward Gunn, who had kept on firing throughout, was hit in the forehead and killed instantly. Pinney pushed his body out of the way and went on firing until further hits on the gun made it unusable. He drove away unscathed. The next day, in a comparatively quiet area, a stray shell landed close enough to kill him.

Major ROBIN HASTINGS

On the morning of 25th November the 1st Field Regiment was in support of a battalion of Sikhs when

Twenty-eight tanks were advancing from the south, 3,000 yards away. They were of the heavy Mark III and Mark IV types, arrayed in lines of four or five abreast, with 30 yards between tanks and 70 yards between ranks. Their disposition was such that all tanks were able to shoot, none masking another. At 2,000 yards this formidable armada opened fire upon the field guns, halting to fire cannon and maintaining machine-gun fire when in movement.

As they came nearer their fire grew accurate, but the 25-pounders remained silent, the men lying beside the guns. The brunt was borne by 52nd Battery, which held the western flank of the position. The battery waited stoically until the tanks were only 800 yards away, and then the men leapt to their feet and opened fire. The guns worked feverishly under the hail of bullets and shells. Men fell fast, but the guns were still served. The tanks surged onward to within 500 yards. There they halted. For ten minutes an intense slogging match—tank against gun, toe to toe—ensued. It was the Germans who called it off. They scrambled off to the west to a hull-down position, where, with turrets and guns alone exposed, they could continue the fight at a more comfortable range. After a further ten minutes' terrific hammering of the guns in the open, the Panzers charged 52nd Battery head on. Half the artillerymen were strewn around their guns and limbers, but their comrades never wavered, smashing back shot after shot. At 300 yards the tanks had had enough. They wheeled and withdrew to the south-east heavily shelled by 11th Battery, which until then had been able to take only a small part in the action.

52nd Battery had sustained 41 casualties in 45 minutes. In all, 1st Field Regiment had 18 killed and 44 wounded. Seven enemy tanks were destroyed and another, which was hobbling away damaged, was finished off by a troop of South African anti-tank guns which made a timely arrival on the scene.

Lieutenant-Colonel DOBREE

The character of the tank battles is well reflected in this passage:

DISASTER

The order went through all the intercoms from commander to crew: 'Driver, advance. Speed up. Gunner, load both guns.' The Honeys positively leapt over the top of the ridge and plunged down the steady incline to the Trigh.[1] I knew my driver, who was getting used to this sort of thing, would have his foot hard down on the accelerator, straining his eyes through the narrow slit before him to avoid the sudden outcrops of rock or the slit trenches that littered this oft-contested terrain. On each side the Honeys were up level with me. That was good. My wrist-watch showed 1 o'clock as I gripped hard on the edge of the cupola and pressed back against the side to ride the bucking tank.

We were half-way down the slope and going like bats out of hell in the bright sunlight before the Jerries realised what was happening. Then the familiar pattern of alarm and confusion and panic-flight away from us at right angles to the road. There was no slackening of speed, and within another minute we had hit the soft sand of the well-worn desert highway and become absorbed into the cloud of dust and that frightened herd of vehicles stampeding blindly northwards.

I had the same intention in my mind as on a previous occasion— to go right through them, turn about and cut off as many as possible, shooting up everything that tried to get past. I put the mike close to my lips and told my tank commanders briefly to start shooting. My own gunner pulled the trigger immediately and within seconds the dust was full of the criss-cross pattern of tracers drawing red lines through the yellow cloud and puncturing the fleeing dark shapes with deadly points. From the turret tops we let go with tommy-guns and revolvers, and every now and again the whip-crack of the 37-mm interjected the staccato chatter of the Brownings. I could still see a Honey or two racing alongside, but what was happening beyond the narrow limits of vision I could only guess. And my guess was that the whole squadron was there. Another minute perhaps, I thought, and then I would give the order to turn about.

Suddenly, through the dust, I saw the flat plane of the ground disappear into space. I yelled like mad at the driver to halt. He had seen the danger only a fraction of a second after I had, and jerked back on the brakes even while I was shouting at him. The tracks locked fast and tore up sand, rock and scrub in a brief and frantic tussle to stop the momentum of the tank. We skidded to a violent

[1] The Trigh Capuzzo, the main east–west track in Cyrenaica.

stop with the front sprockets hanging over a sharp drop that started the descent of a steep escarpment.

The first thing I saw, through popping eyes, ten yards in front and below me, was a motor-cycle combination lying on its side with three German soldiers standing stiffly at attention in a row beside it, their backs towards me and their hands stretched high above their heads. I rejected immediately a quick impulse to shoot them. While my mind was still trying to absorb this apparition I became aware of the astonishing scene at the foot of the escarpment, where it levelled out into a broad wadi. Vehicles of all shapes and sizes were everywhere—some upright and still moving away as fast as they could; others stationary and bewildered; many lying on their sides or backs with wheels poking grotesquely upwards. Dark figures of men darted wildly about.

Even as I watched, a great lorry went plunging down the escarpment out of control; it struck some outcrop and leapt high into the air, somersaulting to the bottom in a fantastic avalanche of earth, rock and scrub and odd-shaped bundles of men integrated with jagged pieces of wood and metal. The concentration of transport in the wadi below was a wonderful target. I said quickly into the mouthpiece: 'Both guns. Men and vehicles. Fire with everything you've got.'

The bullets went zipping inches above the heads of the three immovable figures in front of the tank. They never twitched a muscle. When the 37-mm cannon suddenly went off they jumped involuntarily, but none of them turned their heads or gave any indication that I could see of fear or curiosity. They just stood there, three backs and three pairs of arms while the tracers went streaming in flat, straight lines into the dusty turmoil below. I wondered idly where the rest of the Honeys were, and if they were having as good a time as mine was.

Suddenly there was a fearful bang, and simultaneously I was drenched from head to foot in an astonishing cascade of cold water. For a moment or two I was physically and mentally paralysed. I just could not believe that anything like that could happen. Then realisation came swiftly and terribly . . . the water tins on the back of the tank had been hit. It could mean only one thing. As I looked backwards I was already giving the order to the gunner to traverse the turret as fast as he bloody well could. In one comprehensive flash I saw it all, and the fear leapt up in me. Not fifty yards away a 50-mm anti-tank gun pointed straight at the Honey, pointed straight between my eyes. Beyond it were other guns and then as the dust drifted over the scarp the sight I had dreaded most—a number of motionless Honeys and the huddled figures of black-bereted men crouched on the sand or stretched out in the agony of death.

It took less than a second for the whole scene and its awful meaning to register in my mind. I could see the German gunners lamming the next shell into the breech as the turret whirled. I yelled: 'On. Machine gun. Fire.' In the same moment I saw the puff of smoke from the anti-tank gun and felt and heard the strike on the armour-plating. Quickly I looked down into the turret. A foot or two below me the gunner was staring at his hand, over which a dark red stain was slowly spreading. Then he gave a scream and fell grovelling on the floor. In the top right hand corner of the turret a jagged hole gaped, and through it, like some macabre peepshow, I could see the gun being reloaded. I knew that in another few seconds I would be dead, but something well beyond reason or sanity impelled my muscles and actions.

I leaned down and pulled the trigger, and kept my finger there until the gun jammed. God knows where the bullets went. Twice I felt the Honey shudder and the second time more water came pouring in. When the Browning stopped and my mind leapt about searching for some way to stay alive I suddenly saw the slim chance. If the tank would move at all, and we could drop over the edge of the escarpment, we would be out of sight of those blasted anti-tank guns. I could see them framed in that jagged hole, the gunners working feverishly, their faces strained and vicious. I said urgently into the mike: 'Driver, advance. Over the edge. Quick!'

Nothing. I thought: 'My God, Whaley's had it. We've all had it,' and screamed down into the turret: 'Driver, advance. For Christ's sake advance!' Then I saw what had happened. In falling, the gunner had jerked back on the intercom leads to the driver's earphones. The cords had tightened round his neck, pulling him backwards over the driving seat and half-strangling him. He wrestled frantically with his earphones and ripped them off. He didn't need them to hear my panic bellowing.

I felt the gears engage, and for a split second the world stood still. Then the engine revved, and the Honey heaved forward and dropped with a violent crash over the escarpment. In the turret we were hurled about like corks, and then the bouncing stopped and we rode smoothly down the slope. We were out of sight of the guns on the top of the escarpment, and with a great rush of unbelief I knew we were going to get away with it. The three German motor-cyclists still stood motionless. The tank could not have missed them by more than a few inches, yet they still had their hands in the air. Down in the driving compartment Whaley was wrestling with the sticks to keep the tank on a diagonal course that would take him to the bottom of the slope away from the enemy. When the ground levelled out a bit I ordered him to turn right to run into a little wadi that offered a safe way out to the south. We were travelling with the turret back to front, and I prodded the operator with my foot as he bent over the prostrate gunner and indicated to him that I wanted the turret traversed back to the normal position. While he was turning the handle I could not resist a last backward look at those three men. Incredibly, they were still standing as we had left them. I began to think they had become literally petrified with fright and would stay there down the centuries in some miraculous monument.

So much had happened in a few minutes, or a few hours it might have been, and I had looked so closely into the valley of the shadow, that I found it difficult to return to reality. I just could not fully absorb our situation. I had to grip the hardness of the armour-plating and see the familiar figures of the tank crew to realise that we were still alive, and that we were going to stay alive. The gunner lay there groaning in pain and sobbing in fear. There was nothing much wrong with him, and I shouted at him roughly to pull himself together. My thoughts went out to the rest of the squadron. Where were they? What had happened to them? Were they all dead? It was something I had to find out.

We were chugging along casually through the deserted silence of the wadi. It was uncanny after the tumult and terror just behind us, and the thought kept on intruding that we were no longer on earth, that we were driving in some ghost tank on another level of exis-tence . . . that we were all dead. When I put the mouthpiece to my

lips I was half-prepared to hear no voice come out. The unreality
persisted when the Honey swung right in response to my order, and
moved slowly up the slope of the crest. As soon as my eyes were
above the lip of the escarpment we halted, and the full picture of
horror burst on me immediately.

Not much more than 500 yards away, like a projection on a
cinema screen, lay the battlefield. My eyes lifted to the tall black
columns, leaning slightly with the wind, and followed them down
to the Honeys gasping smoke. Four of my tanks were blazing
infernos; three others just sat there, sad and abandoned. A line of
anti-tank guns, with their crews still manning them expectantly,
lined the edge of the drop. The whole scene was silhouetted sharply
against the yellow clouds of dust which rose in a thick fog from the
wadi below. I could see many men running about between guns and
tanks and vehicles. My heart ached as I picked out the familiar
beretted figures of our own troops, huddled in disconsolate groups
or being shepherded singly by gesticulating Germans.

ROBERT CRISP

*General Auchinleck replaced Cunningham, who was growing despondent,
by Major-General Ritchie, hoping that Ritchie would now execute his
personal instruction to Eighth Army: 'There is only one order ATTACK
AND PURSUE ALL OUT EVERYONE.' Many factors affected
Cunningham: the following episode must have been one.*

BULL IN A CHINA SHOP

Being Monday and a calm, sunny morning, my small headquarters
decided to 'make and mend', or, in other words, do their washing,
using three jerricans of water collected from a forward bir. General
Norrie, accompanied by Mike Carver and his reconnaissance wireless truck, had gone north about seven miles, to General 'Straffer'
Gott's Battle HQ. Into this peaceful scene came a signal from Eighth
Army, telling us General Cunningham was on his way up, in a
Blenheim of all things, for an urgent conference. As I was free, and
concerned very much about the aircraft using our shocking strip,
Jack Napier asked me to collect General Cunningham and take him
forward. Connell was wrestling, grimly but blasphemously, with

his large garments, being clad only in underpants, so I drove the car over, anxiously watched a bumpy but safe landing, collected the General and his one staff officer, and away up to Seventh Armoured Div's dispersed headquarters. While the three Generals cooked up the next battle, I waited round, enjoying the sun. Suddenly someone shouted orders, a whistle blew and the whole outfit started packing up, absolutely on the double. I drove over to Mike Carver and asked, 'What the devil's happening?' 'Plenty,' said Mike. 'Rommel's charging round like a ruddy bull in a china shop, with three or four Panzer columns. Two from up north are heading this way, but Straffer's boys will see them off. By sheer bad luck, a third one coming in from the west fluked a gap in the armoured-car screen, crashing straight on to South African Div HQ and their thin-skinned transport. There's a hell of a scrum starting ten miles west of here, and rolling this way fast! We're beating it with Straffer, and sticking to him. I've told our crew to pack and go east. You'll have to get the Army Commander off smartly!' At that moment all three Generals appeared and mine said, 'Get General Cunningham off in his Blenheim at once!' No time to worry about springs, I drove my precious Ford utility full speed for the landing-ground in a run more crazy than any gazelle hunt. Almost unopposed, driving everything ahead like sheep, about twenty German tanks rolled eastwards, completely disintegrating our rear organisation and, in the course of doing so, having the fun of their lives! We dodged through the thickening mob of runaways, which hurtled across our course, urged on by occasional shell bursts or bouncing tracer. Very fortunately I knew that particular desert area almost bush by bush, because, between speed, dust, and crossing vehicles, navigation was impossible. More by good luck than judgement, we hurtled down the strip to where the Blenheim was revved up, raring to go. The Commander and his staff officer climbed aboard, and off she bumped, clearing a crossing three-tonner by inches! That was General Cunningham's last impression of the forward situation. Small wonder he believed withdrawal into Egypt inevitable.

Brigadier GEORGE CLIFTON, DSO, MC

Eighth Army carried out Auchinleck's orders. Tobruk was relieved, and Rommel repulsed. He was steadily driven westwards beyond Benghazi, and between 1st January and 6th January established himself in a final position at Agheila.

*

This is only a limited impression of a long, ferocious conflict; and perhaps the best comment on Crusader, and indeed on the whole of the fighting during 1941, is:

WAR POET

We in our haste can only see the small components of the scene,
We cannot tell what incidents will focus on the final screen.
A barrage of disruptive sound, a petal on a sleeping face,
Both must be noted, both must have their place;
It may be that our later selves or else our unborn sons
Will search for meaning in the dust of long deserted guns,
We only watch, and indicate and make our scribbled pencil notes.
We do not wish to moralise, only to ease our dusty throats.

DONALD BAIN

1942

Defeat and Victory

In 1884 Ferdinand de Lesseps, builder of the Suez Canal, was elected to the French Academy. In the course of a speech of welcome Ernest Renan said: 'Hitherto the Bosphorus has provided the world with embarrassment enough; now you have created a second, and more serious, source of anxiety. For this defile not only connects two inland seas, but it acts as a channel of communication to the oceans of the world. So great is its importance that in a maritime war everyone will strive hard to occupy it. You have thus marked the site of a future great battlefield.'

Quoted at the beginning of the first volume of *The Mediterranean and the Middle East* series in the official *History of the Second World War*

*The 'future great battlefield' was the line of defences running due south
from El Alamein, a little station on the coastal railway, fifty miles to the
west of Alexandria, where in November 1942 Montgomery achieved the
decisive victory over Rommel which prevented the latter for ever from
breaking through to the Suez Canal. 'Before Alamein we never had a
victory. After Alamein we never had a defeat', Churchill observed that it
might almost be said. But in the months of 1942 preceding Alamein the
Imperial armies suffered many defeats, not only in the desert but also, and
far more disastrously, in the Far East, where the Japanese were fanning out
swiftly in all directions during the first stages of the establishment of their
Greater Co-Prosperity Sphere, which would ultimately embrace vast areas
of Asia and the Pacific. Here the first and unexpected disaster was the fall,
in mid-February, of*

SINGAPORE

Col. Dalley had posted an augmented company of *Dallforce* by the
mouth of the River Kranji, where the Japanese had first landed,
under the command of a tinminer named Harte-Barry. Dalley saw
them during the evening before the assault began and gave them
orders not to retreat. During the visit he noticed that the nearby
Australian machine-gun battalion was looking unhappy under the
bombardment. Australian war reporter Ian Morrison, who was with
Dalley, confessed: 'I was windier that day than I had ever been
during the Malayan campaign. And if I was windy, who had been
bombed and dive-bombed pretty frequently up at the front and
broken in to noise, what must it be like for the young officer who
was going up to the front for the first time? We came across some
Australians in a rubber plantation. They had dug shallow trenches
and were sitting in them. They were jittery, no mistake about it. We
came across a party with a young Australian soldier from one of the
25-pounder batteries who had his leg blown off. His mates did not
think he would live. They were carrying him back to the aid post.
Thunder and lightning began. The uproar of bombardment was
enough as it was without the heavens also taking part. Only six
hours later the Japs landed in that very sector.'

In the morning Dalley went back to his company—and found it,
or what was left of it. One British officer and five other ranks had

fallen back; the remainder of the 200—mostly Chinese—had stood and fought it out against a Japanese machine-gun battalion. 'It was a frightful sight,' he said. 'They'd been blown to pieces. They'd used up all their ammunition. There were no wounded to bring back. They'd stood their ground. They'd had orders to stay and they stayed. And they all died.

'The Australian machine-gun battalion did not stand. They moved back. They were frightened and make no mistake. When I walked back to the road where I'd left my car I went up to Col. Asherton, AIF—a fine chap—and said: "I don't think your chaps are very happy. They aren't liking this very much." I walked round with him for half an hour—he could hold those men when he was around. Their spirits went up at once. I heard afterwards that he was killed very early in the piece. I felt that battalion wouldn't be so good without that particular CO, and that's what happened. They were all new-comers—hardly trained. It was very sad.'

Gunner-Signaller Marshall had a close-up view. His gun battery was placed to cover Tengah Airfield. They did not see the warning Very light—if one was ever fired—and although they had four guns with a range of four miles and 4,000 rounds of high explosive ammunition they did not fire a shot while the Japs were rushing the Island. The first thing they knew was that the enemy had landed and were threatening Tengah Airfield, two miles from their position. Less than an hour later the Australians came down the road from the front line. 'It is the most vivid memory I have of the Singapore campaign,' he said. 'They came moving at a half-trot, panic-stricken. I've never seen anything like it. It was pouring with rain and most of them were clad only in shorts. Few were wearing boots, and some of the men's feet were cut to ribbons—they'd come across rivers, through mangrove swamps, through the bush, then out along the Jurong Road. They'd scrapped everything that could hold them back. They'd thrown aside their rifles and ammunition. We watched them in amazement. We were sorry for them. We realised they must have come through a very rough time and something had got hold of them.

'Some of our chaps gave them boots and we gave them what food we had. We asked what had happened and where they were going. "We're off to the docks," they said. It seemed to be an entire battalion or what was left of a battalion. Among them was one Aussie soldier fully equipped: rifle, ammunition, cape, shirt, shorts and boots. He came across the road to three of us who were standing watching. "What's happened?" we asked him. He looked at his fellow-Australians. "They're finished," he said. He was quite calm. He was a boy of about nineteen, a private. He seemed sorry for his mates. "Can I join up with you blokes?" he asked.

'He came along with us. I don't know what happened to him later but I remember that one chap among the horde. He had control of himself. The others had lost control. They were panting, incoherent, a rabble.

'Behind the Aussies came the Indians. The Australians had come through their lines and the Indians had caught the panic. The Indians were mostly young boys. They were without any officers. They didn't stop. They just went hurrying down the Jurong Road heading for Singapore Town. Naturally we were alarmed. We asked the Aussies what had happened. "The Japs are a quarter of a mile up the road," they said.

'Meantime a Bren-carrier manned by Argylls had been sent up the Jurong Road on reconnaissance, to see if in fact the Japs were on the Aussies' heels. Presently we heard the roar of its engine approaching on the return journey. The Aussies saw it, thought it was the Japs and just seemed to dive head first off the road. "Look out," they yelled. "It's the Japs!" They dived into storm ditches, into the bush, anywhere out of sight. In seconds the road was as clear as if the rabble had never been there.'

KENNETH ATTIWILL

*

There was, of course, much bravery displayed in Malaya and at Singapore as well as that apparent cowardice which often arises simply from lack of firm leadership, ignorance and confusion. Both qualities could also be observed when, after the Japanese captured Rangoon at the beginning of March, the British forces set out on their dreadful 900-mile trek to the Indian frontier. The man who was destined in due course to hurl the Japanese back to Rangoon describes two phases of the withdrawal.

1. THE RETREAT

At my headquarters in the jungle just outside Kalewa I was very worried at the delays caused by air bombing, and the fear that either the Japanese or the monsoon would be on us before we could complete the crossing. Having collected the officer responsible for river transportation, and assured myself that he had done all a man could at the Kalewa end, I started off in the dark by launch early in the morning of the 10th May to visit Shwegyin and see what could be done there. My ADC and I reached the jetty at about 0530 just as it was getting light. A steamer was alongside but loading for the moment was interrupted while the Sappers repaired the pier damaged by a lorry. Followed by my ADC, I walked across the steamer's deck on to the jetty. Just as I set my foot on it a stream of red tracer bullets cracked viciously overhead and at once, from the south side of the escarpment to my right, a terrific din of rifle, machine-gun, mortar, and some artillery fire broke out. It was the most unpleasant welcome I have ever had. Obviously something quite big in attacks was starting and it was already close. What had happened to our outer defences I had no idea; they must have been either by-passed or overrun.

I was not by myself, my ADC having decided rather sensibly that, whatever was happening, I should want breakfast and that he had better fetch the box containing it. Rather put off by my reception, I walked up the track from the jetty, past a number of parked tanks, and turned off right towards Ekin's Brigade Headquarters. A lot of stuff was coming over, all too high to be dangerous, but, judging by the noise, just ahead a proper fight seemed to be developing. I found myself crossing one of the larger open spaces, where, crouching behind every little mound and bush that dotted it, were men of the 7th Gurkhas, the battalion that had arrived the previous night. My inclination to run for cover, not lessened by a salvo of mortar bombs that came down behind me, was only restrained by the thought of what a figure the Corps Commander would cut, sprinting for safety, in front of all these little men. So, not liking it a bit, I continued to walk forward. Then, from behind a bush that offered scant cover to his bulky figure, rose my old friend, the Subadar Major of the 7th Gurkhas, his face creased in a huge grin which almost hid his twinkling almond eyes. He stood there and shook with laughter at me. I asked him coldly what he was laughing at, and he replied that it was very funny to see the General Sahib wandering along there by himself *not knowing what to do!* And, by Jove, he was right; I did not!

It is a funny thing how differently the various races react to such a situation. A British soldier would have called out to me to take shelter and would have made room for me beside him. The average Indian sepoy would have watched anxiously, but said nothing unless I was hit, when he would have leapt forward and risked his life to get me under cover. A Sikh would have sprung up, and with the utmost gallantry dramatically covered me with his own body, thrilled at the chance of an audience. Only a Gurkha would stand up and laugh. . . .

2. THE ARRIVAL

We had already had one or two heavy showers to give us a foretaste of what the monsoon would do to us, when, on the 12th May, it burst in full fury. On that day our rearguard was leaving Kalewa and our main body toiling up into the hills. From then onwards the retreat was sheer misery. Ploughing their way up slopes, over a track inches deep in slippery mud, soaked to the skin, rotten with fever, ill-fed and shivering as the air grew cooler, the troops went on, hour after hour, day after day. Their only rest at night was to lie on the sodden ground under the dripping trees, without even a blanket to cover them. Yet the monsoon which so nearly destroyed us and whose rain beat so mercilessly on our bodies did us one good turn—it stopped dead the Japanese pursuit. As the clouds closed down over the hills, even their air attacks became rare.

A couple of marches south of Tamu we received our first helping hand from India. An Indian mechanical transport company met us, but its recruit drivers had been so scared by stories fugitives from Burma had told them and by the perils of the half-made road, that many of them would not drive any farther south. When ordered to do so they took their lorries into the jungle and hid. This difficulty was overcome by putting beside each driver a man from 7 Armoured Brigade who saw to it that they went where they were told—a last service of this magnificent formation. Then the company was of inestimable value in ferrying wounded and sick and sometimes whole units forward.

On the last day of that nine-hundred-mile retreat I stood on a bank beside the road and watched the rearguard march into India. All of them, British, Indian, and Gurkha, were gaunt and ragged as scarecrows. Yet, as they trudged behind their surviving officers in groups pitifully small, they still carried their arms and kept their ranks, they were still recognisable as fighting units. They might look like scarecrows, but they looked like soldiers too.

Field-Marshal the VISCOUNT SLIM, KG

*

In North Africa, too, the British had retreated. The westward drive of the Crusader offensive reached its high-water-mark at Benghazi, and here Rommel recovered, reinforced, and on 21st January returned to the attack— a successful assault which pushed Eighth Army back to the Gazala Line just to the south-west of Tobruk. Many of the army were captured by the Germans in this retreat. One man, though taken at a later date, speaks for all such prisoners:

Of course we had been guilty; so we went
On, though complaining, yet without arousing
Any emotion that was really meant.
We walked ahead, hypnotised by the horizon:
It wriggled in our sweat, in one round drop:
We did not reach it and we did not stop.

The night fell on us whipping us with sand,
The cold, the dry grains in our nose and nails;
The tickling blankets and the loud command
To sleep or wake or empty filthy pails—
—Words in a language that meant no more to us
Than to a bird the fumbled blunderbuss.

We could not sleep, nor wake. We seemed to touch
A secret manifestation of the truth;
We lay down in the desert and learned to teach

Ignorance to professors: we learned to mouth
Old truths, and to forget them when they hurt,
Hurt us too much: truth became true as that.

We seemed like looking in a dead man's eyes
To see small stars dipped deep in the black pupil,
We'd suddenly and simply realise
How old astrologers could without scruple
Paste our lives on to them and advertise
Their rigmarole as wisdom to the wise.

For they were lying like in a black cup
Tealeaves made out of pure white light might lie
And formed a pattern, and a single drop
Brewed from those fragments of immensity
Could satiate thirst, it seemed, and let us pass
The ghost that most and momently haunts us.

What could have been the banquet of the gods,
I almost wondered, what could it have been
If these stars are the dregs? Are all men besides
Morsels to nibble when the feast is done?
I thought until the thought hardened past pain.
My thoughts grew eyes. They let the stars down in.

So for a long way: but it ended near
Tunis—you know the place? Most of us died
There—but you don't. You never will know where
Tunis pitted the map. It was outside
The squares they plant with pin-marks, beyond the four
Winds' quarters. I lived there. It is everywhere.
          From *The Transparent Prisoner* by BURNS SINGER

                              *

*Though Slim's main body had reached the Indian frontier, other troops,
carrying out rearguard operations, lagged hundreds of miles behind in
Burma—Michael Calvert's Bush Warfare Group, for example. When
they reached the Chindwin river he went for a swim. He was not alone. He
found himself involved in*

A FIGHT FOR LIFE

On the beach, as naked as I was, stood a Jap. A pile of clothes lay near his feet and in my first startled glance I took in the insignia of an officer on his bush shirt. It was the second time within a fortnight that I had come face to face with the enemy at a completely un-expected time and place, and for the second time we were both too startled to speak. I wondered what he was doing alone in that little cove and then I heard more splashing and shouting from the other side of the far promontory. This time the voices were Japanese.

Fantastic as it seemed I could only conclude that he was out with a patrol and had made the same decision as I had, namely to wander off on his own while his men went swimming. I watched him carefully in case he dived for his gun but he appeared to be listening for something. Then a strange gleam came into his eyes and I realised that he had heard my men.

I was baffled. If I yelled for help the Jap patrol would hear me, as well as my own. There were twelve of us but there might be twenty or thirty of them; in that case their superior numbers would give them the advantage if it came to an open fight in the confined cove.

While I was still thinking hard the Jap officer stepped into the river and came towards me. I think his mind must have been working much like mine; he could see that I was unarmed but if he used his gun it would bring both patrols running and he did not know our strength. We were behind the main retreat but for all he knew I may have collected a large band of stragglers. Anyway, he wasn't taking any chances on an open fight which would needlessly risk his men's lives. He preferred to tackle me with his bare hands.

He knew his ju-jitsu and the water on his body made him as slippery as an eel, but I was the bigger and stronger. We fought in silence except for the occasional grunt, and struggled and slipped and thrashed around until we were at times waist deep in the swirling river. It was an ungainly fight, almost in slow motion, for it is extraordinarily difficult to keep balance or move quickly and surely in two or three feet of water. Our breathing became heavier and the Jap got more vicious as he jabbed his fingers at my face in an attempt to blind me. I think it was not till then that I fully realised this would have to be a fight to the death.

I was a trained soldier, taught how to kill with a gun, or a bomb, or a bayonet or even a knife in the thick of a battle. Somehow this seemed different, more personal, as the two of us, naked as we were, fought in the water. Apart from anything else I had come to admire this game little Jap. He had all the guts in the world. He could so easily have called up his men and let them fight it out but he had chosen to protect them by taking me on alone.

Now he was putting up a tremendous show and I was hard put to it to hold him. I pulled myself together. Brave or not, I had to kill him. Or he would kill me.

I was thankful for one lesson I had learned: never to take my boots off in the jungle outside camp. Other clothes can be scrambled on in a moment but boots take time, and time can cost lives. Even on this occasion I had stuck to my rule, which was just as well. I managed to grab the Jap's right wrist and force his arm behind his back. And I buried my face in his chest to stop him clawing my eyes out. Then as he lashed out with his left arm and both feet, I forced him gradually under the water. My boots gave me a firm grip and I shut my eyes and held him under the surface. His struggles grew weaker and weaker, flared again in frantic despair and then he went limp. I held on for a few seconds longer before releasing my grip. Slowly I opened my eyes and for a moment could see nothing except the eddies of water caused by his final efforts to break free. Then his body emerged on the surface a couple of yards away and floated gently off downstream.

MICHAEL CALVERT

*

THE MAHRATTA GHATS

The valleys crack and burn, the exhausted plains
Sink their black teeth into the horny veins
Straggling the hills' red thighs, the bleating goats
—Dry bents and bitter thistles in their throats—
Thread the loose rocks by immemorial tracks.

Dark peasants drag the sun upon their backs.

High on the ghat the new turned soil is red,
The sun has ground it to the finest red,
It lies like gold within each horny hand,
Siva has spilt his seed upon this land.

Will she who burns and withers on the plain
Leave, ere too late, her scraggy herds of pain,
The cow-dung fire and the trembling beasts,
The little wicked gods, the grinning priests,
And climb, before a thousand years have fled,
High as an eagle to her mountain bed
Whose soil is fine as flour and blood-red?
But not! She cannot move. Each arid patch
Owns the lean folk who plough and scythe and thatch
Its grudging yield and scratch its stubborn stones.
The small gods suck the marrow from their bones.

Who is it climbs the summit of the road?
Only the beggar bumming his dark load.
Who was it cried to see the falling star?
Only the landless soldier lost in war.
And did a thousand years go by in vain?
And does another thousand start again?
ALUN LEWIS (Lieutenant, the South Wales Borderers, who
    died in an accident in Arakan in southern Burma in 1944)

*

*In that other land where the valleys crack and burn, the North African
desert, the Long Range Desert Group throughout these months had been
making secret patrols of a thousand miles or more into enemy territory,
quartering the land from Lake Chad to Tripoli. One agent they dropped in
Cyrenaica at the end of April was 'Popski' (the Belgian Lieutenant-
Colonel Vladimir Peniakoff, who later was to form the famous reconnaissance group, 'Popski's Private Army'). As a change from suborning the
Senussi Arabs he decided to spy on a route much used by Axis traffic.*

THE WRONG SIDE OF THE FENCE

It was a busy day on the track that morning: a steady stream of vehicles went by in both directions and from where I sat I could see the faces of the soldiers as they drove by. There is something deeply satisfying in watching the enemy war machine from the wrong side of the fence and this, my first opportunity, gave me much pleasure. A snooper's enjoyment, no doubt, but marred by no guilty conscience; with, indeed, a sense of virtuous achievement and a happy knowledge of having outwitted the enemy. I had never seen so many German soldiers in all my life as I did that morning; watching them I thought: 'Smug-faced fools, you think that the enemy is ninety miles away! If you only knew! He is a stone's-throw away, sitting under a bloody bush and writing down in his book every bloody vehicle of yours.' I had ruled several pages of a notebook in columns with headings: Mark III tanks, Mark II tanks—five-ton trucks with troops—ditto with supplies—staff cars, motor cycles and so on. The right-hand page for westwards traffic, left-hand for eastwards traffic. The density of traffic was about two hundred vehicles an hour, which kept me pretty busy and I filled up the pages, with considerable satisfaction.

By noon traffic became scarcer and I had periods during which no vehicles were in sight. Then the periods lengthened and by two o'clock the road seemed permanently deserted. The sun was overhead, the heat was considerable, I felt drowsy. A lonely truck roared in the distance, appeared round the bend, loaded with German troops, was entered in my book and passed on. I lay back and stretched my legs: my two companions were asleep, their head cloths drawn over their eyes. Then I realised something was wrong: I had not heard the last truck grind up the next rise after it had passed us. I lifted my head and I saw it halted on the track, five hundred yards away. Through my glasses, in the shimmering heat, I saw the men out of the truck, gathered in a bunch. 'Brewing up', I thought. I touched my companions on the shoulder, they woke up without a start and turned their eyes as I pointed. I lay back and 'Abdel Aziz kept watch. Ten minutes later he touched me: I turned on to my stomach and looked through the glasses at two mirage-distorted figures: they came nearer and resolved themselves into two German soldiers. The glasses lowered, I judged the distance to be still quite safe and I said to 'Abdel Aziz and his companion: 'Go back to the sheik's tomb—I shall meet you there later,' and I cocked my Tommy gun. 'Abdel Aziz got up and walked away—he was just an Arab in the landscape, no one would notice him. His companion grunted: 'I am staying,' and we both crawled behind our bush and kept our heads down. The two Germans, a private and a feldwebel, had a rifle and a pistol between them. They were now quite near and seemed to be making for our bush: as they had not unslung their weapons it was likely that they were not suspicious, but still they were making straight for us. Very carefully I shouldered my Tommy gun. Between us and the two Germans was a rather conspicuous small tree, about twenty yards from our bush. I slid the catch to 'single shot', brought the foresight to bear on the feldwebel and decided to fire when he reached the tree. If I succeeded in bringing both men down with no more than three or four shots, I hoped that the others, at the truck, would not notice and I would have time to withdraw unperceived in spite of my (as I thought) conspicuous uniform. The feldwebel advanced with a glassy stare. I drew breath, aimed at the pit of his stomach and started squeezing the trigger. As he reached the tree, however, he stopped, turned away from me, and his companion did the same. I released the trigger hoping that I would not, after all, have to kill these two men that I didn't know. They undid their belts, slid down their slacks and squatted in the shade of the tree.

Lieutenant-Colonel VLADIMIR PENIAKOFF, DSO, MC

★

The torments of war even penetrated to the army waiting in England. At Reigate, for example, the headquarters of Montgomery's South-Eastern Command, there was

STAFF EXERCISE

On one horrid occasion Monty issued an order that all officers at his headquarters under the age of forty-five should parade at 10 am in full marching order carrying rifles and ammunition, and should run for ten miles as a formed body. Rifles were hastily borrowed and equipment scrounged, and we duly formed up and set off, ominously followed by the Major-General Administration in a staff car, by the Director of Medical Services in another staff car, by two Military Policemen on motor-bicycles, and, last of all, by a large Royal Army Medical Corps motor ambulance.

The first casualty was one of the Army Commander's ADCs, who tripped over his own feet going down Reigate Hill and crashed to the ground. We all felt slightly better after that. ADCs are considered rather pampered creatures, though Monty had been known to make his personal staff ride behind or in front of his car on motor-bikes—a proceeding much frowned on by the ADCs' Union, of which I still considered myself an honorary member. Skirting the edge of the town, the rest of us streamed across Reigate Heath in the direction of Betchworth. From time to time some exhausted runner would fall by the way, to be rallied, as we supposed, by the MGA, medically examined by the DMS, arrested, if proved a fraud, by the Military Police, or, if passed as genuine casualty, popped into the ambulance.

After we had crossed the River Mole the pace began to tell, and about half of us broke off and walked, reserving our running for downhill slopes. We arrived at the finishing post only a few minutes after our more athletic colleagues. Next day I was so stiff and had such frightful pains in the calves of my legs that any crippled German could have overtaken me if I had had ten yards' start.

RALPH ARNOLD

And then there was

THE LIGHT THAT FLASHED

The Brass at the War Office seemed to think (perhaps with justification) that we were dismissing the reports of a spy on the Isle of Lewis too lightly. He seemed to be operating a long way down the west coast of the island, towards its boundary with Harris. Every night, regularly at 9.30 pm, he flashed his lights out to sea, presumably to a lurking submarine, which took down his message. The flashed signal was followed by a long, continuous beam, followed in its turn by more intermittent flashes. About 9.40 pm, the operation was complete.

Major N. G. Salvesen, the Security Officer for this Protected Area, and I, his assistant, looked at the map. We looked at the reports. We looked at each other. From our Inverness office it really seemed confoundedly inaccessible. The road appeared to stop at Uig and after that there were only tracks. The local constable from Stornoway had had great difficulty in getting there. In a six-page foolscap report (speaking from memory, the chain of communication was via the Chief Constable at Dingwall—the Scottish Office— the Home Office—the War Office—Scottish Command) he related how he had personally seen the flashing light, but failed to track it to its source. He had spoken to the few crofters and shepherds in the neighbourhood. Most of them had seen it. On one memorable night the Home Guard had turned out, and they had all watched impotently as the spy flashed his signal out to sea. Some of them saw it from a vantage point to the north, others from the south, but as soon as they stepped down from the high ground they lost sight of it.

Salvesen weighed in with an appreciation of the situation. (1), he said, nothing of interest to the war effort was happening in the locality. Therefore (2), he went on, the spy could have nothing to report. In which case (3), he asked, why should a German submarine run the risk of lurking out in the Atlantic night after night? (4), he concluded, if there really was a spy, best leave him where he was, as he could do so much less damage there than anywhere else in the British Isles.

The War Office reacted promptly. A Captain Someone from a top secret department, travelling as Mr Price. would report to us very shortly accompanied by an assistant to investigate the matter. We were to give him all the help he needed.

Mr Price was an amiable chap. He arrived ten days later (having taken some leave first) and without his assistant, who could not be spared for so long at the same time. They had not realised how far away it was. He asked us to lend him one of our Field Security NCOs in plain clothes, and some transport. The only transport available was an army motor-cycle, and so Mr Price, a lance-corporal in sports jacket and flannels, an army motor-cycle, and sundry equipment set sail from Kyle of Lochalsh to Stornoway and duly impressed the natives when they arrived at the scene of operations a day or two later. Mr Price visited the points from which the spy's light could be seen, set up his highly sophisticated direction-finding apparatus, and instructed our lance-corporal how to work it. Bearings were plotted on maps and the light actually pin-pointed. On the following day, with some difficulty because of the remoteness of the spot, the spy was tracked down.

Mr Price told us all about it when he returned to Inverness several days later. An ancient crofter, a man of regular habits, had no indoor sanitation in his house. Every night, before he went to bed, he walked some twenty yards across his land to a kind of cave, swinging his lantern in time with his footsteps. He put it on a ledge while he squatted down, and swung it again on his return. His story was corroborated by the evidence in the cave.

Mr Price reckoned that it was a satisfactory conclusion to a difficult case, even if it had been a long journey (about 1600 miles there and back) to discover a crofter's lavatory.

HAROLD HARRIS (who then was a
captain in the Intelligence Corps)

★

SENTRIES

At the sharp corners of the world, behind
Sandbags or concrete or barbed wire,
Wait the unthinking champions of the mind
Through sombre days or nights of hectic fire;
Without heroics, beautifully uncouth,
Beneath their heavy boots the squelching past
But in their eyes the Future gathering fast
And in their hands unformulated truth.

May these attain to know what they believe,
Live what they know, before the girders part
And chaos drags them under—these naïve
Sentries of the complicated heart.

LOUIS MACNEICE

The sentries of the Eighth Army were caught napping when on 26th May Rommel launched an all-out offensive on their positions along the Gazala Line. A ding-dong struggle followed, with the advantage steadily swaying in Rommel's favour, around defended areas to become famous as 'The Cauldron' and 'Knightsbridge'. The Eighth Army began a long withdrawal to Alamein, and Rommel captured Tobruk at last.

TOBRUK FALLS

Dawn lightened the sky along the bleak escarpment; the night mists lifted. Then the German barrage fell upon the bunkers of the Tobruk perimeter; the desert burst apart in dust and thunder. The Stukas came with the early morning sun. Orange smoke rolled up against the blue sky as the German engineers signalled their gunners to lengthen the range so that they could move in to breach the mine-fields and anti-tank defences. Just before seven o'clock the German infantry followed. Before eight, the *Panzerarmee* was one and a half miles inside the Tobruk perimeter.

Within the falling fortress there were the too-familiar decisions and counter-decisions and time-wasting exchanges of visits between commanders. A counter-attack was ordered: the tanks arrived without the infantry two and a half hours after the German break-through. Only then did the infantry begin to move. By now, two German panzer divisions were driving for King's Cross, where the Via Balbia and the El Adem road met.

Outside Tobruk Ritchie was visiting his corps commanders; at mid-day he learned that 'some enemy activity' was in progress, 'apparently against Tobruk'. He immediately ordered 30th Corps to attack through Sidi Rezegh with all available armour and mobile forces. This move achieved nothing: in Axis war diaries it is hardly noticed.

Inside Tobruk, the defence was disintegrating in scenes of apocalyptic confusion and doom. By four in the afternoon the Germans were on the eastern airfield, and driving straight for the town of Tobruk, with all its stores and installations prepared for the intended British summer offensive. Under heavy German gunfire, demolition charges were blown in petrol, water, refri-gerations and naval ammunition stores. A dark column of smoke towered through the sunshine into the blue Mediterranean sky.

At seven in the evening 21st Panzer had captured the town. Germans swarmed everywhere through the confusion and noise, performing the housewifely function of mopping-up. Some British units held out for a time, others were quickly overwhelmed.

As the debris of his garrison poured past his headquarters, Klopper signalled and signalled Eighth Army. There was no answer. At five o'clock the desperate Klopper had telephoned Brigadier Thompson, the Area Commander, that fortress headquarters was about to disperse, German tanks being close. In the hope of speaking to Eighth Army Klopper nevertheless held on until half-past six, when his headquarters started to pack up.

Now at last came a personal signal from Ritchie:

'. . . You are having a very tough fight today and I see this afternoon some enemy tanks have got through the outer perimeter. But I feel quite confident of your ability to put them out after destroying as many as possible. I am doing all I can from outside to relieve the pressure on you and our power to help you from outside will increase daily. The turn of the tide will come and feel quite sure of inflicting a crushing defeat on the enemy. . . . All good fortune to you personally and the whole of your grand command.'

Dusk fell, and men from broken formations crowded wearily into the precarious security of the western half of the perimeter. In their nostrils was the ubiquitous smell of burning; in their mouths the sour, familiar taste of defeat. Klopper himself had joined 2nd South African Brigade, where he tried to speak to Ritchie on the Army Commander's personal radio-telephone link. But Ritchie was away from his headquarters. Klopper spoke to Whiteley, his Brigadier General Staff, and conveyed the state of the fortress. Whiteley got in touch with Ritchie, then passed on to Klopper the Army Commander's orders to break out tomorrow night; an escape route would be held open.

While Klopper's officers talked and talked endlessly round the questions of whether, and how, to break out, the men settled down to wait with that patient resignation of the soldier, and Klopper himself tried again and again to speak to Ritchie. Midnight passed. At two in the morning of 21st June, Klopper gave Ritchie up, and signalled Eighth Army:

'Am sending mobile troops out tonight. Not possible to hold until tomorrow. Mobile troops nearly nought. Enemy captured vehicles. Will resist to last man and last round.'

At three that morning Ritchie returned to his headquarters, immediately telephoned Tobruk, and found he could not get through to Klopper. Now it was Ritchie's turn to endure anxiety and frustration before a silent telephone. As dawn crept palely up the sky, he paced up and down outside his caravan, waiting. At last he and Klopper talked. Ritchie gave Klopper leave to capitulate if the local situation warranted it. Klopper told him that 'he was doing the worst'. Ritchie ended the conversation with a characteristically generous message:

'Whole of Eighth Army has watched with admiration your gallant fight. You are an example to us all and I know South Africa will be proud of you. God bless you and may fortune favour your efforts wherever you may be. . . .'

That morning, 21st June 1942, a white flag was hauled up over Klopper's new headquarters. It was Sir Claude Auchinleck's fifty-eighth birthday.

CORRELLI BARNETT

THE FLAP

General Gott was in his Armoured Command Vehicle (ACV), the first I had seen. He came out at once and walked a few yards clear of it. 'Inglis has gone to Cairo,' he said, and handed me a letter. It was a short note from General Corbett, then General Auchinleck's MGGS. I remember very clearly the opening sentence: 'The Chief has decided to save Eighth Army.' The note then went on to say that the South Africans would retire through Alexandria and the rest of us down the desert road through Cairo.

I asked what was meant by the first sentence. 'It means what it says—he means to save the Field Army,' the General said. He went on to explain: a general retirement and evacuation of Egypt was in contemplation and Inglis had gone to Cairo to arrange for the evacuation of 2 NZEF rear installations and hospitals; he supposed we would go back to New Zealand. I protested that we were perfectly fit to fight and that it was criminal to give up Egypt to 25,000

German troops and a hundred tanks (disregarding the Italians)—the latest Intelligence estimate—and to lose as helpless prisoners perhaps 200,000 Base troops. Strafer replied sadly that NZ Division was battle-worthy but very few other people were and he feared the worst.

I returned to Division and told Gentry of this unpleasant conversation. We said nothing to anyone else and were both sorely perplexed and depressed. In the evening a provisional order for our retirement arrived from 13 Corps. It certainly envisaged the abandonment of Egypt.

Inglis returned on the afternoon of the 30th, nothing else of importance having occurred in his absence, and I returned to 5 Brigade. He drew a vivid picture of the confusion he had seen on the Cairo road and of the prodigious 'flap' in Cairo itself. This was the time of the famous Ash Wednesday when Middle East and BTE[1] were said to have burned many of their records and the Navy left Alexandria in haste. Paddy Costello, later one of our best divisional intelligence officers, was always very upset that the elaborate draft he had prepared for a handbook on the Italian Army was destroyed at this time. We heard all sorts of peculiar and perhaps libellous stories, such as the one that all the reserve store of binoculars had been thrown into Alexandria Harbour, but despite General Gott's warning I do not remember that we were particularly depressed. We thought it too bad to be true.

Major-General SIR HOWARD KIPPENBERGER

*

The startled New Zealanders had not got hold of the full facts. Auchinleck was in no mood to be whipped out of Egypt. He went up into the desert, took command of the Eighth Army, and during July fought Rommel to a standstill. But his success was marred by occasions when the British armour showed less than a professional competence—occasions such as this, of which a war correspondent was an eyewitness:

With the infantry the British tanks went in . . . and this was another of those heart-breaking mistakes and misunderstandings that kept

[1]It was customary to say 'Middle East', meaning Middle East Headquarters, and BTE, meaning 'Headquarters, British Troops in Egypt'.

cropping up in the midst of the British attacks—the little things that
you could have sworn would never happen, but yet did happen and
made the difference between victory and stalemate.

It was a brand new battalion of tanks from England. The crews
had trained and trained thoroughly but they were new to the desert.
Only three weeks before they had come ashore at Suez with their
Valentines. One wonders if it is a good thing to send troops into
action immediately after they arrive in the desert. The guns will
shoot just the same, of course, but it is not quite like Salisbury
Plain. It is not like manœuvres. If petrol runs out it is not just a
matter of running back two miles down the road and taking the
first left where there is a filling station. Maybe the petrol supply
vehicles do not arrive in the desert. . . . Maybe you have to take a
compass bearing to find the nearest petrol dump, which is just a spot
on the map. Maybe you are not too good at reading a compass and
you miss the way. Maybe the dump has moved when you get to it.

There is no workshop close at hand if a track breaks or a gun
sticks. It's hot and the heat plays tricks with the eyesight. Then again
everything disappears under dust and smoke once the action is
joined, and the best eyesight in the world isn't much good to you
half the time.

Anyway these tanks arrived. The Indian sappers cleared a track
for them through the enemy minefields during the night—that was
the idea of sending the infantry in first. So in they went at dawn,
these fresh-faced boys from England, and they were full of confidence
and courage for this, their first action. Someone gave them the
wrong direction. They missed the track entirely and ran instead on
to the mines and there the German gunners caught them in a cross-
fire. Of the eighty-odd tanks that went out, only a score came back.
Two years of training, months of building, a voyage half way round
the world—then everything had gone wrong in a minute. Because
they were given the wrong direction. And one little Cockney
among the survivors shoved his head out of his tank and said to me,
'We couldn't understand what had gone wrong. We never had a
chance to fire the gun. We couldn't see hardly anything. Shells kept
hitting the tank on both sides and throwing us off our course, but
we couldn't see who was firing them. We heard the other tanks
blowing up all around us. Then one of the officers jumped on

board and squeezed into the turret. He said his tank had been hit, and just as he said that a Jerry shell came clean through my turret on the port side and went round and round until it hit the officer on the back of the head and he fell forward on top of the gunner. There was blood all over the place. I was told to go five thousand yards, but when I looked at my speedometer I had done five thousand five hundred. So I turned round and came back again. I seemed to be the only tank that had got through on my sector so I thought I had better come back.' And he added quite sincerely and simply, 'We'd like to have another crack at them, Sir.' His name, I remember, was Gordon Redford.

ALAN MOOREHEAD

*

On 19th August another tragedy followed, the first major Combined Operation of the war, the raid from the sea on Dieppe. Of the 4961 Canadians involved 3363 became casualties or were captured: of the Commandos 247 out of 1057.

THE LANDING

The story of that blood-stained beach at Puits is a nightmare. Our boat was one of the last to make the beach as we passed close by the eastern headland, with the austere French church with its high steeple on the crest. We sailed in a cloud of smoke under the guns on the cliff-top, most of them anti-aircraft guns that crashed endlessly at our fighters and bombers carrying out more attacks.

Our coxswain tried to take us in to one section of the beach and it proved the wrong spot. Before he grounded he swung the craft out again and we fumbled through the smoke to the small strip of sand which was the Puits beach. The smoke was spotty and the last thirty yards was in the clear. Geysers from artillery shells or mortar bombs shot up in our path. Miraculously we weren't hit by any of them. The din of the German ack-ack guns and machine-guns on the cliff was so deafening you could not hear the man next to you shout.

The men in our boat crouched low, their faces tense and grim. They were awed by this unexpected blast of German fire, and it was their initiation to frightful battle noises. They gripped their weapons more tightly and waited for the ramp of our craft to go down.

We bumped on the beach and down went the ramp and out poured the first infantrymen. They plunged into about two feet of water and machine-gun bullets laced into them. Bodies piled up on the ramp. Some staggered to the beach and fell. Bullets were splattering into the boat itself, wounding and killing our men.

I was near the stern and to one side. Looking out of the open bow over the bodies on the ramp, I saw the slope leading a short way up to a stone wall littered with Royal casualties. There must have been sixty or seventy of them, lying sprawled on the green grass and the brown earth. They had been cut down before they had a chance to fire a shot.

A dozen Canadians were running along the edge of the cliff towards the stone wall. They carried their weapons and some were firing as they ran. But some had no helmets, some were already wounded, their uniforms torn and bloody. One by one they were cut down and rolled down the slope to the sea.

I don't know how long we were nosed down on that beach. It may have been five minutes. It may have been twenty. On no other front have I witnessed such a carnage. It was brutal and terrible and shocked you almost to insensibility to see the piles of dead and feel the hopelessness of the attack at this point.

There was one young lad crouching six feet away from me. He had made several vain attempts to rush down the ramp to the beach but each time a hail of fire had driven him back. He had been wounded in the arm but was determined to try again. He lunged forward and a streak of red-white tracer slashed through his stomach.

I'll never forget his anguished cry as he collapsed on the blood-soaked deck: 'Christ, we gotta beat them; we gotta beat them!' He was dead in a few minutes.

The Germans were in strength on the top of the cliff and poured their fire into the gulch and on the slope which led up to the tops of the cliff crest. A high stone wall, topped with barbed wire, crossed the slope and Royals were dying by that wall.

From our battered craft lying in the centre of this wild concentration of deadly fire I could see sandbagged German positions on the top of the cliff and a large house, with rows of windows, on the left side of the cleft in the cliff. Most of the German machine-gun and rifle fire was coming from the fortified house and it wrought havoc on the tiny beach. They were firing at us at point-blank range.

There was another smaller house on the right side of the break in the cliffs and Germans were there too.

Some of the Canadians were able to return the German fire and they knocked off a number of the enemy. One German in his grey-green uniform toppled from one of the windows in the big house. Some of the less-well fortified positions were hit by fire from anti-tank rifles and Bren guns and Germans there were casualties.

Into the terrible German fire ran the men from our boat and I doubt if any even reached the stone wall on the slope, for mortar bombs were smashing on the slope to take the toll of those not hit by the machine-gun bullets that streaked across the whole beach almost continuously. Now the Germans on the cliff were turning their flak guns down on the beach. Our craft was the only one left.

Somehow, the Royals got the two heavy three-inch mortars in our craft down the ramp, as well as the ammunition, but they were never fired. They fell in the water as the crews were hit. The bottom of the boat was covered with soldiers who had been machine-gunned. The officer next to me, Jack Anderson of Toronto, was hit in the head and sprawled over my legs bleeding badly. A naval rating next to him had a sickening gash in his throat and was dying. A few who weren't casualties were firing back fiercely now from the boat. It was useless for them to try to make the beach. The way those men stood up and blasted back at the Germans, when they could feel even then that the attack at Puits was a lost cause, was one of the bravest things I've witnessed.

The hand of God must have been on that little boat, for we were nosed up hard on the sand and yet when the engines reversed it slid back into deep water as if it had been pulled by something out to sea. In training, many boats used to stick on the beach and we had to get out and push them off but this time by a sheer miracle the craft cleared and slowly, ponderously swung around. There was an opening at the stern and through it I got my last look at the grimmest beach of the Dieppe raid. It was khaki-coloured with the bodies of boys from Central Ontario.

ROSS MUNRO

*

But in North Africa, that August, things took a permanent turn for the better. Fresh troops, abundant supplies and powerful new American tanks were arriving or on their way. And there was a new Command. Alexander took over responsibility for the Middle East: and 'Popski' recalls the first report he received about the man who, under Alexander, was now to lead Eighth Army through a steady series of victories into Tunisia.

MONTGOMERY

At Groppi's I met McMasters, a former CSM of mine in the Libyan Arab Force, and now RSM of a Hussars Regiment, a man who naturally, and rightly, assumed that he and his fellow sergeant majors *were* the British Army, and who entertained an affectionate contempt for all officers. Over drinks he grew enthusiastic about the new commander-in-chief, Eighth Army. Since Wavell had left us, our C-in-Cs had been so dreary that I hadn't bothered to find out the name of our latest acquisition.

'It's a general called Montgomery,' said McMasters, 'a short, wiry fellow, with a bee in his bonnet about PT. The first thing he did when he took over was to order half an hour's physical training for Army Headquarters Staff every morning before breakfast. Tubby brigadiers came out in their vests and *ran*. They heaved and they panted, shaking their fat paunches, for everyone to see, and when they couldn't make the grade they got the sack. Sacked them right and left, he did, all the fat bastards.' McMasters chuckled ferociously.

'A few days ago he visited the regiment. Talked to the officers, then to the NCOs. He told us everything: what his plan was for the battle, what he wanted the regiment to do, what he wanted *me* to do. And we will do it, Sir. What a man!' he concluded with unaccustomed emphasis.

A general who has the courage to sack brigadiers from Army Staff and who knows how to evoke enthusiastic devotion in the hearts of regular sergeant majors will, I thought, have no difficulty in defeating Rommel—or even in winning the war. General Montgomery has had my devotion ever since that memorable conversation. He has met with no rivals, sad to say: I have known clever generals, but none, with the exception perhaps of Freyberg, who knew that battles are won primarily by the hearts of men, and that a few shy stuttered words are not enough to set hearts aflame.

Lieutenant-Colonel VLADIMIR PENIAKOFF

The story about PT is perhaps apocryphal . . . a hangover from Montgomery's reputation in England. But the impression he made on McMasters spread swiftly up and down the line. And his first battle was a model victory. On the night of 30th August Rommel attempted to sweep round the southern end of the Alamein line. His objectives (and there exists a map drawn by his own hand to prove it) were Alexandria, Cairo and the Suez Canal. Montgomery foresaw the move, made comfortable preparations and baulked Rommel firmly and decisively. There was only one critical phase in the battle, when the German tanks turned north, from their eastward advance, towards the ridge which gives the battle its name, Alam Halfa. Brigadier Roberts, commanding the 22nd Armoured Brigade which was waiting for Rommel beside the ridge, described his anxieties:

Now I can see the enemy myself through my glasses. They are coming straight up the line of telegraph posts which lead in front of our position. There is some firing by their leading tanks, presumably at our light squadrons, so I instruct these squadrons to come back—but to take it wide so as not to give our position away.

On they come, a most impressive array. . . . It is fascinating to watch them, as one might watch a snake curl up ready to strike. But there is something unusual too; some of the leading tanks are Mk IVs, and Mk IVs have in the past always had short-barrelled 75-mm guns used for close support work and firing HE only, consequently they are not usually in front. But these Mk IVs have a very long gun on them; in fact it looks the devil of a gun. This must be the long-barrelled stepped-up 75-mm the 'Intelligence' people have been talking about.

And now they all turn left and face us and begin to advance slowly. The greatest concentration seems to be opposite the CLY and the anti-tank guns of the Rifle Brigade. (Eighty-seven German tanks were counted at this time opposite this part of the front.) I warn all units over the air not to fire until the enemy are within 1,000 yards; it can't be long now and then in a few seconds the tanks of the CLY open fire and the battle is on. Once one is in the middle of a battle time is difficult to judge, but it seems only a few minutes before nearly all the tanks of the Grant squadron of the CLY were on fire. The new German 75-mm is taking heavy toll. The enemy tanks have halted and they have had their own casualties, but the situation is serious; there is a complete hole in our defence. I hurriedly warn the Greys that they must move at all speed from their defensive positions and plug the gap. Meanwhile the enemy tanks are edging forward again and they have got close to the Rifle Brigade's anti-tank guns, who have held their fire marvellously to a few hundred yards. When they open up they inflict heavy casualties on the enemy, but through sheer weight of numbers some guns are over-run. The SOS artillery fire is called for; it comes down almost as one right on top of the enemy tanks. This, together with the casualties they have received, checks them. But where are the Greys? 'Come on the Greys,' I shout over the wireless. 'Get out your whips.' But there is no sign of them at the moment coming over the ridge and there is at least another half-hour's daylight left.

Meanwhile some of the enemy have started to work round our left flank and the 5th RTR are in action. . . .

And now in the centre the enemy is edging forward again. The artillery is the only thing I have available to stop them, so we bring down all we can, and again they are halted. And then the Greys come over the crest from the north; they are quite clear as to the hole they have to plug and they go straight in. The light is beginning to fade and the situation in the centre seems to be stabilised. But there is a little trouble on our left; some of the enemy have worked round the 5th Tanks position and are now coming on to our 25-pdr gun lines. . . . Accordingly, since the centre is now a little congested with the Greys in most of the CLY's position I order the CLY (what remained of it) to move round to the left and cover the gap between 5th RTR and the 44th Division's defences. As darkness falls flashes and tracer are to be seen on the left flank; the CLY have met the enemy tanks but have halted them, so we seem secure at any rate for the night.

Major-General G. P. B. ROBERTS, CB, DSO, MC

TRUMPED

The previous fortnight I had spent mainly in a lorry, ringed by telephones, at rare intervals reading Gordon Childe's *Man Makes Himself* (which I had bought in Alexandria), sometimes ordering guns to fire, always with half an eye on the plotting-board spread under a light-proof tarpaulin on the ground below me. On the board half-a-dozen bombers would suddenly be marked, advancing in line abreast across the Cretan sea. By successive plottings we would trace their landfall and see them hiving off to their targets. Two or three would come our way, and I would order the guns to stand to. . . . On one occasion, I remember, only a single enemy bomber was marked on the board and, tired of waiting for more exciting stuff, the telephonists (their receivers strapped to their heads) began playing whist on the board all round the solitary foe. Now and then a fresh plot would come in, and a hurried search would be made amongst the assembled cards for the plot-mark, which would be moved to its new position, and the game without ceasing would appropriately readjust itself. Eventually the bomber arrived over-head, shells bursting about it, and malevolently dropped its bombs just outside. Following the almighty crash, there was a great scatter of bits and pieces over the tarpaulin, and then a piping voice from one of the players—'Now, boys, we can move the f . . . b . . . off the f . . . board and get on with the f . . . game'. Which they f . . . well did, without further interruption. Almost immediately afterwards the aforesaid f . . . b . . . was brought down by one of our night-fighters, and *Man Makes Himself* proceeded evenly to the end of another chapter.

SIR MORTIMER WHEELER (from a letter written at the control headquarters of the anti-aircraft artillery protecting the landing-grounds behind the Alamein Line, 16th September 1942)

*

*On the Burma/India front there were few signs of things taking a turn for
the better. Improvisation was the order of the day: everything was in short
supply. Down in the south 'the Sunderbans, a complicated delta of waterways through which the combined Ganges and Brahmaputra, on a front of
two hundred miles, reach the sea, was an invitation to amphibious penetration'. Slim solved the problem in a characteristic way:*

Based on the existing Army Inland Water Transport Service, which
carried supplies on the river, we formed our fleet of over a hundred
vessels.

We manned it by enrolling the civilian crews of ships in the IWT;
a process that only partially turned them into disciplined Servicemen.
Our officers were volunteers, merchant seamen, amateur yachtsmen,
marine engineers of sorts. These, with the stalwarts already in the
IWT, formed the navigational crews. For manning the armament and
for signalling, we fell back on the medieval expedient of drafting
soldiers aboard. We found an ideal commander for our flotilla,
Lieut.-Colonel Featherstonehaugh, a Regular soldier, who had
sailed before the mast, got a coastal mate's certificate, and had his
wings as an airman. He had led commandos in Norway and was just
the man to handle such a military-nautical set-up and, it must be
confessed, the sometimes queer types that gravitated towards it. The
main armament of our fighting ships was the two-pounder anti-tank
gun; for anti-aircraft defence we relied on Bren guns. Dockyard
maintenance, a big item in so decrepit a fleet, was undertaken by the
workshop companies of the IWT which we established in the various
river ports. They did noble work, but lacked much essential machinery. For major repairs, we had, therefore, to rely on civil firms in
Calcutta.

In spite of all difficulties, we were able, in July 1942, to stage a
grand combined exercise with the flotilla and the RAF. Our fleet,
steaming down the winding channels to the sea, was an impressive
sight—especially its smoke. At the conclusion of the exercise we felt
that, combined with the fighters of the RAF, our flotilla gave us a
reasonable hope, not only of discovering Japanese infiltration, but of
seriously delaying and even checking it. The spirit of the men was
that of the young soldier ship commander who sent the signal,
'Large Japanese submarine reported off mouth of Meghna River. Am

proceeding to sea to engage.' His heaviest armament was a two-pounder, his speed, with the safety valve screwed down, eight knots, and his rickety river steamer was never meant to venture to sea, least of all in the monsoon. The submarine would do eighteen knots on the surface and have a four-inch gun. But he went to look for it!

Field-Marshal LORD SLIM

But a seed was being sown which would soon bear fruit. Orde Wingate arrived in Delhi in the spring, and with the backing of Wavell, the Commander-in-Chief, he spent the summer working on plans for his original and ambitious scheme for Long Range Penetration Groups to operate behind the Japanese lines. This is the impression he created at the time among Wavell's Joint Planning Staff:

Many people came into our office with plans for the reconquest. Some of their ideas were useful: these were carefully noted and filed away for future reference. Some were fantastic and foolish: these we made no pretence of noting, and bowed their originators out of the room. . . . Only in one direction did there seem any prospect of action in the near future. It lay in the person of a broad-shouldered, uncouth, almost simian officer who used to drift gloomily into the office for two or three days at a time, audibly dream dreams and drift out again. When in Delhi, he would make his headquarters in the GHQ library, from which he would borrow a dozen books at a time, to the distress of the librarian. . . . We used to look on this visitor as one to be bowed out, as soon as it was possible to put a term to his ramblings; but as we became aware that he took no notice of us anyway, but that without our patronage he had the ear of the highest, we paid more attention to his schemes. Soon we had fallen under the spell of his almost hypnotic talk; and by and by we— or some of us—had lost the power of distinguishing between the feasible and the fantastic.

Brigadier SIR BERNARD FERGUSSON, GCMG, GCVO, DSO, OBE (who became one of Wingate's column commanders in his Long Range Penetration unit)

Michael Calvert recalls, at a later stage, one of the idiosyncrasies of this ape-like individualist:

He rarely drank any other form of milk except buffalo milk. For this reason he kept four buffaloes at Brigade HQ and the Animal Transport Officer, whose main responsibility was towards our invaluable mules, used to milk them for him.

One day the buffaloes began to get sick, one after the other. Wingate and the Animal Transport Officer tried to help them, but they had no idea what was wrong with the beasts. Wingate put blankets over them and sprayed them with insecticide in case it was something they were catching from mosquitoes or some other bug. But despite the great care lavished on them one of the buffaloes died and the others remained very seedy. Wingate called in the Medical Officer, who declared somewhat testily that he wasn't a damned vet and hadn't the faintest idea what was wrong with the things. Finally, after Wingate insisted that he should do something, the doc gave them injections, presumably a sort of antibiotic. These had no effect and Wingate, in desperation, began dosing them with some of our very small stock of Scotch whisky.

Until that moment we had all been faintly amused by the proceedings and our sympathy was mostly for the unfortunate buffaloes rather than for our commander. But this was going too far and the situation had suddenly become serious. We were not particularly worried at the lack of buffalo milk but we were very concerned at the thought of our vanishing whisky.

Then someone had a brainwave and sent for the local witch doctor from a neighbouring village. He examined the sick animals, who were now very poorly indeed, and after some consideration lit a fire. When it was hot enough he heated up several branding irons, seized one firmly, and approached one of the buffaloes. Then he shoved the red-hot tip of the iron between her legs. The effect of this particular medicine, as one might expect, was immediate. The shocked animal leapt to her feet and began stamping about. Unperturbed, the witch doctor grabbed another branding iron and laid it on one of the beast's flanks. He repeated this, with fresh irons, on the other flank and finally on her shoulder. At each searing touch the buffalo leapt about three feet into the air, but she made no attempt to lash out. Finally, after throwing a pained look at Wingate, she started to graze. The witch doctor nodded, as if satisfied with his treatment, and applied the same doses to the other two. None of them gave us any further trouble.

MICHAEL CALVERT

*

At last, in October, there came to Churchill from North Africa a magic word:

C-in-C to Prime Minister and CIGS   *23 Oct. 42*
'Zip!'

This meant that the long-awaited attack by Eighth Army at Alamein had begun, followed on 8th November by the Anglo-American landings (in Operation TORCH) on the African coast at the western end of the Mediterranean . . . landings at Algiers, Oran, Casablanca and elsewhere. Rommel was now caught in a vice. The ultimate success of these two great enterprises would enable Alexander, in the coming year, to signal to his Prime Minister: 'We are masters of the North African shores.'

The Commander of the Eighth Army describes the problems that faced him before the attack:

ALAMEIN: THE PLAN

Alam Halfa had interfered with the preparations for our own offensive, and delayed us. But the dividend in other respects had been tremendous. Before Alam Halfa there was already a willingness from below to do all that was asked, because of the grip from above. And for the same reason there was a rise in morale, which was cumulative. I think officers and men knew in their hearts that if we lost at Alam Halfa we would probably have lost Egypt. They had often been told before that certain things would happen; this time they wanted to be shown, not just to be told. At Alam Halfa the Eighth Army had been told, and then shown; and from the showing came the solid rocklike confidence in the high command, which was never to be lost again.

The basic problem that confronted us after the Battle of Alam Halfa was a difficult one. We were face to face with Rommel's forces between the sea and the Qattara Depression, a distance of about 45 miles. The enemy was strengthening his defences to a degree previously unknown in the desert, and these included deep and extensive minefields. There was no open flank. The problem was:

First—to punch a hole in the enemy positions.

Second—to pass 10 Corps, strong in armour and mobile troops, through this hole into enemy territory.

Third—then to develop operations so as to destroy Rommel's forces.

This would be an immense undertaking. How could we obtain surprise?

It seemed almost impossible to conceal from the enemy the fact that we intended to launch an attack. I decided to plan for tactical surprise, and to conceal from the enemy the exact places where the blows would fall and the exact times. This would involve a great deception plan. . . .

Next, a full moon was necessary. The minefield problem was such that the troops must be able to see what they were doing. A waning moon was not acceptable since I envisaged a real 'dog-fight' for at least a week before we finally broke out; a waxing moon was essential. This limited the choice to one definite period each month. Owing to the delay caused to our preparations by Rommel's attack, we could not be ready for the September moon and be sure of success. There must be no more failures. Officers and men of the Eighth Army had a hard life and few pleasures; and they put up with it. All they asked for was success, and I was determined to see they got it this time in full measure. The British people also wanted real success; for too long they had seen disaster or at best only partial success. But to gain complete success we must have *time*; we had to receive a quantity of new equipment, and we had to get the army trained to use it, and also rehearsed in the tasks which lay ahead. I had promised the Eighth Army on arrival that I would not launch our offensive till we were ready. I could not be ready until October. Full moon was the 24th October. I said I would attack on the night of 23rd October, and notified Alexander accordingly. The come-back from Whitehall was immediate. Alexander received a signal from the Prime Minister to the effect that the attack must be in September, so as to synchronise with certain Russian offensives and with Allied landings which were to take place early in November at

the western end of the North African coast (Operation TORCH).
Alexander came to see me to discuss the reply to be sent. I said that
our preparations could not be completed in time for a September
offensive, and an attack then would fail: if we waited until October,
I guaranteed complete success. In my view it would be madness to
attack in September. Was I to do so? Alexander backed me up
whole-heartedly as he always did, and the reply was sent on the lines
I wanted. I had told Alexander privately that, in view of my promise to the soldiers, I refused to attack before October; if a September attack was ordered by Whitehall, they would have to get
someone else to do it. My stock was rather high after Alam Halfa!
We heard no more about a September attack.

Field-Marshal LORD MONTGOMERY

ALAMEIN: THE CURTAIN RISES

Standing in the white moonlight on 23rd October in the long
minutes of that last hour before the guns of Alamein opened, I felt a
sudden shock of silence. Not a gun, not a rifle fired. The seconds
ticked on. Never before had this silence happened and it was
happening on this very one evening when it should not have come.
I jumped up the steps into my caravan and rang the CRA to see what
he still had to fill the gaping hole in our common noises. Only our
6-pounder anti-tank guns were not on the move under the Army
plans so he ordered them to shatter this tell-tale quiet. Soon their
staccato cracks broke open the night. We wondered what those at
the receiving end would make of the solid shot that was bowling
and bumping about trenches and plopping into the sandy ridges.
Nothing probably until too late. For us, they brought a little
normality into that strange night.

At 9.40 pm some 500 British guns opened a counter-bombard-
ment to knock out the enemy's artillery on 30th Corps' front. It was
a reasonably successful shoot, damaging and silencing the Axis guns.

There was no roar of cannon, at least none that we heard as the
sound came through the muffling sands below Ruweisat—none even
from our own divisional guns hard by. Wide to the north and south
played the swift flickering lightning flashes, dead white, as if giants
danced a Khuttack war dance whirling their swords about their

heads under the moon. And the sound, too, it fluttered all around us and above us. Many a time I have been in a bombardment, our own and the enemy's, and never have I listened to so seemingly gentle a noise of guns. When I say fluttered, I mean fluttered like a thousand moths—no other. It was hard to believe that 500 field and medium guns close by were pounding the enemy's batteries with shell.

Lieutenant-General SIR FRANCIS TUKER, KCIE, CB, DSO,
OBE (who commanded the 4th Indian Division at Alamein)

THE DEVIL'S GARDEN

The sappers had the simplest brief at Alamein's first night: follow the infantry, clear the mines for the tanks. In the southern corridor the New Zealand rifle companies went first; that foot-itching walk with eyes searching for horns and wires in the sand. Three sapper units would trail them, making four tank roads. The gaps code-named Ink and Boat were Moore's; Bottle and Hat gaps were left to a pair of Army field companies. The CRE in charge of the sappers and supporting Military Police and signals detachments was Lt.-Col. Gilbert McMeekan, a big and vigorous officer who followed Moore's gap in his staff car 'in order to see the troops'. . . .

A few sappers seemed to be utterly alone in a fearful noise as the barrage began and the New Zealanders started forward. McMeekan found the noise 'soothing'. Dust hadn't blotted out the moon yet. There was a No Man's Land of perhaps a mile before the first belt of mines and the 3rd squadron gapping parties walked to within 500 yards of the garden, their sandbagged pilot vehicle driven by Sapper Bill Shaw. Then they waited for the blue light signal from the reconnaissance officer. They had no infantry protection. 'We felt rather lonely and naked,' said Moore afterwards. As they reached the fringe of the minefield, machine guns were turned to them and a few shells fell. The pilot vehicle blew up and provided a splendid target for about ten minutes.

The advance was 20 minutes late and McMeekan found that his communications were valueless: telephone wires were broken by the shelling and wireless was scarcely better. Moore's men worked at first without serious interference, then a heavy machine gun put in a word on their left. Lt. John Van Gruten, a former undergraduate, was sent to silence it. He did.

Bromley Hotchkiss, when he joined the squadron, felt 'a bit of an outsider'. Now he was a corporal. In the gapping of the first belt of mines all his section had been shot away, killed or wounded. He moved the thousand yards to the next field by himself and marked his section's gap. A lorry bringing MPs, wire and marker posts failed to arrive. Hotchkiss found some wire and scrounged posts from the New Zealanders ahead. Then he hung the regulation lamps (green on the safe side of the gap) crouching down below the machine gun tracers, reaching up to the posts like a monkey. The first he knew of his Military Medal was an item in the *Birkenhead News,* sent by his mother.

At the next minefield 3rd squadron were in the very jaws of the assault. The floor was thick with New Zealand and German dead and with anxious casualties. Here, too, was a more elaborate sowing of mines, Italian Red Devils, booby traps, wires inviting the feet. Moore went crawling to find a deviation and almost laid his hands on an S mine's horns. In the left of the two gaps Sgt Bill Stanton, the St Helen's glass-blower, and a strict disciplinarian, took the place of two detector operators who were hit. Moore was feeling a nostalgia for infantry support now, especially when a heavy machine gun began firing accurately from only 70 yards away, and halted the advance. Luckily an alert New Zealand officer noticed this and wiped out the gun post with two of his men.

The tanks were to use the gaps at 4 am. By 3, Moore's sappers were actually in front of the infantry. Bottle gap had been prepared on schedule and Col. McMeekan, his eardrum shattered by a shell's blast, was trying to get the delayed Hat gap open. He was now almost totally deaf and had to give up the driving of his jeep after he failed to hear a Maori sentry's challenge. When another party of Maoris yelled at him McMeekan got out of his jeep and found a trip wire tangled on the back axle.

It was almost six when Moore saw the last marker in the gap. He raced back through the gap to the expanse between the minefields where the Sherwood Rangers' tanks were lined, nose to tail. Moore jumped into the leading turret and shouted to the officers to Come On. The tanks moved immediately, up to the crest of a ridge before the second minefield where they could see Sgt Stanton ready to wave them on. On the ridge, they became silhouettes; the German anti-tank guns in the enemy's main battle position opened up and there was a frightful clang as Moore's adopted tank was hit squarely. He ran back and guided the second tank round the disabled hulk. This one was hit. Moore ran to another. The guns hit it. In the first five minutes six tanks were burning, soon 16 were lost, and the gunfire knocked down marker posts so that more tanks, trying to open out to a flank, went into the minefield.

PHILIP NORMAN

Of the many gallant actions at Alamein certainly one of the most remarkable was the stand made by a small mixed group of 300 men of the Rifle Brigade, the Royal Artillery and the Royal Engineers, with nineteen six-pounder anti-tank guns, in an isolated position, 'Snipe', far in front of the British line. This was attacked throughout a whole day by massed Axis tanks. Men and guns were picked off one by one. At the end of the day the one remaining gun was towed away triumphantly: the position had not been overrun. A subsequent committee of investigation confirmed that twenty-two German and ten Italian tanks were destroyed by this little band. Its commander, Lieutenant-Colonel V. B. Turner of the Rifle Brigade, was awarded the VC and a number of his officers and men were also decorated.

SNIPE

By now it was nearly 11 o'clock in the forenoon and the position had become extremely hot in both senses of the word. The desert was quivering with heat. The gun detachments and the platoons squatted in their pits and trenches, the sweat running in rivers down their dust-caked faces. There was a terrible stench. The flies swarmed in black clouds upon the dead bodies and the excreta and tormented the wounded. The place was strewn with burning tanks and carriers, wrecked guns and vehicles, and over all drifted the smoke and dust from bursting high explosive and from the blast of guns. Six more carriers had been hit and set on fire. The 6-pdrs of Sergeants Hine and Dolling had been knocked out and only thirteen remained in action. Sergeant Swann sent the tough little Hine to take over the gun of Sergeant Cope, who had been hit. Several of the detachments were down to two or three men and officers were manning guns to replace casualties. Other detachments were doubling up. Thus, one of the guns was manned by Lieutenant A. B. Holt-Wilson, Sergeant Ayris and Rifleman Chard—a very tough team who later in the day were to handle their gun with exceptional daring.

But the offensive spirit had firmly seized upon all ranks. The bursting shells that shook the ground and the heavy shot that smashed a gun or carrier, or that took the breath from one's lungs with the vacuum of its close passing, could not shake that spirit. Every kill was acclaimed. At last they had got a weapon that could knock out the panzers. Gone was any thought of 'lying doggo', any conception of mere defence of 'pivot of manœuvre'. The gunners of 239th Battery, who so far had had only one target, buried their head on the spot, manned their brens and rifles and occupied themselves with 'rabbit shooting'. On three sides of the island there was enemy movement of every sort—parties on foot, trucks, staff cars, motor-cycles. Turner, Bird and other officers moved about from gun to gun throughout the morning, so also did Rifleman Burnhope, giving to the wounded, including a few German wounded found in the position, such succour as his scanty medical stores allowed.

The most serious shortage, however, was the shortage of 6-pdr ammunition. Bird and the great-hearted Corporal Francis—the 'young Old Bill' as Bird called him—set about transferring the heavy green boxes from one gun to another by jeep, unconcerned by the heavy burst of fire which this blatant movement invited. The shortage was particularly acute on the south-western sector, facing Hill 37, where Lieutenant Jack's guns were sited.

It was precisely from this direction that another attack was mounted at 1 o'clock, and again by Italian tanks. Believing, no doubt, that there could now be little left of the garrison after so long a drubbing, and having seen no gunfire for some time, eight tanks and one or more Semovente self-propelled field guns (of 105-mm calibre) advanced on the position, firing their machine-guns vigorously.

Here there was now only one gun in action that could bear. It was that commanded by Sergeant Charles Calistan, the finely-built young athlete from the East End of London. He was alone, one of his detachment lying wounded and the others having, on his orders, crawled away to fetch more ammunition. Seeing his predicament, Turner himself and Jack Toms ran to join him. Calistan took post on the left of the gun as layer, Turner on the right as loader, and Toms behind as No. 1.

Turner ordered fire to be held until the enemy tanks were within 600 yards. The sergeant and the two officers then opened a devastating fire. Five of the eight tanks and the Semoventes were hit very quickly one after the other and burst into flames. The three remaining tanks still came on, however, with great spirit, machine-gunning hard, and there were only two rounds of ammunition left.

Toms ran to his jeep, which was a hundred yards away, and quickly loaded several boxes of ammunition from a gun out of action. He drove back with the machine-gun bullets from the three tanks streaming down on him. It was an almost suicidal act. The jeep was riddled and burst into flames ten yards short of Calistan's gun. Turner ran to the jeep. So also did Corporal Francis, who had doubled over from Hine's gun to give a hand. Turner, Toms and Francis lugged the ammunition from the burning vehicle and dragged it to the gun.

At this point a shell splinter penetrated Turner's steel helmet and wounded him severely in the skull. He keeled over sideways beside the gun, the blood streaming down over his eyes.

Toms and Calistan carried on, joined now by Corporal Barnett as loading number. The three remaining Italian tanks, their machine-guns blazing, were now within 200 yards. The silent gun seemed to be at their mercy. Their bullets were beating like rain upon the gun-shield and kicking up spurts of sand in the shallow pit. Calistan, who all this time had been keeping them in his sight with the utmost unconcern, while he waited for the ammunition, laid with coolness and deliberation.

With three shots he killed all three tanks, which added their conflagrations to the other six.[1]

He then coolly turned round and said: 'We haven't had a chance

[1] Calistan, with the DCM and the MM to his name, was later given a commission, but was killed in Italy. He had been recommended for the Victoria Cross.

ABOVE Dunkirk: the beach

BELOW Returned via Dunkirk

ABOVE   North Africa: a typical tank crew

BELOW   North Africa: sharing a waterhole

ABOVE   North Africa: patrol of the Long Range Desert Group (see p. 91)

(see p. 91)

BELOW   North Africa: six-inch gun, Halfaya Pass

ABOVE Tobruk: at ease

BELOW Tobruk: prisoners on lighters in the harbour

ABOVE   Kohima: Garrison Hill (see p. 242)

BELOW   Kohima: Naga village

ABOVE   The Arakan

BELOW   The Arakan: Hill 1301 after capture

Imphal: combing elephant
grass for Japanese

Burma: crossing the
Irrawaddy

ABOVE   Burma: 'the road to Mandalay'

BELOW   Burma: mortaring Fort Dufferin, Mandalay (see p. 306)

Burma: by the Shweli river

ABOVE   North Africa: survivors of 'Snipe' (see p. 144)

BELOW   North Africa: 'naming of parts'

ABOVE   Normandy: typical *bocage* country

BELOW   Normandy: Shermans and Sannerville château

ABOVE   Normandy: the advance to the River Odon . . . an ammunition
lorry explodes under mortar fire

BELOW   Normandy: Shermans near Caumont

Normandy: the liberators . . .
Shermans move up through
Flers

Normandy: the Falaise road

ABOVE   Normandy: Canadian 'Sextons' in action . . . self-propelled
25 pdr. guns

BELOW   Arnhem: some survivors

ABOVE   Italy: mud at Scorticata near the River Rubicon

BELOW   Italy: mopping up Umbertide on the River Tiber

ABOVE   Germany: a 'brew-up' on the road to the Rhine

BELOW   Italy: Popski's Private Army in the Piazza San Marco, Venice

of a brew all morning, but the Eyeties have made us a fire, so let's use it.' He thereupon poured some water into a billy-can, which he set on the bonnet of the burning jeep, and brewed-up some tea. To the wounded Turner, it was 'as good a cup as I've ever tasted'.

This must, without doubt, have been a disconcerting blow to the enemy. An intercept of his wireless disclosed that he was seriously concerned by this island of resistance just before he was to launch his big counter-attack. No further tank activity, however, took place for another three hours, but in the meantime the shelling continued.

Turner, having lain down for a while under a camel's thorn bush near Calistan's gun, insisted, against all persuasion, on visiting his guns once more, but the effort was too severe and he had to be taken down into the small headquarters dug-out where Marten and the wireless were. Even from here he occasionally sallied out to give encouragement and example, but later in the day he began to suffer from the hallucination that he was defending a harbour against hostile warships. On seeing a tank, he would exclaim, 'Open fire on that destroyer.' It was, indeed, a very good simile and an hallucination of the sort that showed the spirit in the man. At length his officers had to restrain him physically.

Brigadier c. e. lucas phillips (an account based
on survivors' personal narratives)

ALAMEIN: THE AFTERMATH

As we advanced, I remembered how we had sat so long during my first action within a stone's throw of the enemy infantry, and I began to look very carefully at the trenches we passed. About two hundred yards from the German derelicts, which were now furiously belching inky smoke, I looked down into the face of a man lying hunched up in a pit. His expression of agony seemed so acute and urgent, his stare so wild and despairing, that for a moment I thought him alive. He was like a cleverly posed waxwork, for his position suggested a paroxysm, an orgasm of pain. He seemed to move and writhe. But he was stiff. The dust which powdered his face like an actor's lay on his wide open eyes, whose stare held my gaze like the Ancient Mariner's. He had tried to cover his wounds with towels against the flies. His haversack lay open, from which he had taken towels and dressings. His water-bottle lay tilted with the cork out. Towels and haversack were dark with dried blood, darker still with a great concourse of flies. This picture, as they say, told a story. It filled me with useless pity.

As the tank went gruffly past, the head of a living man was raised from the next pit; he had not strength to keep it raised, but lifted head and arm alternately, as a man lifts a hat on a stick to draw fire. As we went on moving past, an awful despair settled on his face. I halted the tank, realising suddenly that the driver had not seen him, and had the engine switched off. I got out of the turret and ran to him, hoping that there were no snipers about. I held a two-gallon can for him while he drank the warm, rusty water. Then he said : 'Can you get me out of here?' He was a second lieutenant, I think of New Zealand infantry. His leg was hit in several places below the knee, and covered, like the dead man's wound, with a towel. 'The one that got me got my water-bottle,' he said. 'I've been here two days. I've had about enough. Can you get me out?' His voice broke and hesitated over the words. He suddenly added, remembering: 'Do something for the chap in the next trench,' and seeing my face, 'Is he dead?' 'Dead as a doornail,' said my voice.

KEITH DOUGLAS

ALAMEIN: THE BREAK-OUT

Next morning there was still heavy shelling in the bulge. I went up, but did not enjoy my trip. But the General[1] was certain. He said he had told the Army Commander that the battle was over and had sent a cable to the same effect to the New Zealand Government. In the late afternoon there was a divisional conference. The General said the gap was made to all intents and purposes and next morning we would go south through it and head westwards and north to Fuka on the desert road to cut off the German divisions in the north. The six Italian divisions in the south, without troop-carrying transport, were doomed in any case. We were to load up with eight days' water, rations, petrol for 500 miles, the gunners with 360 rounds per twenty-five pounder and 200 rounds per medium gun.

[1]Freyberg.

This was great news. Monty and I opened our last bottle of whisky to celebrate it.

Next day we did move out. It was quite impossible to move in formed bodies. All we could do was to work our way through the gaps in the minefields in single file, the armour leading. It was all most confused and difficult. . . . At last, in the late afternoon, we found that the way was clear ahead.

The armour was going headlong. Plainly there was a real gap. I abandoned the idea of halting to form up and went on with my head-quarters group, knowing very well that everyone was getting on as fast as possible irrespective of anything I could do or say and we could concentrate from the rear later. A message came for me to go forward and join the General. I went up fast in my staff car, and after passing through Main Divisional Headquarters found him at the very head of the column, happy as a cherub and pointing and smiling gleefully at each group of stranded Italians or abandoned guns that we passed. There were very many signs of complete victory.

Major-General SIR HOWARD KIPPENBERGER

FINALE

After the battle I went to see General Morshead, the Australian commander, to congratulate him on the magnificent fighting carried out by his division. His reply was the classic understatement of all time. He said: 'Thank you, General. The boys were interested.'

Lieutenant-General SIR BRIAN HORROCKS, KCB, KBE,
DSO, MC

1943

'It will take the rest of this year to finish the show in North Africa and give Italy a proper bang. Then, next year, 1944, we had better land in Western Europe and I would like to come home and take part in that. I look forward to leading the Eighth Army into Rome. By Jove, what a party!'

MONTGOMERY TO ALAN BROOKE
16TH FEBRUARY 1943

On the Burma/India front 1943 was mainly a year of waiting and prepara-tion. But all through that year, and the next, and until Japan collapsed, captives from the Empire, both servicemen and civilians, were starving, rotting or dying in prisoner-of-war camps or carrying out forced labour, usually in the vilest conditions, such as

ON THE RAILWAY

Once again time ceased to have any significance, for almost a year no man knew what day of the week nor what week of the month nor even what month of the year it was. It was just 1943 and the Railway. If one were to survive it was essential not to acknowledge the horror that lay all around, still more not to perceive the effect it had upon oneself. It was not wise ever to look in a mirror. Life accordingly evolved into a blur of continuous work, people dying, guards bellowing, heavy loads to be carried, fever which came in tides of heat and cold on alternate days, dysentery and hunger. All those became the normal. Upon them, occasionally, an event super-imposed itself with sufficient violence to be remembered.

There was little scope for planning one's way of life. To preserve my health, I vowed to wash whenever it rained, lying under the dripping edge of the fly, and to clean my teeth every day, using the tooth brush Piddington had given me and ground-up charcoal for powder. Charcoal was also useful as a medicine against dysentery. To preserve some dignity, I vowed I would shave at least once a week if only I could remember the days. To preserve my self-respect, I vowed that whenever necessary I would make the latrines or bust; and to preserve at least some mental agility, I determined to learn off by heart one page a day of Mr Hitler's *Mein Kampf*. As the days succeeded one another for the rest of that black year, this particular vow became increasingly difficult, but I managed never to yield to the temptation of excusing myself from my task—and in return derived a perverse pleasure from the daily assimilation of so much vile prose.

The oldest member of our party died of what looked suspiciously like cholera. Another fell ill and followed him shortly afterwards. We were now six and I found that my limbs no longer functioned very well. There was an angry swelling in my feet which made them look like purple balloons—the toes mere cocktail-sausages attached to them like teats on an udder.

As I looked at them one of the others, pointing at my bloated extremities, asked: 'What's the trouble?'

'Oedema,' I told him.

'Christ!' he said, much impressed; then, cautiously, 'What's that?'

'Swelling,' I told him.

'Silly bastard,' he laughed, 'why didn't you say so first time?'

But, oedema or swelling or whatever the cause, my legs now ceased walking either easily or quickly and whenever any weight was put on my back they folded up. Since Nippon's only object in bringing us all to Thailand had been to put weights on our backs and then get us to carry them elsewhere this condition of mine did not bode well for the future.

And, in truth, things would have gone very badly indeed for me had it not been for the generous help of the men with me. At all times they covered up for me so that the guards did not realise how slowly I worked. And when they had finished their own quota of work then they would do mine, too.

In this respect one Snowy Bernard did most. He was unfortunate enough to have paired up with me when we first started work. Now that my arms seemed to have no strength with an axe he would chop down his own timber, then mine. When my legs crumpled under the weight of carrying the timber—particularly the long bamboos—back to camp, he would deliver his own, then come back and deliver mine. And never was there any suggestion of condescension but only that inexhaustible readiness on the part of the ordinary man to lend a hand whenever it was needed.

And all the time that Snowy and the three other men carried me so steadfastly, I became more and more of a burden. The swelling spread up my legs so that the ankles and knees vanished into two water-filled columns of suet. Then my trunk began to swell with that same ominous suggestion of liquid beneath the skin tissues and even my eyes became merely two slits in a puffy sphere. I was constantly surprised by the slowness of my movements. I was not aware of being slow, but my companions and I had only to start walking and in thirty seconds I was thirty yards behind them. Then Snowy would stop and come back and shove me firmly along until we caught up—whereupon, left to my own devices, I would at once flounder to the rear again.

The guards began to take an unconcealed interest in my condition and daily showed their surprise that I was still alive. '*Ashita mati mati,*' they would say, pointing towards the crop of arms and legs that protruded from the washed-out graves beyond our tent, and drawing a mocking cross on the ground. If I had required any stimulant to prevent me from succumbing to the beri beri that so bloated me those daily jibes by the guards would have done the job perfectly. Nevertheless the morning at last arrived when I found that not only could I not walk as fast as the others, I could not walk at all. This was disconcerting and I decided that I must see an MO. Accordingly that night I left the tent on my hands and knees, eluded the guards, and crawled towards the Headquarters camp. As I covered that quarter of a mile I found myself completely at a loss to understand why babies should spend the first twelve months at least of their lives propelling themselves in quite such an exhausting manner. The moon rose. In the powerful light it shed I decided that Thailand must be the only place in the world where all that moon-beams bring out is decay and mud and the demented high-pitched love song of baboons. My musings on this subject were interrupted by the MO himself, who spotted me ploughing—infant-like—through the mire and wanted to know what the hell I thought I was doing.

I replied that I thought I was coming to see him. He parried this with a question as to whence I came. When I told him he pointed out that that being one of the most cholera-ridden areas in Thailand I was extremely unwelcome and would I kindly stay where I was.

I said: 'What, out here in the mud?' and he replied:

'Yes,' as if that were the most reasonable thing in the world. I was deeply aggrieved and said so. He, however, was adamant and eventually he persuaded me to remove my unwholesome presence altogether by throwing me a small jar. It landed about ten yards up in a pool of slime. I crawled up and retrieved it and, wiping it clean on some leaves, looked at the label. 'Marmite', it read.

'You have beri beri,' he shouted.

'I know,' I replied from the mud.

'Take a spoonful of that a day,' he advised.

'Will it do any good?' I asked.

'Might,' he replied, and, returning firmly inside the palisade of the Headquarters camp, indicated that the subject was closed. I crawled back to our camp, where I found the guards very cross that I had eluded them. I took a spoonful of Marmite and, exhausted, fell asleep.

We were sent down to the river and then given one hundred and twenty pounds each of rice to carry. The track up the mountain, being clay and wet, was murderous. To our surprise we carted the rations not to Kanu but past it to the next camp, about eight kilos up.

Outside Kanu, in the small stream that trickled down from the mountain above, lay a naked man. When asked why he lay there, he pointed to his legs. Tiny fish nibbled at the rotten flesh round the edges of his ulcers. Then he pointed inside the camp. Other ulcer-sufferers, reluctant to submit to this nibbling process, wore the only dressings available—a strip of canvas torn from a tent soaked in Eusol. Their ulcers ran the whole length of their shin bones in channels of putrescence. Looking back at the man in the stream it was impossible to decide, even though he was insane, which treatment was the best.

We reached the next camp, and found it practically deserted—almost all the original inhabitants were dead. There were proud signs of the struggle for survival those men had put up. Carefully constructed latrines, spotless surrounds, an overhead pipeline made from bamboos which brought cholera-free water from its source two or three miles away and hundreds of feet up at the top of the mountain. This pipeline led to a shower-centre with a bamboo floor and separate cubicles (pathetic symbol of man's desire for even a little privacy) and to a cookhouse that was all clean wood and carefully-swept packed earth. All of these were refinements installed after gruelling sixteen-hour shifts of work at the expense of sleep and the re-charging of their energies so vital to the next day's shift. But none of this had been enough—flies carried the cholera germs and mosquitoes the malarial parasites. Starvation and slavery did the rest. Now, as we set out back to our own camp, there were only a few skeleton-like travesties of humanity left and the big fire where they burnt their dead.

These fires flared at every camp where cholera struck. They lighted the way out to work in the dark before dawn: they guided the men back through the dark wetness of the jungle long after dusk. And always, lying round them in stick-like bundles, were the bodies that awaited cremation—bodies at which the returning men peered closely as they came in to see if any of their mates lay among them. And every now and then, as they filed past, came that muttered: 'Half his luck.'

About these fires a strange story was told. At one camp the task of attending to the pyre and of consigning the bodies to the flames was given to an Australian who, being without brains or emotions or finer susceptibilities of any kind, was more than happy in his work.

He stripped the dead of their gold tooth caps; he stole fearlessly from the guards who dared not touch him lest he contaminate them: he cooked what he stole—for one only stole food, or something that could be bartered for food or tobacco, in those days—on the fire where he burnt the bodies. He was a complete moron.

It was his practice before dealing with the fresh batch of bodies that arrived each morning to boil himself a 'cuppa cha' and watch the working party fall-in to be marched away to the cuttings. He liked watching the working parties fall-in to march away because *he* stayed at home by his fire where, even in the monsoonal rains, he could keep warm and do his cooking. Upon one particular morning he sipped his tea out of the jam tin that served as a mug and watched the parade. As he watched he rolled some tobacco in a strip of the tissue that clings to the inside of a bamboo: then, his fag completed, he picked up a body and tossed it easily from yards off (for it was only light) on to the fire. He enjoyed the revulsion this caused. He did it every morning just before the workers marched out. Grinning at them as they glowered angrily, he then shambled to the fringe of the fire to light his cigarette.

As he leant forward to pick up a faggot the body he had just tossed into the flames, its sinews contracted, suddenly sat bolt upright, and grunted, and in its hand thrust out a flaming brand on to the cigarette in the moron's mouth.

With a scream of terror the man who had burnt hundreds of bodies with callous indifference fell backwards, his hands over his eyes. When the workers reached him he was jabbering and mad.

They took him to the hut that housed the sick, an attap roof draped over a patch of mud in which—all over one another—lay hundreds of men. For days he lay there silent, knowing nothing. Then one night he suddenly remembered and screamed, screamed piercingly and long so that, even though it was forbidden, the medical orderly lit a resin flare and rushed down to where he lay to see why he screamed.

RUSSELL BRADDON

*

Early in January a British offensive in the Arakan region of South Burma was moving sluggishly. It stuck, and the Japanese counter-attacked violently with great skill. The British were shattered and demoralised. Slim, now commanding 15 Corps, had to cope with the aftermath.

There was no doubt that the disasters in Arakan, following an unbroken record of defeat, had brought morale in large sections of the army to a dangerously low ebb. Morale was better in the forward combat formations, as most of the shaken units from Arakan had been withdrawn. 4 Corps in the centre, and, I flattered myself, 15 Corps in the south were staunch enough. It was in the rear areas, on the lines of communication, in the reinforcement camps, amid the conglomeration of administrative units that covered the vast area behind the front, that morale was really low. Through this filter all units, drafts, and individuals for the forward formations had to percolate, and many became contaminated with the virus of despondency. In the summer of 1943 there was a depressingly high incidence of desertion from drafts moving up the line of communication. Right back into India rumours were assiduously spread picturing the Japanese as the super bogy-men of the jungle, harping on their savagery, their superior equipment and training, the hardships our men had suffered, the lack of everything, the faults in our leadership, and the general hopelessness of expecting ever to defeat the enemy. Such stories were brought even by drafts from England. It was an insidious gangrene that could easily spread.

Field-Marshal LORD SLIM

For the despondent there was one ray of light. In March Wingate and his Long Range Penetration Group trudged deep into Japanese territory and crossed the rivers Chindwin and Irrawaddy, both in Japanese hands. The military results were negligible, the suffering enormous, and the casualties shocking. Of 3,000 who sallied forth, 2,182 returned to India and of these only 600 were fit for future soldiering. Yet the mere knowledge that British troops could tackle the Japanese on their own terms and on their own ground, the jungle, could fight and win and survive, was a tremendous fillip to morale at the time when it was most needed. Michael Calvert, one of Wingate's column commanders, describes an episode in the withdrawal:

I arranged for a final supply drop near Taunggon, then divided the column into ten dispersal groups, which set off on different routes towards the Irrawaddy and Chindwin.

I took with me the cooks, orderlies, and other administrative chaps and our commando platoon, which was commanded by a young Scot, Geoffrey Lockett, a man after my own heart. Geoffrey, who had been a wine merchant before the war, had to have most of his teeth out just before we went to Burma, and he added to the rather grotesque effect of this by growing a wispy beard. Also, he always insisted on wearing the kilt, in the jungle and out of it. He was quite fearless and the sight of this toothless, bearded and kilted Scot charging at them with blazing eyes must have put the fear of God into many a Jap.

With Geoffrey and the rest of my party I set off south again in the hope of drawing away some of the Japs while the other parties of the column got out of the area. Finally we turned north-westward and after slipping across the Irrawaddy without being challenged reached the railway at a spot some way to the south of Nankan, the scene of our earlier demolitions. I still had some explosives with me and decided to use them here to draw the Japs and help the other chaps.

The enemy were being very careful about the railway line now and we knew there were Japs not far away, but I reckoned we could do our job quickly and slip off in the darkness without being caught. I took Geoffrey with me and we laid the charges; then I felt for my time pencils, which would set them off after we had left. These pencils were in various colours, each colour representing a different length of time between setting the charge and the explosion. I had a

strict rule that before a demolition party went out they should sort
out their pencils and nick them with a knife, so many nicks to each
colour, so that they would be easy to pick out even at night. It was
an excellent rule, but that night I had forgotten to obey it myself!

I sat on the railway embankment with Geoffrey and felt myself
breaking out into a cold sweat as I realised what I had done, or
rather what I had not done. To make matters worse some of the
lookouts had just reported that a group of Japs were close by; they
were an engineer working party building a bridge.

'What the hell do we do now?' I whispered urgently to Geoffrey.

He was completely unruffled by the situation. 'Better light a
match and see what we're doing,' he said.

I wouldn't have put it past him to show his contempt for the Japs
by striking a match without any cover, but I had no intention of
doing this. I looked round in the dim light for a bush big enough to
provide a shield, but the banks had been cleared of thick scrub.
Suddenly I found an answer to the problem.

'Lift up that kilt of yours,' I said, grabbing a handful of time
pencils and the matches.

Even Geoffrey looked startled at this. 'Here, be careful,' he said.
'Watch what you're doing with those things.'

The thick folds of the kilt, held close to the ground, proved a
first-class black-out curtain. I quickly sorted out the pencils I wanted
while Geoffrey muttered away darkly about suing me for damages.
We then crept silently down to the track, set out charges and
retreated rapidly to join the rest of our party. We moved off at
once, west again towards the Chindwin, for the Japs would be
looking for us very shortly and I wanted to make the most of the
time the pencils were giving us. Later we heard the distant but grati-
fying explosions behind us. Geoffrey, walking by my side, chuckled
into his beard and I knew that here was a man who would make his
mark in the jungle war.

MICHAEL CALVERT

*

*Meanwhile in North Africa the Eighth Army, Alamein left far behind,
was pushing Rommel slowly but steadily westwards until, in March, they*

hit the Mareth Line, which ran inland from the Gulf of Gabes ... a series
of fortifications constructed in earlier years by the French to keep the
Italians out of Tunisia. A frontal attack on the Line itself failed; but
Montgomery set in motion a 'left hook' by the New Zealand and 1st
Armoured Divisions, who made a wide curve south and then north,
cutting into the rear of the Axis fixed positions. This move culminated in a
night drive by the armour through a narrow defile on to the hamlet of El
Hamma. Horrocks, who with Freyberg was in charge of the 'left hook',
describes his sensations—

IN THE DARK TOO

It was the most exciting and worrying night of my life. As my small
tactical HQ, consisting of three tanks, took up its position in the
armoured mass, I realised very well that if this attack went wrong,
there was no doubt as to whose head would be on the block. I could
hear the arm-chair strategists in their clubs in London saying,
'Heavens! The man must be mad. Fancy trying to pass one armoured
division through an enemy armoured division. And in the dark too.'
Because that was what we were trying to do.

And, of course, in the cold light of day, viewed from England,
they would be quite right; but in reality it wasn't as mad as it seemed.
The Germans as a rule do not react very quickly to something new,
and in this attack two new techniques were being tried out. Never
before had they been subjected to such devastating low-level air
attacks and they were shaken, or so it seemed. Because the 8th
Armoured Brigade, leading the New Zealand assault with their
Balaclava charge, had not suffered such heavy casualties as might
have been expected. Then on top of this was the unusual employ-
ment of armour by night.

All round was the rumbling of tanks, vague shapes looming out of
the dusk. I started very bravely with the upper part of my body
sticking out of the turret of my tank, but as the advance went on I
got lower and lower until only the top of my head was visible.
There was too much stuff flying about for comfort, though most of
the enemy fire was going over our heads into the area which we had
just vacated.

Then suddenly it was dark, and we halted. This was the most

trying time of all: we couldn't even risk that 8th Army panacea for all ills, a brew up. We just had to sit, deep in the enemy positions, and wait. I got down into the tank to see how my crew, the gunner-operator and driver, were feeling. They were cheerful and completely unimpressed by the fact that they were taking part in a unique military operation: they might in fact have been driving up the long valley at Aldershot. In moments of crisis the phlegm of the British soldier is very reassuring.

This long halt seemed to go on for ever: then a pale dusty moon began to make its appearance. And at last, thank goodness, we were off again. It was just possible to make out the dim shape of the tanks in front and on either side and there was a great deal of ill-aimed firing all round. At times the tanks were crunching over occupied enemy trenches, and we could see terrified parties of Germans and Italians running about with their hands up. But we hadn't time to bother about prisoners.

Our progress was desperately slow. That was my chief worry. If we didn't succeed in getting through in the dark, the situation in the morning didn't bear thinking about. We should be surrounded by the enemy and dominated by the hills on either side of the valley.

The reason for the continuous halts soon became clear: the valley was intersected by wadis, many of which were tank obstacles, and it was not easy for the leading regiment to find crossing places. Some-times this necessitated getting on to a one-tank front. But we steadily rumbled on and this difficult night advance was brilliantly carried out by the 1st Armoured Division. As the night wore on the noise of firing came more and more from the rear, and suddenly I realised that we were through—the impossible manœuvre had come off. It was an unforgettable moment.

Lieutenant-General SIR BRIAN HORROCKS

The Eighth Army was now coming to the end of its run. In mid-April its drive westwards brought it to a dead halt in front of 'the inner keep of Tunisia, the great mountain mass which reared its ramparts around the Gulf of Carthage', the harsh bare ridges and sinister valleys among which the British First Army and their American and French allies had been struggling to reach Tunis since the days of their landings back in November. It was at a little place called Enfidaville that the halt occurred, a point where

*the mountains sheer down to the sea and only a thin strip of flat ground
separates the massif from the Mediterranean. Montgomery first sought,
without success, to 'bounce' the Germans off the heights in the hope of
rushing his armour along the flats. The 4th Indian Division put in an
attack on a feature called Garci, and here the Gurkhas exploited their
traditional skills. A Jemadar of 1/9 Gurkhas went in with*

THE KUKRI

I was challenged in a foreign language. I felt it was not the British
language or I would have recognised it. To make quite sure I crept
up and found myself looking into the face of a German. I recognised
him by his helmet. He was fumbling with his weapon so I cut off his
head with my kukri. Another appeared from a slit trench and I cut
him down also. I was able to do the same to two others, but one
made a great deal of noise, which raised the alarm. I had a cut at a
fifth but I am afraid I only wounded him. Yet perhaps the wound
was severe, for I struck him between the neck and shoulder.

I was now involved in a struggle with a number of Germans, and
eventually, after my hands had become cut and slippery with blood,
they managed to wrest my kukri from me. One German beat me
over the head with it, inflicting a number of wounds. He was not
very skilful, however, sometimes striking me with the sharp edge
but oftener with the blunt.

They managed to beat me to the ground where I lay pretending
to be dead. The Germans got back into their trenches and after a
while I looked up. I could not see anything, for my eyes were full of
blood. I wiped the blood out of my eyes and quite near I saw a
German machine-gun. I thought, 'If only I can reach that gun I shall
be able to kill the lot.' By now it was getting light and as I lay
thinking of a plan to reach the gun, my platoon advanced and
started to hurl grenades among the enemy. But they were also
falling very near me, so I thought that if I did not move I really
would be dead. I managed to get to my feet, and ran towards my
platoon. Not recognising me, I heard one of my men call, 'Here
comes the enemy! Shoot him!' I bade them not to do so. They
recognised my voice and let me come in.

My hands being cut about and bloody, and having lost my kukri,

I had to ask one of my platoon to take my pistol from my holster and to put it in my hand. I then took command of my platoon again.

I met my company commander, who bade me go to the Regimental Aid Post. I said, 'Sahib, there is fighting to be done, and I know the enemy's dispositions. I must stay and command my platoon.' But he firmly ordered me and I had to go. Yet before I went, one of my Bren gunners was hit, and my company commander, although wounded in the neck, took over the Bren gun and continued to fire it. Morcover, the doctor sahib, having bandaged me, refused to allow me to return to my platoon.

JEMADAR DEWAN SING (the Jemadar had a dozen wounds on his head alone: he was awarded the Indian Order of Merit)

*

THE CHIEF OF THE IMPERIAL GENERAL STAFF CONFERS WITH CHURCHILL

During the meeting the PM sent for me. By the time I reached him in the Annex he was in his bath. However, he received me as soon as he came out, looking like a Roman Centurion with nothing on except a large bath-towel draped round him. He shook me warmly by the hand in this get-up and told me to sit down while he dressed. A most interesting procedure. First he stepped into a white silk vest, then white silk drawers, and walked up and down the room in this kit looking rather like 'Humpty-Dumpty', with a large body and small thin legs. Then a white shirt which refused to join comfortably round his neck and so was left open with a bow-tie to keep it together. Then the hair(what there was of it) took much attention, a handkerchief was sprayed with scent and then rubbed on his head. The few hairs were then brushed and finally sprayed direct. Finally trousers, waistcoat and coat, and meanwhile he rippled on the whole time about Monty's battle and our proposed visit to North Africa.

Field-Marshal LORD ALANBROOKE

*

To belong to the Eighth or any other Army is to know the comfort of
comradeship, the solace of solidarity. Even the fighter or bomber pilot, if he
survived his sortie, had a base to which he could regularly return: he
belonged to a unit. But this was a war in which many men, and women,
carried out lonely tasks in enemy territory, for months or even years on end,
with only their own selves or a few others for companions. The agents
dropped into occupied Europe, the coast-watchers in the islands of the Far
East, the organisers of resistance groups and native tribes shared this
solitary experience. One such was Spencer Chapman. In his introduction
to Chapman's reminiscences Lord Wavell wrote: '. . . the neutrality of the
Malayan jungle, as Colonel Spencer Chapman warns us, is armed. He
himself was dangerously ill for two months on end, including a period of
unconsciousness for seventeen days; he suffered at various times from black-
water fever, pneumonia, and tick-typhus, as alternatives or additions to
almost chronic malaria; it took him once twelve days' hard marching to
cover ten miles through the jungle; and he was marching barefooted six
days without food on another occasion.' Chapman describes the kind of life
he led in this account of

A CHINESE CAMP

Next day—New Year's Day, 1943—I was shaking hands with
Cotterill and Tyson. Cotterill had been assistant manager of Sungei
Lembing Rubber Estate, and Tyson, a New Zealander, underground
Manager of PCCL (Pahang Consolidated Concession Limited), the
world's largest open lode tin mine, also at Sungei Lembing. They
had been left near the mine with a transmitter and a Chinese operator
supplied by 101 STS to report on the advance of the Japanese. Late in
January 1942 they had been recalled to Segamat. On the way their
wireless operator, who carried all their money as he did their
shopping and paid their coolies, was murdered and robbed by
another Chinese. They had then worked their way south, mostly by
raft, until they reached the Keratong river only to hear that the Japs
were already in Johore. After this they lived with an old Chinese
couple for a month until they had been invited to join this band of
armed Chinese.

Tyson was suffering from what we imagined to be a bad chill, but
it was probably pneumonia. He was one of those unfortunate people

who become really ill as a result of leech bites; Cotterill told me he had been severely bitten in the small of his back some months before and had never properly recovered. While I was there he grew steadily worse—though even then we had no idea how ill he really was, and on January 8th, much to our surprise and sorrow, he died.

The Chinese in this camp were indeed bandits, but they were cheerful and likeable rogues, and they did not suffer from the political and social inhibitions which made the guerillas in some respects so infuriating to live with. The nucleus of the gang had in pre-war days distilled illicit *samsu* and sold it in Segamat. Under the Jap occupation they found themselves without a job or money, so they had collected some weapons, and, forming a band of about forty, operated against the Chinese *towkays* who were helping the Japs. Cotterill had been asked to drive a car for them on one of their raids, which took place shortly before my arrival at Palong, but he thought it wiser not to identify himself with such activities. He told me they had arrived back with suitcases full of loot—tinned food, suits of clothes, bales of silk, jewellery, and several thousand dollars in cash. They claimed to have made a fair division, as was their habit, leaving the *towkay* with half his possessions to carry on business.

Two hours' march to the east of the river they had a jungle camp which I visited, but when I met them they had moved to a group of deserted Malay *kampongs* in a bend of the Palong river. All the Malays were now living in the jungle with the Sakai, and the bandits were growing swamp paddy and living extremely well on unlimited rice, fish, meat, fruit and vegetables.

Though the food and general standard of living was much more luxurious than in the ordinary guerilla camps, discipline and organisation were non-existent. The leader, who had no control over his men, had taken the wife of a Chinese he was alleged to have shot, and she ran the camp—in so far as it was run at all. Half the men lived with their women in squalid shacks in the jungle edge, while the rest, including the Europeans, slept in a tin-roofed hut out in the clearing. Cotterill told me these men also used to capture Malay women in the jungle by firing over their heads until they stopped. Nearly half of them were heavy opium smokers; unlimited *samsu* was available, and free fights not uncommon. It was almost impossible to sleep at night, as the men took it in turn to puff at the opium pipe and the drug made them extremely garrulous and talkative. I have always wondered what it is like to smoke opium, and longed to try, but I desisted, not because I was afraid of becoming an addict but so as not to lose face with the guerillas, who would be bound to hear of it.

In spite of their lack of organisation, the bandits were first-class guerilla material, and thirsting to 'have a crack' at the Jap. They were, moreover, well able to do so, being better armed than any camp I had hitherto visited, though they had already—before Cotterill and Tyson joined them—thrown away several boxes of grenades, not knowing what they were. They had four machine-guns, ten Tommy-guns, thirty rifles, and an almost unlimited supply of ammunition, which they used to blaze off at trees—being extremely gratified if they succeeded in hitting one. But they had no military knowledge—and admitted it—and were consequently the best pupils I ever had. Our lecture-room was a Malay mosque, and as Ah Ching could not understand their dialect and they could not speak Mandarin, I had to address them in Malay, having carefully learnt the more difficult words from Cotterill beforehand. . . .

The week I spent at this camp was one of my happiest in the jungle.

F. SPENCER CHAPMAN, DSO

*

There were also

MEDITERRANEAN MISSIONS

Air operations on the scale we were now arranging from Derna were something quite new. Neither the RAF nor the army had produced any foolproof or as far as I know any other kind of guide as to how they should be handled. Somebody had to know what aircraft were available, what sorties they could make and what loads they could carry, and work out a programme of sorties which fitted our needs into this picture, arranging for the people and the loads to be on the spot at the right time, and, above all, settling priorities. It all sounds very simple, but it called for infinite tact and a specialised skill of a high order. This skill was about to be tested by the doubling of the aircraft we could use. Keeble was fortunate in having to run this side of the work an ex-employee of the Nottingham corporation tramways called Wigginton, who in a few months had built up a well-deserved reputation for running special air services. He ended up in Europe by being responsible for operations of this kind throughout the theatre and then came out to do the same for us in South East Asia.

The training school on Mount Carmel, Military Establishment 102 as it was called, was another impressive achievement. It had been started originally in 1940 by my rhyming slang friend. It had then been used for training some of the Hagana in 1942, when it looked as if Egypt might fall and it was thought the Hagana might provide a 'left behind' force. But later that year a large quantity of arms and equipment was stolen. It was believed that the culprits were members of the Hagana. Relations between SOE and the 'Friends' were broken off entirely. Since then the place had been working to capacity under a series of instructors who had had experience in our schools at home. All our operational officers and men had passed through it, and had good cause to be grateful for what they learned at ME 102. Among other things they will not forget, nor will I, was the astonishing knowledge of European firearms of a Polish instructor called Stanislav Lazariewicz who was, I suppose, one of the greatest experts on this subject in the world. There was another remarkable Pole at the parachute training centre not far away at Ramath David known to us as Andrew Kennedy. His real name was Koverski and he had a wooden leg. He used to accompany every party as they emplaned for their first jump, and Andrew would always be first out of the aircraft. The theory seemed to be that if a Pole with a wooden leg could jump, so could you. It worked with outstanding success.

Keeble was fortunate also in having some exceptionally able people in the field. Bill Deakin and Bailey in Yugoslavia, Billy Maclean, David Smiley in Albania; Eddie Myers, Monty Woodhouse, John Stevens, Tony Andrews and John Harington in Greece, to say nothing of the party in Crete which included Tom Dunbabin, a Fellow of All Souls, and Paddy Leigh-Fermor—these were men of quite unusual calibre, though not all of them had been picked by

Keeble. As has been seen he planned to supplement them by many others. His idea also was to place each of the areas under an officer, preferably a professional soldier of Brigadier's rank. Eddie Myers was already a Brigadier, and two further Brigadiers had been selected, Armstrong for the Mihailović liaison and 'Trotsky' Davies for Albania. There was talk too of sending another exceptional man of this rank to Tito, though this project worked out rather differently in practice. There were also some remarkable people working in the country sections. To mention only a few there were Hugh Seton-Watson, Francis Noel-Baker, Philip Leake and Mrs Hasluck, who was to give invaluable tuition to everyone who went to Albania. There was however one cuckoo in the nest. One of the most efficient and hardworking men in the Yugoslav section was James Klugman, now a leading member of the Communist Party of Great Britain.

BICKHAM SWEET-ESCOTT

*

Though these clandestine activities were proceeding apace all around the Mediterranean during 1943, the same was not true of the efforts of the British First Army and its American allies in the mountains and valleys of Tunisia. After the landings in November 1942 a slender British force had struck boldly for Tunis itself and the coup de main *only failed within a few miles of the city: it failed because a vigorous build-up of Axis forces in their bridgehead round Tunis swiftly surpassed what could be delivered to the Allied spearhead, placed as it was at the end of a long line of communications from its Algerian bases, which, in turn, had to be fed from Britain and across the Atlantic. By the end of 1942 the British Chiefs of Staff stated that 'far more intensive measures are necessary if the Germans are to be driven out of Tunisia, and if, indeed, we are to avoid defeat'. By mid-February, the* Official History *observes, the whole Allied front was 'a sprawl produced by circumstances'. The small British force, under-equipped and ill-supplied, and lacking adequate cover in the air, had thus to fight, and did fight, many a bloody battle, sometimes won but more often lost in the face of superior odds. Battles such as this, described by a parachute officer:*

DEATH RIDGE

The Germans began their attack against the centre and northern positions of the 1st Battalion on Death Ridge. Then, at first light, lorried infantry were seen deploying at the level-crossing about half a mile to the north, and a heavy attack came in against the north-western end of the ridge, with another down the valley towards Tamera station. 'T' Company on the northern edge were at last surrounded and lost heavily during many hours of concentric attacks, but they held on stubbornly. Eventually the survivors were relieved in the late afternoon by a counter-attack led by Colonel Pearson himself with all immediate battalion reserves, clerks, wireless section, cooks and stretcher-bearers, who drove the Germans off the northern end of the ridge.

Another attack at midday against the southern end was held by the interlocking fire of the 1st and 2nd Battalions. The Germans tried to penetrate into Cork Wood, but were finally stopped on the northern and eastern slopes, and so heavy were their losses that they made no further attempt that day.

With the virtual loss of 'T' Company it was now impossible for the 1st Battalion to hold the whole of Death Ridge, particularly the exposed northern end, so it pulled back its line to the more densely wooded southern slopes and had to resign itself to the enemy occupying the slightly higher half.

In our counter-attacks separate groups could not keep touch in this dense jungle-like country, so we used to form up in an extended line, with three or four paces between each man. Then at a signal from the centre the force would move forward, beating the thickets as it went. Our camouflaged clothing and helmets were peculiarly suited to this type of country and practically invisible over a few yards. Invariably the German infantry had had no time to dig in, and as the noise of shouting and beating approached they usually slunk away through the undergrowth in twos and threes, firing wildly. Then, above the final bedlam of war-whoops and pot-shots, 'Ho——Ma-homet!' the battle cry of the 1st Brigade, would ring out and echo round the wooded slopes, as the line closed and the Germans ran.

'Ho——— Ma-homet!' was one of those inexplicable things which suddenly take root; within a few hours it was in common use throughout the whole brigade. Possibly it was derived from the long-drawn-out cry of the Arab muezzin from the hill-tops and mosques of Bou Arada, calling the Faithful to prayer—a sound which puzzled our men for a while, and which they used to mimic. For the Germans it was the knell of doom, heralding a determined counter-attack and thickets erupting green-clad men roaring to the charge. It was no idle reputation that the British paratroops won in the Tamera valley.

PETER STAINFORTH

As Montgomery was feeling his way cautiously towards the Mareth Line, Rommel saw the opportunity for a swift thrust into the vitals of the Allied position in Tunisia, by which he hoped to inflict considerable damage before having to turn east again to face Montgomery. In mid-February he attacked with units of the Afrika Korps and the 10th Panzer Division in the area of the Kasserine Pass, a door to the Allied rear. He shattered and demoralised the Americans who took the first impact of his armour and pushed on to the furthest point of his penetration, where a small British force carried out a classic 'thin red line' action, one of the most crucial of the whole campaign in north-west Africa. They were aided by regiments of American artillery who went straight into their firing positions after a forced march of several hundred miles. This little group was called Nickforce after their commander, Brigadier Nicholson; it fought the dramatic battle of

THALA

At dawn on February 21st Nickforce consisted of HQ 26 Armoured Brigade (17th/21st Lancers and 2nd Lothians) with some 60 Valentines and Crusaders, one company 10 Rifle Brigade, F Battery and 2nd/5th Leicesters. The enemy having gained the Kasserine Pass was expected to resume his advance either on Tebessa or Le Kef. We now know that he intended to go flat out for Le Kef, which was not only a large army maintenance area but also TAC HQ First Army. There was nothing between Nickforce and Le Kef.

Brigadier Nicholson, who had only assumed command of this

force at 0300 hours, ordered 2nd/5th Leicesters to occupy the high
ground south of Thala and directed 26 Armoured Brigade to hold
the enemy off from the Thala position at all costs until 1800 hours,
by which time 2nd/5th Leicesters would be dug in with minefields
laid. Brigadier C. A. L. Dunphie, commanding the brigade, fought
a successful delaying action throughout the day and by 2000 hours
most of his brigade had withdrawn through 2nd/5th Leicesters.
Suddenly an apparently orderly situation changed violently. The
leading German tanks, following the withdrawal closely, broke
through the Leicesters' position—F Battery found themselves in
action at short notice and here is their story, as told by their battery
commander, Major C. Middleton.

'At first light on February 21st the Armoured Brigade, with
17th/21st Lancers on the right and 2nd Lothians with F Battery in
support on the left, were in position astride the road about 20 miles
east of Thala. The Leicesters were moving on to their position. It was
a bright, sunny day and during the morning a certain amount of
activity was observed. German infantry could be seen getting out of
vehicles, but they were well outside the range of our guns. At about
one o'clock a German tank attack developed, with SP guns in support.
They were engaged and the armoured regiments, already much
reduced in strength and armed with 2-pdr Valentines only and a few
Crusaders with 6-pdrs, were leap-frogged back during the afternoon.
Observed shooting was extremely difficult at this stage owing to the
dust and the almost continuous smoke screen put down by the
armoured regiments. The battery was at the same time leap-frogged
back troop by troop, and about 30 minutes before dusk it passed
back through the Leicesters' position and went into action about
1,500 yards in the rear. There had only been time for the very
briefest of reconnaissances by the CPO and troop leaders and by the
time the guns got into action it was dark. The position was extremely
cramped, for guns were sometimes only 20 yards apart and no more
than 150 yards separated the two troops, T Troop being in the front
with V Troop behind them. At dusk the armoured regiments
passed back through the Leicesters' position and went into leaguer.

'Less than an hour later, while subsection meals were being got
ready and the digging of slit trenches and preparations for the night
were going on in the dark, some tanks came up the road and stopped,

the leading one no more than 100 yards from the battery position. The situation was confused, some of our vehicles were lost and looking for their units, and the night was dark; but the identity of these tanks was suspect. Sergeant Ainslie, No. 1 of the nearest gun, went forward to reconnoitre and heard German voices. In the dark he got close up and found that the leading tank had apparently broken down with mechanical trouble. As he got back, a Bren carrier drove unsuspectingly up the road towards the leading tank, which opened at point-blank range and brewed it up. A small plan was made to deal with the immediate situation. Captain J. S. Pirie was to fire a Very light over the German tanks while Sergeant Ainslie laid his gun on the leader. Lieutenant J. G. Bagnall was to discourage any German from showing his head out of the turret by opening on him with a Bren. The first Very light misfired, but the second one was successful, and Sergeant Ainslie knocked out the leading tank with his first shot. It burst into flames. This stirred the remainder of the tanks into activity and they attempted to withdraw, firing as they went. Another tank was knocked out almost immediately by Sergeant Ainslie's gun and a third, which came off the road and moved round in front of T Troop's position, was dealt with by Sergeant Laurie. He and his detachment were taking cover from the small-arms fire in their shallow slit trenches when the silhouette of this tank was seen passing across the front of the gun position about 50 yards away. Sergeant Laurie immediately jumped up, laid, loaded and fired his gun himself and knocked out the tank. The remainder of the tanks withdrew back down the road and sat on the high ground firing their machine guns, with tracer, indiscriminately down the road. At the same time a fierce exchange of firing broke out away on the right, where German tanks had penetrated into the leaguer of 17th/21st Lancers, and a number of tanks on both sides were knocked out in a confused engagement in the dark.

'The situation was now highly obscure, but the one thing that was clear was that there was to be no withdrawal from this position. It soon became obvious that the Leicesters' position was no longer held and that the actual front line was T Troop's line of guns. There was a great deal to be done, and not much time to do it. Slit trenches had to be dug for each gun, arrangements made for local defence and

the two guns on the right of the road moved to the main battery
position. The command post, too, was re-sited by a small bridge at
the side of the road close to the guns. When daylight came the
position was not going to be healthy, as the guns were in a hollow
overlooked from the high ground about 1,500 yards ahead. In
addition, the road from Thala on to the gun position was completely exposed and so the quads were ordered to dump all their
ammunition and, together with the remainder of the vehicles, get
clear of the position by dawn. At any moment the position might be
attacked by infantry.

'By first light each gun and command post had a slit trench, and
Captain I. Buchanan (a Canadian officer on attachment) had been
established in an OP on a pimple to the left of the position. The area
was shelled at frequent intervals throughout the morning and
several tanks which appeared on the crest about 1,500 to 2,000 yards
away were engaged furiously over open sights. When AP ran short,
HE 119 'cap-on' was used. It is doubtful if any of the tanks were
actually knocked out but they were certainly discouraged. OPs were
also engaged over open sights. No infantry attack on the position
developed during the day, but the shelling was heavy and obviously
directed from the ridge in front, and casualties amounted to one
killed and thirteen wounded, including Captain Pirie, who had been
an inspiration throughout. During the day the battery was greatly
heartened by a visit from the BRA, First Army, Brigadier Parham,
who insisted on visiting each gun. While he was there a German
motorcyclist with sidecar advanced down the ridge in front and
after having been greeted with a hail of ill-directed small-arms fire
was knocked out by a gun. Too late, and to our great regret, we
discovered that he was a medical orderly who had clearly lost his
way.

'The road from Thala was under shellfire and during the day the
quads had to run the gauntlet several times to bring up more
ammunition. The evacuation of casualties was undertaken volun-
tarily by Gunners Kerr and Peters, the driver and wireless operator
of one of the troop leader's trucks. They worked untiringly, often
under shellfire, and succeeded in getting all casualties, both our own
and those of other nearby units, back to the ADS at Thala.

'Another highlight of the day was Captain Buchanan's OP work.

Practically all the time his line was out of action, as it was repeatedly cut by shellfire, but he was able to carry on sending fire orders by "voice control", which he enlivened with suitable words of encouragement. When his voice failed him he engaged enemy OPs with his rifle and claimed several hits. By the end of the day he could no longer speak. We were told later that his running commentary had been a great encouragement to a company of the Rifle Brigade who, unknown to us, had been in a position on our right.'

The Company Commander of C Company, 10th Rifle Brigade, Major R. B. Fyffe, wrote of this action:

'The enemy now held the high ground overlooking the F Battery and C Company positions and throughout the day both units were subjected to heavy artillery fire. From time to time the guns of F Battery were hidden in an enemy stonk and it was almost unbelievable that their crews could remain alive. No sooner, however, did the enemy shelling slacken than the Gunners leapt from their slit trenches and carried on with their interrupted programme, firing like mad until they were again doused by the enemy. This went on, it seemed to us riflemen watching, continuously; and the way in which the Gunners served their guns was a sight which will always remain in our memories. Their battery commander also was outstanding, sometimes moving about amongst his guns unflurried by the enemy stonks, and sometimes scrambling up a hill behind them, whence he yelled fire orders and shouted encouragement to his magnificent teams. From time to time an ambulance came up to the battery position to take away the wounded, but F Battery never failed to respond to their commander's calls.'

As a result of the action the battery was awarded three MCs, one DCM and three MMs. . . .

Le Kef was saved. Had the enemy got through, their occupation of this city, even if only temporary, would have seriously disturbed the First Army plans and delayed the final offensive on Tunis.

General SIR CAMERON NICHOLSON, GCB, KBE, DSO, MC

After this action Rommel conferred with Field-Marshal Kesselring and, as the former recorded in his Papers, *they agreed that a continuation of the attack 'held no prospect of success and decided to break off the offensive by stages'. The thin red line had held: and a few days later, on another part of the front, 155 Battery of the Royal Artillery and the 5th Hampshires made a similar 'last stand', as gallant as any in the annals of the British Army. This was at*

SIDI NSIR

By the end of February 1943 a long withdrawal in front of the Eighth Army had convinced the German High Command that their best hope of successful and conclusive operations in North Africa lay in an all-out offensive against the First Army. They planned therefore to break through to the vital centre of communications at Beja and, by continuing the drive westwards, to isolate the northern wing of General Anderson's widely dispersed British, American and French forces: and so to Algiers!

Leaving 15th and 21st Panzer and 90th Light Division to hold General Montgomery, they moved 10th Panzer Division with great secrecy via Mateur into the mountainous area west of that town. To this force they allocated a group of Messerschmidts and, more potent still, 501st Heavy Tank Company, consisting of their entire resources of the much vaunted and as yet untried Mk VI Tiger tanks. These tanks were reputed to weigh 90 tons and to combine the advantages of impenetrable armour and a huge gun.

For the opening phases of this attack they selected Sidi Nsir, a detached locality in the hills 12 miles east of Hunt's Gap, Beja, a wild country of stony djebels and barren valleys. The force at Sidi Nsir consisted of the 5th Battalion the Hampshire Regiment and 155th Battery (Major Raworth) of 172nd Field Regiment RA; its object was to gain time and act as an outpost to the main force of 128 Infantry Brigade, in support of which the remainder of 172nd Field Regiment were deployed astride the main road at Hunt's Gap, covering Beja.

155th Battery had arrived in North Africa towards the end of January after a swim in the Mediterranean, their ship having been sunk by a German submarine. They lost all their equipment, but only a few men, and with remorseless drive and energy were re-equipped and in action three weeks later—just in time to meet 10th Panzer Division at Sidi Nsir, and in time, too, to fight with the battalion with whose name their own will be imperishably linked, the 5th Battalion the Hampshire Regiment.

On February 25th the Divisional Commander (Major-General Freeman-Attwood), the CRA (Brigadier Rigby) and the Commanding Officer of 172nd Field Regiment made a special visit to Point 609, the predominant OP at Sidi Nsir, and stayed there for two hours without seeing any signs of enemy movement or activity. From this OP one can see right down to Mateur, and with a telescope on a fine day can distinguish the windows in the houses; but there are huge valleys and reverse slopes hereabouts behind which a large force could remain concealed.

That night an abnormal number of green and white Very lights were seen, and by dawn the mountains and valleys all around were alive with the movement of troops, guns, tanks and infantry columns.

Soon after 6 am on February 26th F Troop came under fire from mortars behind Chechak Ridge and replied with artillery fire. From this moment until dark, F Troop and to a lesser degree E Troop and the command posts, cooks' shelters, etc., were under increasingly heavy mortar fire. At 7 am enemy tanks attempted a direct assault down the main road from Mateur. F Troop engaged them, No. 1 gun over open sights. Three tanks were hit and the road was blocked very conveniently just where it passed through a protective minefield. No. 1 gun remained in action in spite of mortar and machine-gun fire. Captain Lawrence had decided to stick to his observation post on the Chechak ridge. Later his bravery in an attempt to escape from prison cost him his life.

At 9.40 am Point 609 was heavily attacked by infantry. Communications were broken, WT sets smashed by enemy mortars and all lines cut. Lieutenant McGee was wounded and taken prisoner. (He subsequently escaped, reached the British lines in Italy and had the desperate ill-fortune to be drowned on his way back home.) From this moment on, the battery had but secondary 'eyes' overlooking the Mateur road, which must have been packed with enemy tanks and vehicles.

At 10.15 the CO visited Major Raworth on the gun position. F Troop was then under observation at a range of about 800 yards, and the track leading down to the command post was under very heavy and accurate mortar fire, rounds falling every three seconds or so. On all eight guns the CO found the detachments full of cheerful and determined courage. Lieutenant Taylor and Sergeant Henderson (both of F Troop) in particular stood out by reason of their undaunted offensive spirit and the inspiring example they set. Sergeant Henderson was the No. 1 of No. 1 gun, specially placed on the top of the slope to deal with enemy tanks trying to use the Mateur–Sidi Nsir road. Taylor was the only officer on F Troop position, and he fought there until he was killed.

At this time Messerschmidts attacked from a height of about 200 feet and raked the gun positions with machine-gun and cannon fire. A number of vehicles were burning along the road Sidi Nsir–Hunt's Gap, some of them filled with ammunition and ammonal; but the risks were ignored by officers and men alike as they cheerfully salvaged and carried the shells throughout the action. The wounded acted stoically; none grumbled or complained.

By noon enemy tanks (reported to number 30) and infantry had wormed their way into positions around the flanks of the guns. All this time the battery was completely occupied in engaging enemy infantry, machine guns and mortars, which were closing in on the Hampshire company positions.

The battery fired as many as 1,800 rounds per gun during that fierce, relentless day. Bren guns claimed four Messerschmidts—a triumphant reward for days and days of patient shooting on the balloon range at Lydd before leaving England.

The gallantry of the infantry, isolated on the tops of stony djebels, was superb. Both artillery and infantry were equally determined not to let their opposite numbers down.

At 3 pm a column of enemy infantry penetrated between Hampshire Farm, two miles or so to the west of the Sidi Nsir–Beja road, and the gun positions, and no more ammunition could pass. Twenty minutes later, under covering fire from some 13 tanks in hull-down positions (firing MGs and guns), more tanks attempted to advance down the main road. A Panzer Mk VI was leading. This was hit three times by Sergeant Henderson's gun. A smaller Panzer Mk IV tried to pass, but this in turn was knocked out by No. 1 gun. Yet a third tank was set on fire by the same gun.

The enemy held back, shelling and machine-gunning the positions, particularly F Troop, which was more easily spotted. Both troops were now in action against enemy tanks over open sights. But the tanks in hull-down positions had a great advantage over our guns and engaged them one by one, setting on fire ammunition dumps, killing or wounding the detachments and eventually smashing up the guns themselves.

At four o'clock another attack was put in from the Mateur road against F Troop's southern flank. Sergeant Henderson smashed up the leading tank, but immediately afterwards he and his entire detachment were knocked out by a direct hit. (Sergeant Henderson recovered later in an enemy hospital.) The tanks then came on over the ridge in front of F Troop, who still had three guns in action and engaged the enemy at ranges of from 50 to 10 yards with Lieutenant Taylor, the fitter, cooks and all survivors running from gun to gun and servicing each in turn.

At this stage the slope of the ground, which is steep and convex, gave the gunners some much-needed help, for the attacking tanks were handicapped by their limited ability to depress their guns. F Troop fired for over an hour more before they were finally silenced. Then the tanks moved down the road past F Troop and surrounded E Troop.

At 6.30 pm Bren guns and at least one 25-pdr of E Troop were still in action against the enemy tanks at point-blank range.

A press report of the next day quoted what was stated to be an eyewitness account from the company sent out to try to link up with the defenders of Sidi Nsir. It read:

'A battery of 25-pdrs fought most heroically. The guns continued to fire when the ammunition in the gunpits was ablaze; the last surviving gun knocked out two tanks with its last two shots at ten yards' range and the last man still on his feet was seen jumping from the gunpit and running towards the tanks with a bomb in his hand.'

No doubt there was an element of exaggeration in this tale, as in many which followed after, but it gives some picture of the dogged determination with which this grim fight was fought to the end.

At length the tanks smothered the gun position with machine-gun and gun fire, and any man who moved was at once riddled with bullets. Some tanks went round the position swivelling on their tracks and crushing in the slit trenches.

At 5.51 pm the last message came back over the wireless, 'Tanks are on us', followed a few seconds later by the single letter 'V' tapped out in Morse.

Many, both German and British, thought that the battle was over. But in fact it had scarcely begun. One third of the guns of 172nd Field Regiment had been lost, but a precious 24 hours had been gained and the gallant action of 155th Battery had instilled a healthy measure of caution into the enemy, whose one real chance of success lay in speed.

At dawn on the 27th, headed by a group of Mk VI tanks, the menacing columns moved westwards along the winding, narrow, single-track road to Hunt's Gap. But long before the enemy reached Hunt's Gap he was being pounded continuously by a heavily reinforced artillery which had made full use of the 24 hours' respite to establish extra 'eyes' in the mountains, as well as large dumps of ammunition. The road by which the enemy advanced stretched mercilessly for miles and, as luck would have it, it rained and rained and rained. It was as if the enemy had walked deliberately into a carefully baited trap. His heavy tanks floundered in the mud. They became trapped on a narrow road from which they could not turn back. Their drivers were panicked by concentrations of artillery fire from a daily increasing weight of field guns, until eventually they themselves completely blocked their only route of advance.

Then, for ten days, field and medium guns hurled thousands of shells upon them, smashing their tanks and vehicles on the road and mowing down their infantry when they tried to get round over the barren hills. The gunners of 153rd and 154th Batteries took a remorseless revenge for their comrades of 155th who had died at Sidi Nsir. . . . And when at long last the enemy gave up the bitter struggle, some 30 to 40 of his tanks, including ten of his very limited force of Tigers and 50 to 60 other vehicles, lay smashed along the road to Hunt's Gap. One prisoner stated that on March 1st his company went into battle over 200 strong and came out on March 5th with a strength of 45.

Brigadier W. D. MCN. GRAHAM, DSO, OBE
(who commanded 172nd Field Regiment)

*

*Though it was often the case that men from the same regiment were fighting
in both the First and the Eighth Armies, these two formations differed
widely in experience, in discipline, in dress. When in April the two armies
meshed, and a fatal ring closed round the Axis outpost in Africa, it was not
unnatural that each felt certain reservations.*

GREEK MEETS GREEK

Englishmen at war often seem to have enough energy to spare from
fighting the enemy for use in disparagement of their friends. Since
the Regiment was represented in both, the meeting of the First and
Eighth Armies cannot pass without comment. From the point of
view of the Eighth Army an impression of this meeting is given
quite clearly by Paddy Boden:

'Here we saw for the first time the British troops of the First Army.
It was interesting to compare the difference in outlook, technique
and appearance between the members of the two armies. The first
and most obvious differences were those of appearance and technique. First Army lorries were all painted dark green and brown,
and when in harbour were parked in huddles, making the best use
of any available cover. Eighth Army transport was painted the colour
of sand and the drivers continued to rely on dispersal as the best
protection against air attack. There is little doubt that the best
solution would have been a compromise between the two methods,
both of which were carried to absurd extremes. The officers and
men of the First Army were readily distinguishable from those of
the Desert Army by their dress. The former were more or less
correctly dressed, and, more often than not, wore steel helmets as a
matter of routine. In the Eighth Army it was almost unheard of for
an officer to wear battledress trousers, and steel helmets were worn
only on very rare occasions. More important than these relatively
superficial differences were the differences of outlook.

'For nearly three years the Battalion had been fighting in the
Western Desert, more or less isolated from all contact with England,
which could be reached only by air and round the Cape. Other units
had, of course, arrived from England more recently, but these new-
comers quickly identified themselves with and assumed the habits of
the 'veterans', doing this either as a matter of policy or purely from

a natural desire not to be different. One example of an officer quickly adopting 'local' dress was General Montgomery, who was to be seen one day very soon after his arrival in the desert in August, 1942, at the Headquarters of XXX Corps wearing a khaki drill jacket and Sam Browne belt.'

Major ROBIN HASTINGS

*

But whatever their differences, the death-blow for the Germans in Tunisia was struck by a combined force of two infantry and two armoured divisions drawn from both armies, under the overall command of General Horrocks. He sent in a blitzkrieg *assault running straight through to Tunis from*

MEDJEZ EL BAB

This country was entirely different from the desert where I had spent the last nine months. It looked far more like England, with its growing crops and small hills broken by the mountains on either side. But to see the country meant visiting the forward units who held positions overlooking the Medjerda valley. This is not as a rule a popular procedure with the forward troops, to whom there is nothing more irritating than too brave generals who refuse to take the normal precautions and stand upright, wearing a red cap, in the front line, thus inevitably inviting retaliation from the enemy artillery—the shells descending on the heads of the unfortunate troops usually after the general has gone. During the First World War we used to have a notice-board in our trenches bearing the words, 'Please remember we *live* here.'

On this occasion I removed my red cap and explained to the troops that I would take every precaution, but that I simply must see the country. If after my departure they were shelled—well, I was sorry, but it was the fortune of war.

The more I saw of this country the more convinced I was that here was a wonderful opportunity to employ the type of attack which, given the right sort of terrain, can be irresistible. This was to advance on a narrow front in great depth, so that there are always more men and more tanks to maintain the momentum. This endless procession, when seen from some enemy trench which is being steadily shelled (we had one gun to every seven yards of front) and attacked from the air, must surely strike despair into the hearts of even the stoutest of defenders. So I decided to attack on a 3000-yard front with the two infantry divisions followed by the two armoured.

Zero hour was 3 am on 6th May. On the previous afternoon I moved into a small command post which had been dug into a hill reasonably close to the front line. Some hours later I was sitting with my feet on the table, sipping a short drink and reading a novel, when the canvas screen which served as a door was pushed aside and in came General Alexander, who must have had a long, exhausting drive to get up to me.

Obviously dusty and tired, he said rather testily, 'You don't seem to have much to do.' I looked at him in surprise and replied: 'If I had anything to do now, Sir, we should have lost tomorrow's battle before it ever started.'

Nevertheless I much appreciated his visit and he impressed on me the importance of speed and of not allowing the enemy to draw us off from the direct route to Tunis.

I never felt so confident about any battle before or after. Everything went like clockwork. The two infantry divisions punched the initial breach, and at 7.30 am I was able to order the two armoured divisions forward. By midday we were through the crust and the tanks were grinding their way forward down the valley towards Tunis. It was a most inspiring sight to see these two well-trained and experienced armoured divisions being used in a role for which armoured divisions were specifically designed—to exploit a breakthrough deep into the enemy's heart. They worked like efficient machines, aircraft, guns, tanks, infantry and vehicles each fitting into the jig-saw of battle in its proper place.

I do not claim this as a great feat of generalship; it was nothing of the sort. I was merely fortunate to be in command of a battle in which victory was a foregone conclusion.

Lieutenant-General SIR BRIAN HORROCKS

'TUNIS HAS FALLEN'

At Kilometre 9 all Tunis broke into view—the wide bay, flanked by mountains, the spreading town, one of the largest in Africa, not much harmed by bombs but smoking now with a score of large fires. We stood poised on the summit for a moment before we dipped down into the suburbs. I remember thinking over and over again as I stood in the rain, 'Tunis has fallen.' That simple thought seemed to be quite enough in itself, as complete as a curtain falling on a play, and if one had any sense of triumph I do not remember it. I can recall only a sense of relief and gratitude.

Someone, the retreating Germans probably, had piled brushwood round a bungalow and it was burning brightly. In all directions there were fires and occasional explosions. Clearly the enemy was destroying his dumps before he got away. More and more houses appeared. The crew of a tank had pulled into a piece of waste land and the crew were boiling a pot of tea with a ring of curious Arabs squatting around them. . . .

Looking around I saw I was again among the Desert Rats. The Red Jerboa in the red circle was painted on the battered mudguards, the most famous symbol in the whole Desert War. And the men in the vehicles were the Eleventh Hussars, the reconnaissance unit that had led the Eighth Army across the desert since Wavell's time. With them were the Derbyshire Yeomanry, the men who had led the First Army through all the hard fighting in Tunisia, and they carried the symbol of the mailed fist. . . .

The vehicles had pulled up and at the head of the line a British officer stopped us. 'No farther,' he said. 'There are German snipers down the street. Wait until they are cleared up.' We waited in the rain but no firing sounded and one or two of the armoured cars moved on again. In his excitement my driver tried to get ahead of the armoured cars but I held him back, as we were already third in line and the only unarmoured vehicle on the spot except for Keating's jeep. We waited until two tanks and a Bren-gun carrier had gone ahead and then we followed.

Quite suddenly the Avenue de Bardo sprang to life. Crowds of French people rushed into the street and they were beside themselves in hysterical delight. Some rushed directly at us, flinging themselves on the running-boards. A girl threw her arms round my driver's neck. An old man took a packet of cigarettes from his pocket and flung them up at us. Someone else brandished a bottle of wine. All the women had flowers that they had hastily plucked from their gardens. A clump of roses hit me full on the mouth and there were flowers all over the bonnet of the car. Everyone was screaming and shouting and getting in the way of the vehicles, not caring whether they were run over or not. A young Frenchman, his face working with excitement, hoisted himself on to the roof of our car with a Sten gun in his hand. He screamed that he was an escaped prisoner and something else in French I did not catch, but I pushed him off, not sure whether he was friend or enemy. There were Germans walking about all over the place. They stood gaping on the pavements, standing in groups, just staring, their rifles slung over their shoulders. A Bren-gun carrier shot past us and it was full of Germans whom the Tommies had picked up, and in their excitement the crowd imagined that these Germans in the British vehicle were British and so they threw flowers at them. The Germans caught the flowers, and they sat there stiffly in the Bren-gun carrier, each man with a little posy clutched in his hand.

The double doors of a big red building on the right-hand side of the street burst open and at first I could not understand—the men who ran out, scores, hundreds of them, were British, in flat steel helmets and British battledress. Then it came to me—they were prisoners whom we had rescued. They stood in an undecided group for a moment on the sidewalk in the rain, filling their eyes with the sight of us. Then they cheered. Some of them had no heart to speak and simply looked. One man, bearded up to his eyes, cried quietly. The others yelled hoarsely. Suddenly the whole mass of men were swept with a torrent of emotional relief and wild joy. They yelled and yelled.

Handing out cigarettes we caught their story in broken phrases. 'Four hundred of them, all officers and NCOs . . . due to sail for Italy today. Another big batch of them had sailed yesterday.'

There was an Italian lying in blood at the doorway and I asked about him. A major answered. 'He and another Italian were on guard over us. An hour ago a German armoured car went down this street and they put a burst of machine-gun bullets through the door, hoping to hit us. They didn't care about the Italian sentries and they hit this one in the head. He's dying. His friend went crazy. He rushed off down the street shooting any German he could see, and I think they killed him.'

We drove on again. On our left there was a tall and ancient stone viaduct and piles of ammunition were burning at the base of the pillars. A railway line ran beside the road. On our right there was a four-storied red building, a brewery. We were just level with this when the shooting started.

It started with a stream of tracer bullets, about shoulder high, skidding across the road between my vehicle and the armoured car in front. We stopped and jumped for the gutters. The crowd melted from the street, the cheering died away with a sort of strangled sigh. After the first burst there came another and another, and soon there must have been half a dozen machine-guns firing at very close range. The trouble was that one had at first no notion of where it was coming from. This was my first experience of street fighting, but I felt instinctively I wanted to get up against the wall. There were five of us in our car, Austen, Buckley, the driver and Sidney Bernstein, none of us with arms, and we groped our way along one of the side walls of the brewery.

The shooting now was continuous. Three lads suddenly jumped out of the nearest armoured car with a Bren-gun. They dashed across the road, flung themselves down on the railway line, set up the gun and began firing. The Germans from the Bren-gun carrier had also jumped into the ditch beside the railway and they lay there on their backs, each man still holding his posy.

Looking up, I saw a line of bullets slapping against the brewery wall above us. As each bullet hit it sent out a little yellow flame and a spray of plaster came down on top of us. At the same moment my driver pointed up. Directly above us two German snipers were shooting out of the brewery, and we could see the barrels of their guns sticking out of a second-storey window. As yet the Germans had not seen us. Since at any moment they might look down, we crawled back to the main street. Keeping pressed against the wall, we edged our way from doorway to doorway until we reached the building where the British prisoners were kept. It was raining very heavily. There was now a second wounded man on the wooden floor. All this time the engine of our stationary car was running and the windscreen wipers were swishing to and fro. It was in a very isolated position and directly in the path of the shooting.

After ten minutes or so the firing eased off. The tank had let fly with a couple of heavy shells and that had sobered up the snipers. We began to edge back to the brewery, hoping to get our car before it caught fire from the tracers.

A German with blood pouring down his leg popped out of a doorway in front of me and surrendered. We waved him back towards the British prisoners. Two more Germans came out of a house with their hands up, but we were intent on getting to the car and took no notice. At the corner of the brewery two sergeants, one American and the other British, who were staff photographers, ran across the open road to their vehicle, grabbed their tommy-guns and began firing. They were enjoying the whole thing with a gusto that seemed madness at first. Yet I could understand it a little. This street fighting had a kind of Red Indian quality about it. You felt you were right up against the enemy and able to deal with him directly, your nimbleness and marksmanship against his. The American was coolly picking his targets and taking careful aim. The young Frenchman with the Sten gun turned up, and I realised now that he had been warning us about these snipers in the first place. He led the two sergeants into the brewery, kicking the door open with his foot and shooting from the hip. They sent a preliminary volley through the aperture. Presently the three of them came out with the two snipers who had been shooting above our heads. They had wounded one.

The sergeants then offered to cover us while we ran for our car. My driver was quick. He whizzed it backwards up the street, and we ran to the point a quarter of a mile back where the rest of the British column was waiting.

ALAN MOOREHEAD

*

Now that General Alexander was able to signal back to Churchill 'We are masters of the North African shores', the first stepping-stone selected for a return to occupied Europe was Sicily. On the eve of the main assault a small party was landed on Sardinia by submarine and parachute to aid the RAF in the destruction of German torpedo-bombers on the island's airfields which might otherwise damage the Allies' invasion convoys. The landings were successful, a number of planes were destroyed, and the party sought to escape. One of the saboteurs was John Verney.

CAPTURE AT TERTENIA

We always walked in single file. After ten minutes Brown said from the rear: 'We are being followed.'

'Are you quite sure?' I whispered, and kept walking.

'Three men, about a hundred yards behind.'

'We'll walk faster. Don't look round yet, but when I say, glance back casually and see if they've dropped behind.'

We lengthened and quickened our stride, but after some minutes Brown said the men were gaining on us.

'All right, we'll pretend to rest by the road. Make a business of off-loading the packs, as though it was a natural halt. We'll soon see what they want.'

The three men came up to us and appeared friendly. Three ordinary peasants. Were they from the cart? In which case, where had it gone, because we could not hear its wheels, nor did it come in sight after five minutes.

I told the men we were Germans from Tertenia marching to Villapatzu; the old story. It came out quite slickly now. And the men seemed to accept it. But I wasn't happy about them, or about the story. I didn't know that there were any Germans in Tertenia. And it was suspicious that the men should have followed. And where was their cart? I tried hard to convince myself—and the others—that all was well. I refused to believe that anything could go wrong just when everything ought to have been nearly right. But I blamed my folly for having stuck to the road with more bitterness than I can describe.

I tried to chat naturally to the men about water. Could we get a drink anywhere? They led us to a spring, hidden in the bushes near the road, which we would certainly have missed. They seemed over-fond of us, unanxious to get on their way home and to leave us. I said we were tired and would sleep a while by the spring before continuing, and begged them, with how much politeness, not to bother to wait. . . .

The mosquitoes round the spring were bad and the three men

warned us not to stay or we might catch malaria. I countered that we had anti-mosquito cream. At last, to my relief, they showed signs of moving.

Then we heard the cart approaching. The men promptly pressed us to come back to the road and drink some wine. No, we didn't care for wine; we just wanted to stay and sleep. 'Thanks very much all the same, please, please don't wait for us,' and so on.

The men returned to the road to the cart. We looked about desperately for a good line of retreat, but the ground near the spring was boggy; we sank in to our knees and obviously we couldn't escape far without being heard or seen. But was this, after all, a trap? I could not, dared not, believe it was. There was still no apparent danger, nothing tangible to fear. Which was what made the incident so nightmarish.

The cart stopped and we could hear low voices of men talking. Unable to bear the suspense, I left the bushes and joined them. I said I had changed my mind and would like to buy their wine. They produced a small Italian army bottle of it, for which I gave them a 500-lire note. They laughed delightedly, all piled on the cart and drove on. I listened to their laughter growing fainter and fainter and felt better. I rejoined Brown and Fry and told them that they had only been simple peasants after all, who had sold a pennyworth of wine for a pound and were chortling with joy at my expense. I believed the explanation because I wanted, desperately, to believe it. Then, allowing time for the cart to get well ahead, we started off down the road again.

I intended to leave the road and find cover as soon as I could, but the landscape on all sides was barren and open. There was no hope of reaching Alberu—all that mattered now was safety for the next day, if there was a next day. The premonition of calamity stifled me, try how I would to be optimistic. And when Brown whispered that we were still being followed I was not really surprised. I just felt rather sicker at heart than before.

There was only one man, who might of course be a different one; it MIGHT be only a coincidence. . . . We tried to outwalk him again and failed and stopped again by the roadside, this time pretending to urinate. The man caught up. I thought I recognised him, but I could not be sure. He did not speak but walked over to a shepherd who appeared with his flock suddenly nearby. They had been resting for the night by the road. I walked over, too, and asked him if we had already met at the spring. He denied it. The shepherd looked at me strangely, I thought. He was carrying a gun. Neither paid me any attention and went on talking together.

We waited and the man walked off, up the road ahead of us. The shepherd sat down with his flock. We followed the man until a bend placed him out of sight of us. Then we turned up the hill into some scrub, hoping that if he was hostile we might give him the slip. And at the same moment we heard the horses' hooves—how many horses we couldn't tell, but they were galloping down the hard road. And they grew louder and louder very quickly.

I saw now, only too clearly, what had happened. The peasants on the cart had sent back to Tertenia for help while they stuck to us.

We dropped our packs and crawled up the hill among the bushes. We might yet get away. I hoped the horsemen would ride on till they caught up the man. But the latter was running back down the road. As the *carabinieri* came round the bend we heard him shouting to them to stop—no doubt pointing in the direction we had taken. The shepherd appeared on the skyline above us, so it was useless to try and climb the hill undetected. We dived on top of each other into the thickest bush. There was still a chance the search would carry on up the hill, if they didn't find us at once.

We lay there while the *carabinieri* and peasants searched all round. They passed and repassed our bush without spotting us. I began to have hopes, however faint. I wondered whether we should have thrown grenades when the *carabinieri* were on the road instead of bolting and hiding. Now we were so cramped we could not even reach our revolvers without stirring the branches. A man was standing five yards away. We lay and prayed the search would move a little farther on, to give us time to relax our aching muscles. A twig moved, a leaf rustled; the man noticed. Before we knew it, we were the centre of an excited mob, shouting, firing their rifles in the air, pulling us by the limbs, seizing our arms and possessions, screaming orders at each other and at us—an experience which might have seemed almost amusing if we had not felt so bitterly humiliated.

JOHN VERNEY

★

SICILY: GOING IN

'We are going in now!'

The crew chief was bending over me with his mouth close to my ear. The other members of the stick were rousing themselves, making a final check on their jumping equipment and sitting forward expectantly on the edge of the bucket seats, taut and apprehensive of the ordeal ahead. There was a grotesqueness about their shapeless bodies, distended by a heavy load of equipment, harness and bulky statichutes: they looked like the rubber Michelin man, in the darkness of the cabin, weird and unearthly and quite in keeping with the present tense situation.

'Stand up!'

My voice sounded very weak and far away amid the roar of the plane. We lined up facing the jumping door, and the crew chief took up his station alongside it. Holding the corners of the door firmly I took a look out.

The sea was racing beneath our wings, only a score of feet below. At first there was nothing but an expanse of rolling waves heaving like a pulse; then the plane banked steeply and altered course, and I saw the coast—an ominous shadow between sea and sky.

Suddenly we heard the guns ahead—the furious crackle from the quick-firing pom-poms and the deeper intermittent crack of the heavier barrage. At once terror gripped me as I braced myself to meet the inverted red-hot rain. I had had no experience of flak, and those fountains of red and orange tracer looked quite appalling. There is something specially disturbing about being shot at from below—one's body seems to be much more vital when attacked from that direction.

The searchlights caught us for an instant when we were about three miles out. The cabin was suddenly filled with a blinding light but this dimmed almost immediately and we were back in the twilight of the moon. Two swords of light were probing out to sea, but our plane eluded them and rushed on towards the shore. The beams were now off our line and searching for the next flight coming in.

Little blobs of light were reflected on the inside of the fuselage and slowly passed diagonally upwards towards the tail. The aircraft swerved violently, and immediately there was the high-pitched crackle of the 20-mm cannonade. A bewildering flicker of tracer sizzled past us. I saw what seemed to be a galaxy of coloured globes floating leisurely above the land. They peeled away from a dark mass, which I took to be a hill, and danced towards us like a swarm of angry bees rising from an upturned hive. They curved over, coming faster every second, then they were flaming comets roaring and crackling about the plane in streaks of light. We were running through the curtain of light flak—an interlocking apron of tracer shells flicking up in intricate patterns of gold, red and white.

The plane suddenly rocked and quivered as though the Titans were slamming the metal sides. Crash! Crash! Tiny particles of steel pattered against the fuselage. Two 88-mm shells had burst above and behind our tail.

Wham! Our world suddenly turned upside down and then blew up with a roar, opening a yawning chasm beneath our feet. Everything was momentarily black . . . revolving planets . . . plunging meteors . . . the sound of tinkling glass . . . the acrid smell of high explosive. Then my vision cleared, and we were lying together in a heap on the matted floor.

We scrambled to our feet very dazed and shaken and seized with a wild desire for self-preservation. We calmed down a little in a second and sorted ourselves out. The overhead anchor cable—mercifully not in use—was cut and was trailing in the centre of the fuselage. All the windows on the starboard side were broken, and moonbeams peered through a dozen ugly gashes above our heads.

Then we were across the coast, and there was land beneath our feet, so close that we seemed to brush the tops of the olive trees as we swept inland. The heavy flak ceased abruptly, and even the rain of 20-mm died down a little. We rose to clear a slight fold in the ground and dropped into the trough beyond. We hopped over an embanked road and swerved to avoid a large obstacle in our path. Then the floor of the fuselage tilted abruptly to an alarming angle, so that we had to hang on tight to avoid being flung into the well of the tail; and the tune of our engines changed to a high-pitched shriek as airscrews clawed frantically at the sky. The plane bucked suddenly as we flattened out.

Green light! and my batman hit me on the thigh as the signal to jump. The next moment I was dazzled by the blast of the slipstream and plunged downwards with the air buffeting my face. After the inferno of flak and the pandemonium inside the aircraft I was overwhelmed by the unexpected stillness. My parachute had pulled me up with a jerk, and now there was no sound except for the wind rustling in the dark, silken shadow above my head. I felt afraid my floating body might provide an individual target for the enemy gunners, but my confidence grew as I sank lower towards the shadows and the comparative safety of the ground.

I glanced quickly about me to get my bearings. For some reason I could not see the river and I remembered to look for the fires from the bombing of Catania airfield. Then for the first time my brain took in the burning landscape; the whole area was a confusion of twingling fires and tongues of flame. Haystacks were blazing and patches of dried-up grass were roaring fiercely, while over all hung a thick haze of smoke.

Before I was fully conscious of what was happening I landed heavily on my back in a gully ten feet deep, having struck its wall with a force that knocked all the breath out of my body and left me gasping among the reeds. For some seconds I lay and sobbed for air, incapable of unravelling myself from the silken cords.

Something warm was pouring down my leg, and my fingers encountered a wet patch. I must have been hit, I thought. Then I found that the water bottle beneath my smock had burst and been flattened by the impact.

I crawled to the lip of the gully, then grabbed my pack and Sten and set off up the dropping zone with the moon on my right, to look for our six containers. I had only gone fifty yards when I found three lying among the stubble of a freshly cut cornfield, the marking lights giving out a ghostly blue glow. Clarkson joined me a moment later, and we hoisted one on high, so that the rest might rendezvous at the light. The whole plain was silent except for the crackling fires, so I gave the rendezvous sign with my torch down the dropping zone. After a minute or two the men began to collect until finally the stick was complete.

While the others hunted around for the two remaining containers and our collapsible trolley, the sergeant, my batman and I had a look to see where we had landed. I climbed an embankment cautiously and found an unmetalled road on the top. Then I saw the winding ribbon of water peeping through a deep screen of rushes and knew that this was the Gornalunga and that we had landed on the right place.

PETER STAINFORTH

'I AM THE ENEMY YOU KILLED, MY FRIEND'

My men came up from the beaches singing and hailed us cheerfully; they were glad to find that we, too, were alive and that death had as yet driven no wedge into our unity. We formed up and set off along the track, that swung suddenly seawards and continued along the cliff's edge, until we came to a group of huts enclosed with a wooden palisade. A skirmish had been fought about the hutment and pieces of our own and the enemy's equipment littered the trodden ground. The gate into the palisade had been blown down and a Sicilian family was huddled together in the centre of the enclosure. The grandmother, whose toothless face was withered like a mummy's shrunken skull by sun and labour, and the mother knelt with the children kneeling before them, their hands raised in supplication to the Virgin Mary; and the father, his lips also mumbling a prayer but his eyes fixed on our every movement, stood in the middle with an arm round the neck of a shabby, moth-eaten donkey, clearly the one possession for which they were prepared to die. A small boy, the only other male, with tears streaming from his wide fearful eyes, guarded the animal's other flank, and as we stepped through the gate to search the buildings, his fingers convulsively clutched its lousy hide. They were bundles of rags; poor scarecrows, riddled by disease and undercut by starvation; and angular bones and stringy flesh showed through the gaps in their clothing. We felt ashamed that we had been the cause of their terror. A few filthy blankets and a tin or two were strewn about the earthen floor of their living quarters but there was not a stick of furniture or a single decency. The whole place stank of excreta and it was as much as we could bear even to glance into the huts. We left the family still praying about their donkey, but a corporal, turning round in the gateway with a curse, tossed a packet of cigarettes into their midst. Others followed suit with more cigarettes and bars of chocolate.

We found at the next hutment along the track a second donkey, undefended this time, which we attempted to harness into a cart, but the girths broke immediately and rather than manhandle our considerable weights of weapons and ammunition any longer, we piled them into the cart and took it alone. The track, narrowing and winding tortuously between a cactus hedge and the cliff verge, was just wide enough to take the width of the cart. As we rounded a corner, we suddenly came on the corpse of an Italian soldier sprawling out and blocking the way. His open mouth was twisted into a coarse grimace and his body was stiffened into a taut arch. The hedge was too high to lift the body over, but it had to be moved if we were to pass. While I wondered how this might best be done, the corporal who had thrown the first packet of cigarettes levered it forward with his foot until it tumbled like a heavy branch over the cliff and fell without altering its attitude on the rocks below. The track widened out again and, where it turned abruptly inland to run uphill through a vineyard, the body of one of our own men lay stretched out. His pallid face, which seemed to have been coated with grease, was empty of all expression, and the flies, singing sharply in the rising heat, crawled as thickly as currants over his skin. A gascape had been thrown across his body and we raised it to hide his face, but as we moved it we saw that his bowels had been torn out. We covered his face with a rag and hung his helmet on an upright bayonet to mark his resting place.

The sun beat down intolerably and as we toiled up the tracks, quickly petering out into the vineyard's soft dust, its rays could almost be heard to vibrate shrilly like telegraph wires on an empty English road in mid-summer. Half-way up the sloping vineyard, towards the white cubic farm buildings on the crest, we were passed by a middle-aged woman walking quickly down towards the sea. Her blue and white striped dress flapped about her erect figure with the vigour of her movement as though it had been caught in the wind, and the loose end of her kerchief fastened over her coils of black hair trailed out like a streamer behind. She stiffly averted her face from us to conceal not the tears that ran from her unblinking eyes but the look of implacable hate and contempt into which her features were set. Two coastguards had been bayoneted in their post by the man whose face we had covered up, and the hurrying woman, who may have been wife or mother, was going too late with a handful of bandages to tend their wounds.

DOUGLAS GRANT

DOLCE FAR NIENTE

The men of the Eighth Army enjoyed Sicily after the desert. It was high summer; oranges and lemons were on the trees; wine was plentiful; the Sicilian girls were disposed to be friendly. It was very hot and the mosquitoes were unpleasant; indeed, they were a menace since they were the malarial type. Our medical discipline was not good as regards the regular parades for taking preventive medicines that are so necessary in such conditions; we suffered almost as many casualties from malaria as we did from enemy action. We were all used to the heat; but whereas the desert was dry, Sicily was humid.

The men in back areas discarded all possible clothing and some even took to wearing the wide-brimmed Sicilian straw hat. I well remember an incident that occurred one day as I was driving in my open car up to the front. I saw a lorry coming towards me with a soldier apparently completely naked in the driver's seat, wearing a silk top hat. As the lorry passed me, the driver leant out from his cab and took off his hat to me with a sweeping and gallant gesture. I just roared with laughter. However, while I was not particular about dress so long as the soldiers fought well and we won our battles, I at once decided that there were limits. When I got back to my headquarters I issued the only order I ever issued about dress in the Eighth Army; it read as follows: 'Top hats will not be worn in the Eighth Army.'

Field–Marshal LORD MONTGOMERY

But for the British, Canadian and American troops slogging their way over the island Sicily was not all top hats and oranges and lemons. There was much bitter fighting and many casualties before the occupation was completed. The following running commentary, by a captain of the Green Howards, on an attack on Mount Pancali gives the flavour of a myriad local conflicts:

WHAT A MORNING!

08.30 The guns open up, and we move forward into the open. 6th Battalion on our right are going to have a grand-stand view of the attack.

09.00 At the foot of the hill at last. Looks bloody steep from here. I stop the artillery over the wireless; we're not going to get into our own barrage. There are big boulders as we climb. The men are splendid, climbing up grimly not knowing what to expect at the top. I move over to the right to search for Nigel's (Lt. N. Mounsey) platoon but cannot see them. We reach a ledge just before the summit and pause for breath, and then I hear 'Pedestrian' shout: 'Follow me, 11 platoon', —and I find myself on the top.

We have been covered during the climb by steep slides and boulders, but now machine-guns open up all round. The ground now is flat but covered with rocks. A miserable Boche crawls from behind a boulder about ten yards in front shouting the inevitable 'Kamerad'. He could have killed me twenty times over as I stood there, but he is too shaken to press the trigger. I run past him—gosh, this is great fun now! Bullets are whining everywhere, but our blood is up—we are shouting, swearing, cheering—it's easy, they're giving themselves up—they've had it! Except that on the right there's no sign of Nigel, and a lot of fire is coming from behind that wall. I see Boche moving, but now away— they're advancing in the copse where I think Nigel's crowd is—three spandaus open up on us, and I drop just in time. I look round. Gosh, I've only one section with me! The rest of the Company has swept forward. I can hear the CSM yelling encouragement to them. Geoff is quiet, and looks bad, he was hit in the thigh, but staggered on to the top to collapse in a hail of bullets.

I am as excited as hell, and get a Bren to open up towards the copse, and Jerry quietens down. I must be excited now as I do a damned silly thing—I zig-zag forward under cover of the Bren—only half a dozen Boches there at the most I should think—two blokes say 'Good luck, Sir', and a voice says 'I am coming with you, Sir'. Grand troops!—it's Cpl. Kendrick. We dash forward amongst the spandau lead, our Bren silences one machine-gun.

Another twenty yards, then more spandau, and a dash for cover behind a big boulder—I turn round to see Kendrick shot clean through the throat. I grab his tommy and loose off the magazine. Poor Kendrick! Courage evaporates. I hug the ground and pray; then Jerry starts shelling us. I shout back for a smoke screen on the copse. The first smoke bomb lands nearer to me than to the copse, and I shout a correction, only to find that the mortar crews have been knocked out. I lay there nearly half an hour sweating. Presently the Boche get browned off and come out with their hands up—about thirty of them, armed to the teeth. What a morning!

Captain K. A. NASH

*

At 0430 on 3rd September Montgomery's leading troops of the Eighth Army crossed the Straits of Messina and landed on the Italian mainland. This preliminary probe of 'the soft under-belly of Europe' was the beginning of a continuous advance from the southern and northern shores of the continent which would not cease until the final defeat of Germany in 1945. And on 9th September the Fifth Army, a combined Anglo-American formation under Lieutenant-General Mark Clark, started to come ashore on the west coast of Italy over the beaches of Salerno while to the south the 1st Airborne Division arrived at Taranto. But before the Allied landings the most intensive secret discussions had been proceeding in an endeavour to persuade the Italians to surrender. Eisenhower's Head of Intelligence describes their outcome:

THE HOPED-FOR EFFECT

Castellano had been given until midnight on 30 August to reply to our proposals, and from 26 August the clandestine radio was manned constantly. Very few at Allied Force Headquarters knew what was happening, but the excitement amongst those who did was intense. Douglas Dodds-Parker (later Colonel Dodds-Parker, MP) was in charge of the signals arrangements and I recollect vividly my tremendous relief when about late afternoon on the 30th he received a message through the radio link to say that Castellano and Montanari would reach Sicily the next day. The conversations in Lisbon had not failed. Our confidence in Castellano was justified. Even the Zanussi episode had not confused matters.

We left for Sicily by air on 31st August with high hopes for quick results, but when we met Castellano and Montanari at a camp specially prepared for us near Alexander's headquarters, things looked less hopeful. Castellano read from a document which said that if the Italian Government had been a free agent it would have accepted our terms, but that the situation had now materially changed. The Italians drew attention to a big increase in German troops in Italy since the Lisbon negotiations. The very existence of Italy was now threatened. In view of this Castellano insisted that his Government should be told exactly where in Italy and in what strength the Allies would land. As Mr Murphy wrote to President Roosevelt: 'It is a nice balance in their minds whether we or the Germans will work the most damage in Italy. They are between the hammer and the anvil.'

We had already decided that for security reasons we could not give the Italians precise information. We could only keep impressing on Castellano that we intended to land in force; that whatever he said or did Italy was doomed to become a battlefield; that we would declare an armistice before we landed but that we could not give any exact information of our intentions and plans until shortly before the landings took place. We felt that we had done all we could to persuade the Italians, and Castellano was told late in the afternoon of 31 August that he and Montanari must return to Rome immediately to consult their Government and obtain a final decision. We added that whatever the decision it would not alter the plans of the Allies, in spite of the consequences for the Italian people, and we pointed to his native Sicily as an example of the devastation that could be caused by bombing. The Italians left for Rome that night in their own three-engined Savoia. It had been a hot and sultry afternoon and the negotiations had been long and complicated. All our nerves were on edge, and we could do nothing but wait. I took the opportunity of the pause to pay a rapid visit to Algiers.

We did not have to wait long. Very soon we received an urgent communication from the Italian Government to say that the Allies' terms were acceptable, and that the delegation would return to Sicily immediately. Once again we were to be disappointed. Castellano blandly maintained that although the Italian Government had accepted the terms he was still without authority to sign anything. The position was becoming ridiculous. The invasion was due to take place in a few days' time and many of our plans were based on reaching some kind of agreement with the Italians. We held a council of war and came to the conclusion that one hope of a speedy solution would be to get General Alexander, the highest ranking officer in Sicily at the time, to intervene. He agreed and, in the most resplendent military uniform he could lay his hands on, booted, spurred and bemedalled, he made a formal call on Castellano.

He was a formidable and imposing figure as he introduced himself to the Italians to whom his name was already a legend—a fact on which we were banking. He expressed his satisfaction at learning that they were now, at last, prepared to sign the armistice terms. When they declared, rather sheepishly, that they could do no such thing, he burst into a torrent of angry words and indicated, in Hitlerian manner, that his sorely tried patience was now at an end. He gave the wretched Italians such a sound lecture on the disgraceful manner in which they were endangering not only our own military operations but even the future of Italy, that they immediately promised to reconsider the whole matter and convey General Alexander's message to Rome. He ended by warning them that a refusal might mean the bombing and possibly the destruction of the Italian capital.

All this had the hoped-for effect. Castellano, after consulting with his colleagues, despatched a last message to Badoglio asking that he be given at once the necessary authority to sign the armistice terms. Atmospheric conditions were bad and messages were delayed, but at long last the interminable waiting came to an end. At 4.30 pm on 3 September the Italians received full authority from their Government to sign the surrender.

Major-General SIR KENNETH STRONG, KBE, CB

*

As the Eighth Army slowly made its way up the east side of Italy, 'Popski',
with his handful of jeeps, roved far ahead into country still in Axis hands,
passing back information and creating alarm and despondency. One of the
many episodes in which he was involved was that of

COGNAC FOR MAJOR SCHULZ

I called to a little man who had been standing by for a long time
waiting for his turn to speak, shy but less dim-witted than those
other boobies. The first thing he said was:

'I know the quartermaster officer in Gravina, Major Schulz, the
one who buys supplies for the officers' mess. His office is in the piazza,
the third house to the left of the trattoria, the one with the double
brown door. My name is Alfonso.'

His words gave new life to my poor brain, dazed by so many
hours of fruitless gossip.

'Alfonso,' I said, 'please tell those people who are still waiting that
I shall talk to them tomorrow.' I took him by the arm and we sat
down side by side on a stone. Alfonso had sold cheese, eggs and wine
from his farm to Major Schulz, he had been in Gravina the day
before and had noticed many things; he offered to go again and try
and find out what I needed. Eventually we evolved another plan.
First Bob Yunnie with four jeeps set off to watch the Potenza–
Gravina road. He found a suitable hide-out on a height opposite the
small mountain-top town of Irsina, close enough to the road to read
the number plates of the passing vehicles. He organised the familiar
routine of road-watching, and I pulled back three miles to a deserted
railway station on the Potenza-Gravina line. From the station
telephone I rang up Major Schulz: I had a long struggle to get
through but eventually I got on to him. Speaking Italian mixed with
a few words of German I told him, with a great show of secrecy,
that I was the quartermaster sergeant of an Italian headquarters in a
town which had recently been evacuated by the Germans. I had, I
said, the disposal of eight cases of cognac which I would like to sell
if he would offer me a good price. We haggled a good deal about
the sum. When we had finally come to an agreement I said that for
obvious reasons I didn't care to deliver the goods by daylight. If he
would wait for me in his office that night at eleven o'clock I would

drive up with the drink in a captured American car. Would he give
the word to the control post on the Spinazzola road to let me
through without asking questions?

Major Schulz was a simple soul: he may have had scruples about
buying stolen goods, but he wanted the cognac badly for the general's
mess, and I had made free use of the name of his predecessor,
Hauptmann Giessing, with whom, I said, I had in the past made
several similar deals. (The relevant information came of course from
Alfonso, a good schemer with an observant mind.) He agreed to
my dubious request and promised to wait for me that night.

With Cameron we stripped our jeep and loaded in the back some
compo-ration boxes, weighted with stones. At ten to eleven the guard
on the road block lifted the barrier for us and waved us through, and
at eleven exactly we pulled up on the piazza opposite Major Schulz's
office. Cameron and I grabbed each end of one of our cases, went
past the sentry, up the stairs straight into the office, where Major
Schulz dozed at his desk. Woken by the thump of the case on the
floor, he opened bleary, drunken eyes and gazed at us uncertainly.
Cameron didn't give him time to wonder at the nature of our
uniforms, but hit him smartly on the head with a rubber truncheon
—a gift to us from SOE. Schulz passed out and slumped in his chair.
Cameron went down stairs for another case—while I went through
the papers in the room. By an amazing stroke of luck, open on the
desk lay the ration strength of the units of the First Parachute
Division and attached troops which were supplied by the distributing
centre in Gravina, dated September 12th, 1943. While Cameron
brought up the remaining cases I collected more documents out of
the files. We placed a quarter-full bottle of whisky, uncorked, on
Schulz's desk (the poor man deserved a reward), and walked out
into the street. The German sentry was idly examining our jeep—
moved by an impish gust of Scottish humour, Cameron, the sedate,
shook him by the hand, pressed on him a packet of 'V' cigarettes,
said:

'Good night, good German,' and we drove off.

Two hours later, from a fold in the hills, Beautyman tapped out:
POPSKI TO AIRBORNE STOP TOTAL STRENGTH ENEMY FORMATIONS
OUTSIDE TARANTO 12 SEP ALL RANKS 3504 RPT THREE FIVE ZERO FOUR
MESSAGE ENDS

On the 0900 call I received:

AIRBORNE TO POPSKI STOP PLEASE CONFIRM TOTAL STRENGTH ENEMY
FORMATIONS TARANTO PERIMETER NOT MORE 3504

I knew that Intelligence had put the figure much higher. Slightly
piqued, I fell to the temptation of showing off and, having by now
sorted out the papers I had stolen from the unfortunate Schulz, I
composed a lengthy signal which ran to four or five messages and
took the rest of the day to encipher and transmit. It went something
like this:

POPSKI TO AIRBORNE STOP CONFIRM TOTAL STRENGTH ENEMY 12
SEPTEMBER ALL RANKS 3504 RPT THREE FIVE ZERO FOUR INCLUSIVE
OFFICERS 441 STOP LOCATIONS FOLLOW GINOSA OFFICERS 61 ORS 500
MATERA OFF 72 ORS 570 ALTAMURA OFF 83 ORS 629 SANTERAMO OFF
58 ORS 469 GIOLA OFF 92 ORS 755 GRAVINA OFF 75 ORS 140 STOP
ORDER OF BATTLE FOLLOWS ONE PARACHUTE DIV 19 RGT D COY O.C.
LT. WEISS INITIAL W.G. GINOSA B COY LESS ONE PLATOON O.C.
HAUPTMANN SCHWARTZ INITIAL ILLEGIBLE GINOSA . . .

and so on: Major Schulz had filed his strength returns with care.

With this flourish I considered that my first mission was completed, and I turned my mind to investigations much further afield.

Lieutenant-Colonel VLADIMIR PENIAKOFF

*

*When the Allied armada arrived off the beaches of Salerno the German
16th Panzer Division, which had moved across from Bari a few days
before, was already on the alert. 'Within hours of the announcement of the
armistice the beach defences were manned and covered by well-sited
machine-gun positions and several mobile batteries of 88-mm guns in the
hills behind Battipaglia. In accordance with their doctrine of striking as hard
as possible at any invading force at the moment of landing, small groups of
tanks were moved up close behind the actual beach defences. "Alarmzu-
stande II" had been ordered at 1600 hours 8th September by the division
when a report was received that thirty-six ships with destroyer escorts had
been sighted twenty-five miles south of Capri.' This was the prelude to
what was nearly an Allied disaster, and the death-knell to any hopes of
surprise for Operation*

AVALANCHE

Northwards we fared across the Tyrrhenian Sea, line upon line of
LSTs, with larger ships and cruisers between us and the invisible coast
of Italy, and a busy screen of destroyers, anti-submarine trawlers and
motor launches all about us. During the night there had been gunfire
over Sardinia away to the west. From the bridge beside the commander, the scene was picturesque but quiet, ordered and intelligent.
A signal was climbing the mast of the leading ship, and I put out my
hand for the code-book. Spelling out the signal with unaccustomed
eyes I wrote on the pad ITALY HAS SURRENDERED, and turned to the
commander. 'Do you see what I see?' I said to him. He took the
book from me, glanced at it, and replied, 'Yes, I expect so. Now
what are we going to do?' I picked up the megaphone and ordered
all hands aft. Army and Navy packed in below the bridge, and I told
the news. There was a moment's pause, then a wild burst of cheering
that was echoed from ship to ship as the word spread. The cheering
died and I again put up the megaphone. 'Well, that's that. Now I
am going to ask you to do a little thinking. What does Italy's
surrender mean to you and me? It means just this. It means that,
instead of a reception committee of a few half-hearted Italians on the
beach at Salerno, we shall find a first-class German armoured corps
with its back well up. We shall beat it, but tomorrow's battle will be
a trifle tougher than it might have been. Each one of us . . .' They
dissolved slowly into serious little discussion-groups.

In the gathering darkness we altered course and, leaving the
commander on the bridge, I went down to his tiny cabin under-
neath, took off my boots and immediately went to sleep. . . . A penetrating jolt, as though the ship had struck a rock, nearly threw me
from the bed and a second jolt brought me to my feet. We had been
closely straddled by two bombs, and as I climbed to the bridge hell
was let loose. Rocket-ships were hurling blazing salvoes at the
unseen coast; monitors, cruisers and destroyers were blasting the
blackness and intensifying it by their lightning flashes. The first
landing-craft, including one of my light batteries, were groping
shorewards. The flickering night was alive with hidden activity.

Dawn, after a sudden faint start, grew slowly amidst the mist and smoke. Detached fragments of mountain began to appear in the intermittent rifts; I remember the greedy delight with which my eyes, mountain-starved by two years on African desert, feasted momentarily upon a jagged crest of the Apennines. Now we were zigzagging towards the beaches, evading the black, sinister mines which, loosened from the sea-bed around us by our devoted mine-sweepers, clustered like fishes' eggs among the waves. And now we were under shell-fire. In front of us a landing-craft with tanks aboard slowly rolled over and sank. A destroyer coming inshore to the rescue was likewise hit. Then the Navy closed in and gave the offending battery everything. (When I visited the spot later in the day, I found the German guns knocked to all points of the compass and their plucky crews splashed about them.) Meanwhile, another German battery, four 88-millimetres, had got the range of our craft over open sights as we moved slowly in, awaiting our turn at the beach. The captain of the next landing-ship beside us was killed by a direct hit on the bridge. Another ship beyond was struck forward and received a number of casualties. Our turn was next. The rounds came over in sharp salvoes and bracketed us with perfect precision, sending showers of spray over us as we changed course cumbrously to vary range. The troops lay flat on deck or were mildly screened in the hold. The naval commander and the brigade commander on the bridge took it in turns, salvo by salvo, to stand and watch the beach ahead, making the usual fatuous and self-conscious jokes which are appropriate to such an occasion and taking turns ceremoniously also with the single tin-hat which we shared. At length the awaited signal flashed to us from the beach; the commander signalled 'full speed ahead' and we struck the beach fairly and squarely. Sprigge, RNR, had brought us in to a nicety.

It was a long, fidgety but interesting battle. It had one rather particularly uneasy moment on the seventh day (15th September) I remember, when an expected infantry brigade failed to arrive from Tripoli and left our line very thin on the ground. The right flank of 10th Corps was in fact penetrated by the enemy and an ugly situation was in the making. At midnight I was called up by the corps commander and ordered to collect an emergency force of all available gunners to fill the gap as infantry. In the course of half an hour some four hundred of my artillery-men, armed with an assortment of Bren-guns, Tommy-guns and rifles, were assembled from all quarters in the vivid moonlight, formed into a hollow square for a rapid appreciation of the situation from their brigadier, and marched off in groups to the broken front line. One group, under Major Sir Basil McFarland, redoubtable ex-mayor of Londonderry, came quickly into action; the gap was sealed, and next day 'Gunner-force' was creditably relieved for its proper duties by reinforcements brought in by sea and air.

SIR MORTIMER WHEELER (who as a brigadier was then
in command of the 12th Anti-Aircraft Brigade)

A COMPLETE LACK OF PLAN

Fusilier Needham had spent the night in the wood. At first light he crawled for half a mile with his group of wounded down a ditch towards a field, from which they heard German voices. They retired, but as they reached a road they were challenged by a German sentry. They ran as fast as they could, with the crackle of small arms and bullets whistling about them; they were between the lines and at last running in the right direction. Mortar bombs were falling around; then, to their chagrin, British troops also started firing at them. Needham was conscious of an explosion and felt himself tossed through the air. When he next woke up he was about to be loaded aboard a Bren-carrier; from the pain in his stomach, he realised that he had been wounded again. The Bren-carrier rattled down a lane leading to the beaches, but had not driven far before hitting a mine: both tracks were blown off and the occupants hurled into the road. A passing lorry rescued them; they were later transferred to an ambulance, which took them to a casualty evacuation ship and thence to a hospital ship bound for Algiers.

As he lay on a stretcher, the Fusilier looked back over his recent days' fighting, recalling the things which have remained in his mind ever since. The salient points went through his head in quick flashes:

What appeared to be a complete lack of plan. We were never shown any details, only rough notes, and everyone thought the landing would be easy.

The way American soldiers appeared on the beach when we were under heavy fire; they were carrying weighty kit-bags, had no shovels, and told us they did not expect any fighting.

The terrible scream of German dive bombers and my pleasure at watching one smash into the ground just in front.

Seeing a large factory disappear into dust, together with its German garrison, as a broadside from a ship tore into it.

The hypnotic attraction of tracer bullets as they came towards me so slowly, suddenly to speed up and crack by.

The terror on an Italian farmer's face, as he cried and asked for help for his wounded wife. As I and another helped him he told us in broken English how both his sons had died in Africa. We took his wife into his house, and upon opening the bedroom door found a German officer on the bed, dead, with both legs blown off.

The good temper and help given by other Fusiliers—to the extent of crawling under intense fire to help and to pass cigarettes and food.

How I missed a cup of tea and hot food.

The terrible smell of death—I can still smell this now!

Watching a man lying down with six bullets in his stomach, groaning in agony as he slowly died; I felt sweat all over me, even though it was cold.

How the time and days passed—it seemed all so quick afterwards.

Fusilier D. NEEDHAM of the 8th Royal Fusiliers,
as reported by HUGH POND

*

INTO NAPLES

Leaving my cumbrous armoured car to follow, I threaded rapidly in a jeep along the broad street beside the docks, which were clogged with the capsized hulls of Italian warships and merchant-men. There was still intermittent firing in the further outskirts of the city, but all Naples was afoot to welcome us with flowers and strange varieties of Union Jack. At one point, where the Germans had overturned a number of tramcars across the road, I slowed down to negotiate the obstacle. The crowd surged forward and a man thrust a leaflet into my hands. It had been printed, manifestly at the risk of his life, when the Germans were still in occupation, and is one of my more treasured relics. It reads thus:

Brothers,

After thirtynine months of war, pains and grieves; after twenty years of tiranny and inhumanity, after the innocent victims of the most perverce gang at the Government; today, September 8th. 1943, we can cry at full voice our joys our enthusiasm for your coming.

We can't express with words our pleasure, but only we kneel ourself to the ground to thank God, who have permit us to see this day.

With you we have divided the sorror of the war, with you we wish to divide the day of the big victory.

We wish to march with you, until the last days against the enemy N.I.

We will be worthy of your expectation, we will be your allied of twentyfive years ago

> Hurra the allied
> Hurra the free Italy
> *The committee of antifascist*
> *ex*
> *fighters of the big war*

SIR MORTIMER WHEELER

After the capture of Naples, on 1st October, the Allied armies on both sides of Italy were faced with a long slog from river to river and mountain to mountain. As Churchill put it, 'there was always something else'. The ferocity of the countryside was matched by the ferocity of the enemy.

TEDESCHI

To the 11th Hussars *(moving north from Vesuvius: Ed.)* almost the only redeeming feature of the next few days was the astounding reception accorded them by the Italian people, from whom the arrival of their

Daimlers never failed to evoke wild acclamations and the showering of food of every kind. But local support did not stop short at that: the Italians would frequently come forward with a plentiful supply of accurate information about the Germans, and they would not hesitate to jump aboard the armoured cars to show the way. On the very first morning an unknown patriot in Marigliano gave his life in running out to warn a scout car of 'B' squadron that enemy tanks were round the corner, and when he fell his wife picked up his rifle and went forward, vowing to kill some of the hated *Tedeschi*. That same village also saved Trooper Wills from capture when his White scout car was hit and burned, hiding him as the enemy came to search the houses, and eventually smuggling him out to safety.

Active opposition to the enemy by armed civilians was also a marked feature of the fighting on the Naples plain, despite the shocking reprisals with which the Germans tried to stamp it out. 'A' squadron met the first results in the burning town of Acerra, where a quickly organised guerilla band had tried to cut off some of the retreating Germans. Here some of their tanks returned to mow down the civilians, and Sergeant Green's Troop saw one of them direct machine-gun fire on local volunteers who were filling up a blown-up ford to get the armoured cars across. In a neighbouring village, as 'B' squadron passed through, the inhabitants were burying ten of their men who had been lined up and shot. Just after the armoured cars had gone, more Germans suddenly jumped over the cemetery wall and shot down the crowd with Tommy guns as they stood beside the graves.

Brigadier DUDLEY CLARKE

*

After the Italian surrender and the Allied advance many Allied prisoners were moved from camps in Italy to detention north of the Alps: many, in various ways, escaped, to lie doggo with the aid of peasants or to join the bands of partisans who operated in the mountains.

A DASH FOR IT

From somewhere at the head of the queue a shot rang out. The shuffle of feet, the subdued murmur of fifteen hundred-odd voices, changed abruptly to an eerie silence that lasted a few seconds. One or two shouts, then silence again, and then the conversations started up with forced unconcern.

'One of the Yugoslavs made a dash for it. A sentry shot him dead.'

The message, whispered back along the line, added an extra chill to the night air. 'I saw it happen,' said a voice near me, later. 'A big dark chap, with a sort of white cotton scarf round his neck.' Later again, we filed past the dim shape, a pair of boots protruding from under the sack, a warning to anyone who might be contemplating a similar dash. 'This is all just a bad dream,' I said to myself over and over again, fingering the scrap of paper in my pocket with Kempster's sister's address. Then I was quietly sick.

Some time after that, around 11 pm, Amos, Mark and I squeezed into a cattle truck with thirty others. The floor reeked faintly of sheep, or it may have been goats. The sliding door rattled shut and was bolted from the outside. Once used to the dark, I could see a glimmer of sky through an open ventilator under the roof on the opposite wall. Soon afterwards the journey to Germany began. For a while we shunted forwards, then backwards. Half-dozing I wondered if we were heading for Rome after all, but I had little idea of time or distance. Then, in a more purposeful fashion, we moved forwards, to the north, and I fell soundly asleep.

When I woke the train was stationary. The headache had vanished and, as often happens, I now felt exuberantly well. Amos was shaking my shoulder, whispering something about taking a look. We scrambled cautiously to our feet and picked our way among bodies to the ventilator. He was tall enough to be able to peer out and reported that we were near a steep bank, that a German sentry was walking up and down the line, and that the night was fairly black.

The train might start again at any minute and there was no time to collect clothes or provisions. He gave me a leg up and I hung for a few seconds half in half out of the ventilator, listening for the sentry's steps. They were moving away. I lowered myself quietly to the track, scrambled up the bank and threw myself down in a muddy field that was planted, I vividly remember, with beans. A few seconds later Amos himself lay panting beside me. And after a long minute the train moved off.

As it receded we could hear someone plunging clumsily about in the beans near us. We pressed our faces and bodies in the earth, imagining that we'd been spotted and were being searched for by an Italian peasant or a German soldier. We were being searched for, but by neither.

'Ah, there you are,' said the man, joining us.

'Christ, Mark, who asked *you* to come?' I said, but under my breath.

JOHN VERNEY

★

Many of the escaped prisoners endured severe sufferings in the winter mountains, often short of warmth or food or shelter. But these were as nothing compared with the sufferings of the fighting troops during the last month of 1943, as they inched up to the famous Gustav Line which, carefully constructed by the Germans right across Italy to defend Rome from the south, and centred on Cassino, was to baulk the Allied advance until the following May. An indelible impression of the conditions in which the fighting continued is given by the historian of the Queen's Own Royal West Kent Regiment, in an account based on war diaries and the recollections of those who were there:

The Italian winter had now set in with snow on the hills, grey skies, strong winds and heavy rain. North of Torino near the coast the river Sangro, swollen with rain and snow, ran five feet deep and a hundred yards wide between steep banks. Across the river, level farm-land extended for over a mile. Then there rose an escarpment 150 feet high, and beyond that an upward slope to a ridge on which stood the villages of Fossacesia, Santa Maria and Mozzagrogna. On this ridge the Germans had prepared their main defensive positions, which included machine-gun nests connected by tunnels, pill-boxes, houses reinforced by concrete and deep shelters. Anti-tank and anti-personnel minefields covered all approaches; one of the most troublesome of the mines for the infantry was the small schu-mine, which would blow off the foot of anyone who trod on it. This immensely strong position, called the Gustav or Winter-Line, extended the whole width of Italy and was designed to stop the Allied advance once and for all. . . .

Patrols had already discovered that the river was only lightly defended in accordance with German custom. It was now decided to extend the patrolling across the river in order to find out as much as possible about the enemy; to deny the Germans access to the river; and at the same time to protect reconnaissance parties of Sappers and armoured formations.

Major J. D. Forman, who was now second-in-command, was placed in charge of patrolling in the battalion. As 'Patrol Master' he established his headquarters in a farmhouse on the Torino Ridge with a magnificent view across the river. From this he briefed patrols to clear the mines; reconnaissance patrols to discover what positions the enemy were occupying; patrols to draw fire from these positions and thus find out their strength; fighting patrols to destroy these positions when their strength was known; and patrols to protect RE and tank reconnaissance parties. An average of ten patrols or 60 men were in this way sent across the river every twenty-four hours. A patrol diary was kept, and each patrol was carefully cross-examined on its return. The information obtained was collated by the Intelligence Section and shown on a large panoramic sketch of the area.

The first task was to lift the mines which the Germans had carefully laid on all the tracks across the level farmland and in all the possible approaches to the escarpment. Even a worse obstacle than these was the River Sangro. Indeed, during the first few days the river presented greater difficulties than the enemy. For, to begin with, the Germans attempted to contest the control of the river area by fire by day and by patrolling at night; but they soon gave this up and were content merely to defend their positions on the escarpment. On the other hand the river was at first not very difficult to cross, but later it was often necessary to swim it. In fact to cross it became a most precarious undertaking, because it varied in depth and rate of flow according to the amount of rain and snow that had fallen in the hills. Several men were drowned because of an unexpected rise of the river, and it thus became necessary to re-test each crossing-place before it was used a second time. It was found that the best way to cross was for a patrol to wade out into the middle of the river, each man firmly gripping the man in front of him, and then to turn upstream to face the flood until a shelf of firm shingle was reached. The troops would invariably be wet through at the outset of every patrol, with a consequent loss in fighting efficiency.

Lieutenant-Colonel H. D. CHAPLIN

Such conditions can undermine the morale of the best of men . . . even those of the gallant 2nd New Zealand Division.

BLACK MORNING

25 Battalion relieved the Twenty-first which had had no break since we crossed the Sangro a month earlier and was now very weary and, when the relief was completed, about 2 o'clock on Christmas morning, 6 Brigade took command of the sector. I met the battalion, trudging slowly out to its billets after daylight, and thought that I had not seen men so exhausted since Flanders. Every man was plastered with wet mud up to his neck and their faces were grey. Nevertheless I got smiles and cheerful words from every officer and every platoon. From all but one.

There was no response whatever from one platoon. The eighteen men passed me silently, their faces utterly expressionless, and none replied when I spoke to them. I was startled. A few hours later the battalion commander came in with a stern set face and gave me the reason. These men were under close arrest because they had refused to go into action. Only the platoon commander and four men had gone in. Such a thing was unheard of in the Division and the CO was heartbroken.

It was a sad business. Charges were laid, a court martial convened, and the cases were heard a week or two later. It appeared that during the afternoon before the attack the platoon sergeant warned his officer that the men would not go in. The company commander was informed. He relieved the platoon, which was in fire-pits in a reserve position, and brought it back to a farm-house to be rested. In the evening he spoke to the men in a firm and soldierly fashion and when he left was satisfied that he would see them on the start-line. Zero hour was at 4 am, the men were to be awakened at 3 am to have a hot meal at the company cooker, and then to move a few

hundred yards to the start-line. At 3 am the platoon commander
went to the door of the room in which the men were sleeping, called
out 'Shake a leg', and went back to complete his own preparations.
When he had finished and had his meal, only four men arrived at the
cookhouse, there was no time left and he went into battle with them
only. The others were found by the RSM still wrapped in their
blankets after daybreak and were at once put under arrest.

At their trial some maintained that they had not heard any call and
had simply overslept. Others, more candid, admitted that they had
made up their minds not to go into the attack. They all had good
records, the sergeant a particularly good one, and the platoon had
behaved well in the previous month's operations and had had eleven
casualties. They were all convicted and received sentences of one to
two years' imprisonment, the NCOs being in addition reduced to the
ranks. There was no sympathy for them in the battalion but I felt, as
did the General, that there would have been no trouble with a more
understanding platoon commander and confirmed the sentences
with reluctance. There was no doubt that these men had been
severely tried, but no more than their comrades who went forward
to their duty on that black morning.

                         Major-General SIR HOWARD KIPPENBERGER

                                    *

*Though the Mediterranean war, and to a lesser degree that on the India/
Burma front, were the focus of attention for the Empire throughout 1943, it
should not be forgotten that every month saw training steadily progressing
in Great Britain for the men who in 1944 would land in Normandy, while
manifold preparations and experiments were in hand to produce devices
which would assist those men ashore when D Day finally arrived. Of the
latter one of the most significant was the formation and training under
General Hobart, a pioneer of armoured development, of the 79th Armoured
Division which devised, tested and learned to use the variegated types of
specialised tanks whose aid when D Day came was inestimable . . . flame-
throwers, tanks to clear minefields, bombard tanks to destroy concrete pillboxes, bridge-laying tanks and so on—the 'Funnies'. Among this motley
assembly were the DD tanks—armour which could be launched at sea,
swim ashore, and come into action immediately on the beaches.*

PERILS OF THE SEA

Nigel Duncan, by this time a colonel, had the task of running the first launchings from LCTs under the auspices of the Sea Wing—a typical Hobart centralised school of instruction. Formidable difficulties intervened, for not only were unknown aspects being investigated, but the demands of secrecy became totally prohibitive when a nearby beach at Sokes Bay suddenly swarmed with hordes of workmen, constructing strange caissons (parts for the great artificial harbour called Mulberry). Until a new secluded beach could be found, GHQ Home Forces forbade launchings. The DD instructors were Canadians—men of sterling qualities but fretting under the restrictions imposed by secrecy—and some there were whose experience in inland waters inhibited them against the perils of the sea.

Anyway, no launchings had taken place before Hobo came down to see for himself, and Duncan, backed by a wealth of experience of his General, philosophically rode out the passing storm. At dinner that night Hobart concentrated his attentions on the Chief Trials Officer and the naval officer in command of the LCTs. By 1 am, as Hobo recalled, 'after dint of drinking too much spirits', everyone had been persuaded and he called down the table, 'Nigel—we launch tomorrow.'

Next morning an LCT, with seven Valentine DDs on board, breasted a six-inch sea to the accompaniment of warnings by the trials officer that the conditions bid fair to lead to fatalities. At last, the first tank drove down the ramp, cocked its tail in the air and slid into the water—then drifted helplessly when the driver found it impossible to engage the propeller. In next to no time a naval launch secured a towing line but, taking up the slack with a jerk, pulled the DD on to its beam and sent her to the bottom, fortunately leaving the crew swimming on the surface.

The next launch proved successful but was followed in quick succession by two more partial failures and then a total stoppage when the fifth tank jammed in the door of the LCT. So far Hobo had viewed the trial with objective interest, although clearly not pleased, but chatting with the crew of the sunken tank his patience ran out.

Hobo: 'What member of the crew were you?'

Soldier: 'The driver, Sir.'

Hobo: 'Did you have any difficulty getting out?'

Soldier: 'Oh, no, Sir, none.'

Hobo: 'Did your escape apparatus work?'

Soldier: 'I don't really know, Sir. You see the oxygen bottle was empty.'

Duncan says that by the time they reached shore he felt depressed and shaken. They lunched unhappily and then out of the blue, as he got into his car, Hobo remarked, 'Well, I'm sure it will go all right. Now look, you've got thirty chaps there and each has got to do six launches as commander and six as driver and he has got to do it by day and night as well.'

Duncan reckoned this at about three thousand launches and, remembering the speed of launch for only five tanks in the morning, said, 'I don't honestly think we can do that.' Then quite suddenly the whole aspect changed as Hobo patted Duncan on the shoulder saying, 'Of course you will—you'll find it will work out all right.' A month later DD tanks were leaving the LCTs at one every fifteen seconds.

Major KENNETH MACKSEY, MC
(who served in 79th Armoured Division)

There was another form of liquid refreshment for those who were thinking about how to get back into Europe. The man who was responsible for the blueprint for the Allied re-entry, COSSAC (the Chief of Staff to the Supreme Commander . . . that is to say, the man who tried to plan D Day before its Commander, Eisenhower, was definitely appointed) describes it.

THE 'BLACK HORSE' PLAN

I asked particularly for an outstanding Canadian officer to be my own Military Assistant, a request to the fulfilment of which General McNaughton gave his particular personal attention. The man he chose, Major Roly Harris of the Queen's Own Rifles, not being immediately available, he temporarily lent me Major Peter Wright of the Royal Canadian Engineers, and it was through him that the COSSAC Staff acquired an entirely unofficial, most beneficial, though somewhat unorthodox, accretion to its strength. Peter Wright had been billeted for some time in the Baker Street neighbourhood, and in the course of the long winter evenings had become a regular at the 'Black Horse' in Marylebone High Street. The clientele of the 'Black Horse', like that in every other pub in the British Isles, took a keenly intelligent interest in the course of world events and were in the habit of debating nightly the proper steps that should in their opinion be taken to accelerate the downfall of the enemy. This was in their view clearly being delayed at this time only by incompetent leadership, by vested interests or by other similar well known obstacles to progress. At the time when Peter joined me the 'Black Horse' Plan for the invasion of Europe was already far advanced, and he kept me abreast of developments. He and I had not collaborated for long before we found ourselves confronted by one of the many insoluble problems that continued to crop up. Peter's ebullient sense of humour produced the suggestion that the question be referred to the 'Black Horse'. I agreed, and from this the habit grew up of consulting from time to time, naturally without their knowledge, the thoroughly representative body of opinion that congregated at this hospitable bar.

Lieutenant-General SIR FREDERICK MORGAN, KCB

*

The great battles in the Mediterranean, and the imminence of a Second Front in north-west Europe, naturally distracted attention from 'forgotten units' like those Australians who were struggling against the Japanese in damp, disease-ridden jungles to defend their homeland. The following episode therefore makes a fitting finale to the year 1943:

CRASH AT THE ERAP RIVER

On the 21st October the commander of the 24th Battalion instructed Captain Peck to fly to the newly-cleared Boana airstrip and look after the lines of communication to the forward company. Peck left Nadzab in a Piper Cub at 11.30 am on 23rd October, but when it did not arrive at Boana during the next three hours, some anxiety was felt. Although patrols searched along the probable route of the

plane, nothing further was heard until the night of 28th October
when the doctor boy of Dzenzain reported to the 24th Battalion's
adjutant with a message handed to him by a native child. The
message, signed by Peck, was:

'To 24 Aust Inf Bn. Badly burnt both legs, broken jaw, 2 bad
eyes. Picked up by party of natives. Pilot killed and buried. Boy
starting 4 day trip Sunday. Might make it.'

The natives carrying Peck on a stretcher were met at Old Munkip
by medical officers on 29th October. Although very weak, he was
able to tell his story of the devotion and compassion of the mountain
natives. The plane, flying through heavy rain, had crashed into the
mountain, killing the pilot instantly and throwing Peck into a stream.
He walked down the stream and slept in a hut during the night. On
the morning of the 24th he could not walk and so began to crawl,
but had gone only a few yards when natives found him.

Having found the crashed aircraft the natives had removed and
washed the pilot's body, buried it, and placed his gear in a hut
contructed over the grave. Thinking that there was too much gear
for one man the natives began to look for another. They soon found
Peck, washed him, tended his injuries and carried him to a village.
In case he should die Peck gave his rescuers a letter so that searchers
would not think the natives had killed him. On the 25th he wrote
the message which was received at Boana three days later. At first
the natives were frightened to send a runner or move Peck because
they feared the Japanese were in the area. The appearance of two
police boys on the 26th reassured them, however, and they carried
Peck out from the wilderness of mountains, arriving at Badibo on
the 28th.

Many other Allied servicemen in the island campaigns owed their
lives to the natives who rescued them from the gloom of jungles and
the horror of wounds. Doubtless many lost or wounded Japanese
soldiers had been similarly treated. Reduced to fundamentals, it was
the kindliness of the native which often caused him to guide the lost
and succour the wounded so tenderly.

An epilogue to the Peck story resulted from the Americans'
determination to recover the bodies of their dead for re-burial in a
cemetery before eventual removal to the United States. On 13th
November a patrol from the 24th led by Corporal Knight and

including three men of the battalion, one police boy, and 13 natives left Nadzab with a casket to recover the body of the pilot, Lieutenant Harry H. Dunham. On the third day the patrol met the tul tul of Souse who led them to the Erap River, gleaming some 3,000 feet below. A hand and rail bridge had been built that morning by the tul tul. Knight commented:

'A first class job had been done, hand rail and all. Then we looked up at this sheer face of rock. . . . It was about 14 feet high, the natives had built ladders and placed them against the rock. A great job had been done so up we went. How they got the casket up is beyond me. They had big pieces of vine which they took out in front with about 6 boys on it pulling all the way, with 6 or 7 boys behind pushing. It was marvellous. We never thought such a thing was possible.'

After this crossing the patrol climbed 8,000 feet, sometimes on hands and knees and sometimes using more ladders which the natives had prepared. When the exhausted Australians reached the village of Norwal on the top they found a new hut with beds built for them.

At Norwal the patrol met a native called Gartan who had found Peck. Knight had some difficulty in persuading natives to accompany him to the plane two hours and a half away as the track was so dangerous. The route led round a patch of rock running around the side of a mountain without any track. The patrol feared to slip into the river so far below, but when 'Marys' ahead made footholds the rock was safely negotiated. Finally a sheet razor-back with a track only a foot wide led precipitously down to the Erap. Cutting its way through scrub, climbing over landslides and wading waist deep in water the patrol finally came to the pilot's lonely grave close to the river. Knight reported:

'They had planted flowers around the grave which was very decent of them. . . . The natives had put leaves over him to keep the dirt away. They think of the least little things.'

The plane itself was still poised on a rock hanging on its left wing and one wheel 30 feet over the river. The natives did not like Private Gee venturing into it as it might fall into the river below; Gee entered the plane along a limb, but when the tul tul pointed to the gathering storm and explained the danger of the Erap flooding between its cliffs, which were 300 feet high, the patrol hastily gathered its possessions and the casket and body and began the terrible climb out of the river area.

On the 17th the patrol had labour set-backs after leaving Gartan's village. These natives could carry no farther. They had already carried out Peck. Knight later explained how this had been overcome:

'Things looked black for us. Then the doctor boy came up and said his baby was sick. A mosquito had got him so Private Gee said he would go and see what he could do so he took some atebrin with him but when he saw the baby was only a month or so old he knew it couldn't take an atebrin. The doctor boy seemed to think he could but they tried by different ways but all failed so Private Gee hit on a great idea. He told the doctor boy to tell his wife to take it then the baby would get the effect of it. Well he had to show the doctor boy what he meant so he got the baby, put it on the breast of its mother and then the doctor boy woke up. He was very pleased and gave us some boys for our trip after dinner.

'The remainder of the patrol was uneventful.'

DAVID DEXTER

1944

The year of the great battles

Warre is the conflict of enemies enraged with bloody revenge, wherein the parties opposite carry their lives in their hands, every man turning prodigall of his very heart blood, and willing to be killed to kill. . . .Wee wonder now and then at the sudden death of a man; alas, you might there see a thousand men not only healthy, but stout and strong, struck dead in the twinckling of an eye, their breath exhales without so much as, *Lord have mercy upon us.* Death heweth its way thorow a wood of men in a minute of time. . . . Every battell of the warriour is with confused noise and garments rouled in blood. Death reigns in the field, and is sure to have the day which side so ever falls. . . . A day of battell is a day of harvest for the devill.

WILLIAM HOOK, *New England's Tears* or *Sympathy from the New World,* a sermon preached in New England on 23rd July 1640. Hook, late Vicar of Axmouth in Devon, had emigrated across the Atlantic. In 1944 Great Britain and America joined hands across the sea to liberate Western Europe.

During 1944 the 'conflict of enemies enraged with bloody revenge' took the
form, on land, of three massive operations . . . in Italy the Gustav Line was
cracked, Rome fell and the Allies struggled northwards; on the eastern
frontiers of India a Japanese invasion was repelled; and in north-west
Europe the armies of liberation advanced from their D-Day landings on the
Normandy beaches to the threshold of the German Reich. The curtain rose
in Italy, where on 22nd January British and American troops landed at
Anzio, north of the Gustav Line; the plan being that the Line should be
broken at Cassino to enable the beach-head troops to link up with their
brother divisions bursting through the mountains and, in their company, to
thrust the Germans out of the Italian capital. All at first went wrong; and
for many weeks there followed, at Anzio and Cassino, some of the bloodiest
fighting of the whole war. At Anzio the bridgehead settled down into a
siege situation of constant attack and counter-attack.

I took stock of our weapons. We had only about a dozen grenades
left between us, four bren magazines, and six tommy magazines. I
knew from the air photographs we'd studied at B Echelon that there
must be another spandau post to be cleared between the Moletta and
ourselves. I told Macdonnell to follow me down a track towards the
fringe of bushes that overlooked the sea.

'Our usual game, I should think,' I said to him. 'Chuck a grenade,
then in with the bayonet.'

It was not long before we found the position.

'Got your grenade ready?'

Macdonnell nodded. 'You'd better take my tommy,' he said. 'A
bayonet and a Jerry rifle won't be much use.'

We crouched low. 'Right,' I whispered.

Macdonnell threw the grenade. We waited, counted the seconds.
Nothing happened.

'Damn,' he said. 'I must have forgotten to take out the pin and
that's my last.'

All that was left to do was to run up, there and then, and spray
them with the tommy.

Two small and very terrified Germans were huddled in the trench.
Once more my tommy was choked with sand; it was the third time
that morning. One of the Germans fired wildly up at me with his
rifle, at a range of about six feet. I felt the scorch on my shoulder.

'Quick,' I said to Macdonnell. 'I've been hit. Tommy's jammed.'

We looked round. A German came out with his rifle pointed at us, and we bolted back among the bushes to our hedgehog.

'All right, let me get that beggar,' said Macdonnell.

He threw himself down by a bren that had been covering us, and opened up as the German appeared round the corner. It looked as if we'd got him, and he staggered out of sight.

That meant another bren magazine gone. If we didn't get more ammo soon, we would be in serious danger.

'Bishop,' I said, 'you'd better report back to Company HQ that we've taken our final objective. Tell them that I've only eight men left, counting you, and we're dangerously short of ammo. Tell them about the Jerry post still being occupied. I think it's a case for tanks. Come back as soon as you can.'

I hated to see him go. Since Steamboat's we had felt a special understanding. I only sent him because he was reliable.

Manvers said: 'There's another Jerry crawl trench along here, Sir. Can I finish them off with the piat? We've still got two bombs.'

We came to a pile of sand, camouflaged with branches of tamarisk. Manvers aimed carefully. It was the closest range I'd ever seen a piat used.

'That'll finish 'em off all right,' said Manvers, as a huge geyser leapt up with a shattering roar.

We found the place quite empty. Manvers was bitterly disappointed.

'What, no bods?' he said.

We returned to our shack and waited for Bishop's return with news from HQ. My wounds were beginning to throb. I went out and was sick in the bushes.

Suddenly I saw a figure crawling towards us, waving feebly with one hand. Its face was pewter-coloured. I stared, then realised it was Bishop.

'Water,' he croaked.

'My God,' said Dopey. 'He's lost a leg.'

We bent over him. Dopey gave him a drink and removed his helmet. Bishop's leg had been blown off just below the knee. . . . There seemed to be no blood, although his bone was exposed.

He was trying to move his lips. I bent down and heard: 'Jerries still there. Spandau. Had to warn you. . . .'

RALEIGH TREVELYAN

ANZIO DERBY

In these static conditions, with nowhere safe for troops to go, there was little to do off duty until beetle racing suddenly arrived. This caught on like wildfire, particularly among the Gunners and at Divisional HQ. Elaborate totes were constructed and really large money changed hands on bets. A champion beetle might fetch as much as three thousand *lire* or more, and as a thousand *lire* in those days was £2 10*s*, it was no mean price to pay for an insect. Runners were plentiful, for beetles seemed to be one of the chief products of the beachhead. Dig a slit trench, leave it for an hour, and the bottom would be black with beetles all trying to get out. The system of racing was simple. Various colours were painted on the beetles' backs and the runners were paraded round the ring in jam-jars. Just before the 'off', or I suppose I should say when they came under starter's orders, the beetles were placed under one glass jar in the centre of the 'course'. This was a circle about six feet in diameter. At the 'off' the jar was raised and the first beetle out of the circle was the winner. A difficulty arose when, for some reason or another, it became necessary to change a beetle's colours in quick time; but at one Gunner meeting the problem was solved by attaching small flags to the beetles' backs with chewing gum.

Major F. C. M. REEVES

*

THE MONASTERY

When General Tuker, commander of the 4th Indian Division, learned from the Americans that Monastery Hill was the key to the Cassino position: when he saw with his own eyes how it dominated the battlefield, and buttressed the entire system of mountain defences: when he felt, like everyone who experienced it, the almost hypnotic way in which the Monastery on its summit commanded every approach; he sent a routine request to Fifth Army Intelligence for all available information about this building.

The Intelligence Branch of Fifth Army had little to offer. So General Tuker, a determined and methodical man, carried out one of the strangest acts of generalship of the war. He summoned his car, drove to Naples, and spent the greater part of a day combing the bookshops of that city until at last he found what he wanted. That night he sent a memorandum to his Corps Commander, General Freyberg. This memorandum is not only a concise appreciation of the situation as it struck the man most concerned—the General whose division had to attack the Monastery Hill feature: it is a revealing insight into the character of General Tuker. This was the memorandum:

1. After considerable trouble and investigating many bookshops in Naples, I have at last found a book, dated 1879, which gives certain details of the construction of the Monte Cassino Monastery.

2. The Monastery was converted into a fortress in the nineteenth century. The Main Gate has massive timber branches in a low archway consisting of large stone blocks 9 to 10 metres long. This gate is the only means of entrance to the Monastery.

3. The walls are about 150 feet high, are of solid masonry and at least 10 feet thick at the base.

4. Since the place was constructed as a fortress as late as the nineteenth century it stands to reason that the walls will be suitably pierced for loopholes and will be battlemented.

5. Monte Cassino is therefore a modern fortress and must be dealt with by modern means. No practicable means available within the capacity of field engineers can possibly cope with the place. It can only be directly dealt with by applying blockbuster bombs from the air, hoping thereby to render the garrison incapable of resistance. The 1,000-lb bomb would be next to useless.

6. Whether the Monastery is now occupied by a German garrison or not, it is certain that it will be held as a keep by the last remnants of the garrison of the position. It is therefore also essential that the building should be so demolished as to prevent its effective occupation at that time.

7. I would ask that you would give me definite information at

once as to how this fortress will be dealt with as the means are not within the capacity of this Division.

8. I would point out that it has only been by investigation on the part of this Division, with no help from Intelligence sources outside, that we have got any idea as to what this fortress comprises, although the fortress has been a thorn in our side for many weeks. When a formation is called upon to reduce such a place, it should be apparent that the place is reducible by the means at the disposal of that Division or that the means are ready for it, without having to go to the bookstalls of Naples to find out what should have been fully considered many weeks ago.

FRED MAJDALANY

THE RECEIVING END

Tensely we waited in our holes for the bombs to drop. Then they came. The whining scream of their approach, the roar of their explosions and the noise of the aircraft themselves mingled with echoes flung back from the hills to produce an indescribable and infernal bedlam of noise. The whole earth quaked and shuddered under the impact. Then—a sudden silence. Hardly had the dust settled a little than I dashed out to visit the other two strong-points. I stumbled blindly about in a welter of craters. From somewhere a voice shouted: 'All's well!' and then the next great wave of air hulks loomed into view above me.

I could not go back. I remained where I was, and the flood-gates of hell opened once again. We could no longer see each other; all we could do was to touch and feel the next man. The blackness of night enveloped us, and on our tongues was the taste of burnt earth. 'I'll come again,' I said, felt my way towards the exit and rolled out into a crater. I had to grope my way forward as though in a dense fog, crawling, falling, leaping; as I reached my post, another wave was on the way in. The men pulled me head over heels into our hole. Then down came the bombs again. A pause, and once more I groped my way across the tortured earth. Direct hits—here, here and here; a hand sticking out of the debris told me what had happened. When I got back, the men read in my eyes what I had seen.

Lieutenant SCHUSTER, No. 7 Company, 3 Parachute Regiment

Yet even amid the maelstrom of Cassino there were moments of almost idyllic peace.

OBSERVATION POST

If the morning was clear we could see the Garigliano shining in the moonlight as it bent in and out, appearing as a series of tiny dots. Often the valley was hidden completely by drifting smoke from the generators at the station, so that I looked out over billowing clouds to the Monastery, which stood gleaming in the early sunshine. Behind soared Monte Cairo, six thousand feet high, its gullies streaked with snow, which ran down from its white pyramid. Gradually the mist thinned out as the wind veered, and in a few minutes the whole valley was clear.

At this time of day visibility was at its best. I looked down on the near part of the valley so vertically that it seemed to be spread out like a map: the river curved, each bend easily identifiable, the railway, roads and paths stretched like tapes, the farm buildings dotted among the trees and tracks in chessboard fashion. . . .

The relief signaller came up at mid-day with the lunch and crawled down a specially constructed shady gully, at whose entrance was a colourfully worded notice surmounted by a skull and crossbones. In the hot weather the early afternoon was the worst part of the day: one's head drooped, it seemed impossible to keep one's eyes open; the only movement was when an emerald lizard streaked over the hot stones. Then, later, a slight breeze rustled the silver leaves of the olive trees overhead, the rank, brittle grass quivered, and it was possible to concentrate again. But there were always noises to break up the day: the infantry below singing and clattering with their mess-tins; the unexpected bray of a donkey or the peck of a bird breaking a snail-shell; the sounds of guns and mortars—constant 'shellreps' to be sent back; the characteristic woof, blare and following moan of the 'sobbing sisters', which gave themselves away by their quick, fiery streaks shooting into the air; the shriek of our own close-range shelling, which seemed to skim over our heads with only a few inches to spare—once or twice those inches were missing and there was a loud crash behind us, up there on the top of the ridge.

Later in the day the sun struck across the valley slantwise, seeming to pick up all the motes in the atmosphere, so that, first, distant belts of trees and then nearby houses would be completely shrouded by haze. It was at its worst at sunset, when the valley was flooded with brilliant golden light, silhouetting the distant hills but hiding everything else completely—except the forward slopes of Trocchio, where one felt conspicuous and naked. . . .

When it was dark I would take an hour off to go down to the 'OP House' for dinner. A roaring fire would be burning in the great open hearth, several figures crouched over a long row of tins which hung from a rod spanning the width of the hearth; the fire caught their faces, tingeing them an even more brilliant colour than the sun and wind had been able to achieve. Soon after nine I would be on my way up again, the moon perhaps non-existent and the fireflies even more brilliant as they flitted across the faces of the rocks—tiny sparks of intermittent light. With a full moon I could read even the smallest details of a map.

Captain R. L. BANKS

THE KILL

At a quarter to six the earth trembled, and once again the shells started pouring overhead so thickly that at times you fancied you could see them. At the same time another lot of guns began to pound Monastery Hill in support of the Polish attack. In next to no time dust and smoke and yellow flame enveloped the Monastery itself, so that when our Dog and Baker Companies passed through Charlie Company on the stroke of six it was hidden from view. This was the kill. We were going in for the kill. The Poles were sweeping round from the right; we, two and a half miles away in the valley, were on our way to seal it off from the left. It shouldn't be long now. And once we had cut the Highway the very qualities that had made the Monastery an impregnable bastion for so long would turn it into an equally formidable death-trap. For so long the guardian and protector of its garrison, it would round on them in its death-throes and destroy them.

Compared with the previous day, we had a fairly easy advance. There were some snipers and one or two isolated machine-guns, but they didn't seem disposed to resist very strongly, and by ten Baker and Dog, assisted by fresh tanks, were nicely settled on Bluebell, another thousand yards on. We were ordered to push on as fast as possible. So Baker and Dog advanced again to the final objective line, 'Tulip', twelve hundred yards further on. And Able, Charlie and Command Post pushed on to the area just cleared by Dog and Baker. By four o'clock in the afternoon Dog and Baker both signalled that they were established on 'Tulip'—both had OPS directly overlooking Highway Six. Both asked permission to carry on and cut the road and search beyond it. We were ordered to stay where we were, however, as the exact position of the Poles was not known and mistakes might occur if we both started milling around by the road. We dominated it from where we were. We had done what was required of us. We were to stay where we were until we had further orders. The job was nearly done.

During the night Dog and Baker were told to patrol as far as the road. Not till the following morning were we allowed to send anyone beyond it. By that time it had ceased to be a military feat. It was a formal ceremony. So John sent a special patrol of three corporals, all holders of the MM. They crossed the Highway and carried out a careful search of the gullies and ruined buildings on the far side of it, but the only Germans they could find were dead ones. Their time was not wasted, however. Each returned with a Schmeisser gun, a camera, a watch and a pair of binoculars of impeccable German manufacture. An hour later the Poles entered the Monastery. As so often happens when great events are awaited with prolonged and excessive anxiety, the announcement of the fall of Monte Cassino was rather an anticlimax. It was Thursday, 18 May. The battle had lasted a week. The job was done.

FRED MAJDALANY

*

Meanwhile, in the Far East the curtain had also been raised on the long-drawn-out finale of the Japanese 'March on Delhi'. The first move was another British attempt to push forward down south in the Arakan, which was baulked in February by a vicious and effective Japanese counter-offensive. The British and Indian troops were bypassed and units surrounded. But this time there would be no retreat. Fostered by the new technique of air supply they stood fast, fought in their positions, and repelled the Japanese. 'This Arakan campaign', says Slim, 'judged by the size of the forces engaged, was not of great magnitude, but it was, nevertheless, one of the historic successes of British arms. It was the turning-point of the Burma campaign. For the first time a British force had met, held and decisively defeated a major Japanese attack.' Of the air supply Slim also observes:

I made one attempt to interfere with Snelling's arrangements. 'Wouldn't it be a good idea,' I said, 'to put a case of rum in every fourth or fifth plane so as to make sure than when the stuff is shoved out the chaps will really search for it?' Alf Snelling looked at me in the slightly pitying way professionals look at amateurs. 'Sir,' he said, 'I have *already* given orders that a case of rum should be put in *every* plane!'

There was tragedy amid victory. Of his men Slim remarks, 'How some of them died will be for ever a black blot on the so often-stained honour of the Japanese Army.'

THE ADMINISTRATIVE BOX

Bursts of rifle and automatic fire broke out about three hundred yards from Box Headquarters. These were accompanied by more shouting and then screams and cries for help. I heard a voice say in the darkness: 'Good God, they've got into the hospital.'

This was a dreadful thought, as there was very little that could be done until daylight. The defenders were a section of West Yorkshires and twenty walking wounded armed with rifles. It would be sheer folly to send in an infantry attack to drive out the enemy. Only the West Yorkshires were available and they did not know the geography of the hospital, nor would they be able to distinguish between friend and foe in the dark. To call on artillery and mortars was out of the question as our own men would be killed.

I got on the telephone to Munshi to send in a patrol to try and find out what was happening, but the carrier that was sent was driven off by grenades. Clearly the enemy were in greater strength than I had expected. We could only wait for the day to come and take what comfort we might from the fact that the wards, theatres and resuscitation installations were dug down. In the darkness the Japanese might miss them; otherwise, when they discovered that they had entered a hospital, they might take what prisoners they could and leave the remainder. . . .

The full details of what had happened we learned later from the pitifully small number of survivors of the thirty-six-hour ordeal, which was only ended when A Company of the West Yorkshires drove the enemy out. The Orderly Medical Officer, Lieutenant Basu of the Indian Army Medical Corps, was lying on a stretcher in the medical inspection room, resting, when a group of men rushed in from the dispensary at about 9 pm. One man seized his arm, while another threatened him with a bayonet. '*Aiyo*', they ordered, 'Come on.'

Basu was taken to the Japanese commander, who was in the darkened officers' ward busily scribbling notes. Through an interpreter, the questioning began. 'What is your name? What is the name of this place?'

The next question made it clear that the Japanese knew they were in a hospital, and therefore what followed was done quite deliberately and in cold blood. 'How many patients are in this hospital?' they asked. 'How many of them are British officers? What other personnel are there?'

Basu stalled as best he could. 'I am here for three days only,' he said. 'I don't know much about the organisation here.'

'What army units are posted here? How many of them are British and how many Indian?'

'I am a doctor,' said Basu. 'I am interested in medicine, not military tactics.'

At this, one angry Japanese soldier brought the point of his bayonet against the doctor's head as though to finish him off unless he answered the questions more satisfactorily. But the Japanese commander cut in brusquely: 'Show us to the telephone.'

Basu thought quickly. 'It would be dangerous to go near it,' he said. 'There is a machine-gun post just beside it.'

'Then show my men to the operating theatre and the laboratory,' ordered the Japanese officer.

Basu could not get out of this. But he took them to the small theatre which was used only for minor operations. As bad luck would have it, while the Japanese hunted round the theatre for anything they could lay their hands on in the way of bandages and cotton wool, they came on three of the hospital officers asleep. They were awakened and made prisoners. With Basu, they were taken back to the commander for further questioning. It was quite clear that the one piece of information the enemy were particularly anxious to discover was where the supply depot was situated. Basu kept up his pretence at ignorance: 'I don't know; I tell you I'm only here for a few days. I've been too busy looking after patients to find time to visit the supply depot.'

All the officers had their hands tied tightly behind their backs and they were taken to join the British and Indian other ranks, who had been trussed in a similar painful fashion.

The Japanese officer pulled out his sword, waved it over their heads threateningly, sheathed it and withdrew.

The purpose of this melodramatic gesture became clear almost at once. It was intended to cause the maximum alarm to the Indians as an inducement to make them desert to the Japanese to save their lives. The offer came almost immediately.

A man whose appearance suggested he was Indian was brought in.

'There is no need to worry,' he assured the Indians. 'No need at all to worry. You will be taken to Rangoon to join the Indian Independence League.'

'What is your native country?' Basu asked him.

'I come from Maungdaw, in Burma,' he answered.

Later that night, the five Indian medical officers were taken to the dispensary and ordered to pack up drugs for the Japanese. They were particularly interested in quinine, morphine, anti-tetanus and anti-gas–gangrene serum. They wanted to know what was in every phial. Those they did not want they threw to one side. Sally, in 9 Brigade Headquarters, could hear the bottles breaking.

When the Japanese had taken all they wanted, they drove the medical officers back to the watercourse where the rest of the captives were seated in acute discomfort because the bindings on their wrists were cutting into the flesh. Those who asked for water were jabbed with a heavy stick by a Japanese sentry.

The following morning a carrier pushed through the bushes towards the medical inspection room and one Japanese soldier dragged the trussed British other ranks out in front so that they should receive the first burst of fire. When the automatic gun of the carrier opened up, the prisoners desperately tried to find shelter, but they were handicapped because their hands were lashed behind their backs. Some of them were killed and others were wounded. The Japanese looked on grinning. They, too, had suffered casualties. They selected six of the Indian soldiers and ordered them to help to carry seven wounded Japanese.

The stretcher-bearers struggled southwards through the jungle the whole of that day. When night came, the Japanese cooked food for themselves but gave none to the Indians. Next morning, still having had nothing to eat, the Indians were given packs to carry and it was not until the early hours of the following morning that they reached their destination. This was the Buthidaung Tunnel, where there were about a thousand Japanese living. The tunnel was used as a store for arms, ammunition, guns and transport. During the day, six Indians came to see them. 'You need not worry,' they told them. 'You will have trouble for a few days, but then you will be sent to Rangoon to work. Our major will fix things and you will not be tortured by the Japanese.' One of their visitors, a Madrassi, said: 'There are now 400,000 followers of Subhas Bhose. In two months we shall reach Chittagong.'

Seven days later, the six Indian soldiers were taken out of the tunnel, ordered to strip off their clothes beside a sixty-foot-deep gorge, and then were shot by a Japanese officer and five men. Four were killed and their bodies were kicked down the gorge where already more than twenty bodies lay decomposing. One of the Indian soldiers, a RIASC ambulance driver, was shot through the right arm, left shoulder and right hand by the Japanese officer and managed to fall down the gorge without being kicked. At the bottom he discovered that the sixth member of his party, a labourer, although badly wounded, was still conscious. When the Japanese had gone, he helped the other man to move across the gorge, but after a hundred yards the labourer lost consciousness and he had to leave him. Five days later, after living on water and leaves, the ambulance driver staggered into the regimental aid post of 3/14 Punjab Regiment, one of 9 Brigade's units.

Meanwhile, back at the hospital in the Box, the Japanese raiding party had completed their crime. Wounded prisoners received no attention. Those who cried out were shot or bayoneted. Men lying helplessly in bed were killed. In one shelter were a British lieutenant, a major of the Gurkhas and a Signals sergeant. They were being tended by a captain of the RAMC. Four West Yorkshires, whose defence post was overrun in the attack, joined them. When day came, they lay still so that the Japanese might not notice them. During the morning they heard a shout outside and the RAMC Captain asked: 'What do you want?'

The shout—it sounded like 'You go'—was repeated. The Captain shook his head and lay down again. 'Who is it?' asked the Lieutenant.

'It's a Jap,' said the Captain. At that moment one of the Japanese soldiers appeared and shot him through the right thigh. The Captain shouted: 'I am a doctor—Red Cross—I am a medical officer.'

The Japanese shot dead the Captain, the Gurkha Major, two British soldiers and a mess servant. The Lieutenant and the three surviving British soldiers lay still. They stayed like that all day, and when darkness came they managed to leave the hospital and find the safety of the nearest West Yorkshire post.

A British private of the RAMC—one of a party of twenty—survived to describe his experience. He was tied by his neck to another man— as they all were—kicked, cuffed and cracked over the head by rifle butts, and used as a shield on top of a trench by the Japanese when the carrier attacked. Just before dark on February 8 a Japanese officer told the twenty men: 'Come and get treatment.'

They were taken along a dried-up watercourse to a clearing with a running stream. Through the whole hot day they had been allowed only two bottles of water between them. And now they stood by the stream. But they were not allowed to drink. The Japanese opened up at them with rifles. Seventeen of them were killed. That night Lieutenant Basu and nine men who had been wounded when a mortar exploded near them lay in a watercourse, some dying, some crying for water. The Japanese shot one man and bayoneted another who cried too loudly. Just before they left, the Japanese stood in front of them, their rifles ready.

'We are Red Cross people,' said Basu—he and another doctor both had their stethoscopes slung round their necks. 'We are doctors and hospital workers. We have nothing to do with actual warfare.'

Most of them wore Red Cross badges on their arms. It made no difference. The Japanese shot them all.

Lieutenant Basu was shot at twice. He was left stunned. At first he was not sure whether he was alive or dead. He felt at his ear, but there was no blood on his fingers. He could still see and his thoughts became clear once more. He realised how vulnerable he was lying there still alive. So he reached out to the body of one of his dead friends and put his hand on the wounds until it was covered with blood, and then he smeared the blood over his face and head and down his shirt front, so that the Japanese would think he, too, was mortally wounded. He slipped groaning into a trench, and there he spent the night.

On the morning of February 9 the West Yorkshires cleared the Japanese out of the hospital. Their task was made all the more difficult because the enemy had camouflaged their machine-gun posts cunningly with stretchers in the wards and theatre. Fortunately, before the attacks began, most of the wounded had been removed from the hospital to a dried-up watercourse lying to the north. As it was, we found in the hospital area the bodies of thirty-one patients and four doctors—doctors whose services were to be desperately needed in the days to come.

Lieutenant-General SIR GEOFFREY EVANS, KBE, CB, DSO

*

On 5th March came the next move on the chessboard. As in 1943, a Penetration Force under Wingate set off to establish itself deep in Japanese-occupied Burma. But this time a far larger formation was to fly in, set up strongholds, and using these as bases inflict 'the greatest possible damage and confusion on the enemy in North Burma'. The primary aim was to cut the communications of the Japanese facing the Chinese army (under an American General, Stilwell) far away to the north.

TAKE-OFF: BURMA

The Dakotas taxied into position. The two ropes were fixed. Everyone was very quiet as the roar of the engines died down and we waited for zero hour. I was standing on the airstrip with Wingate, Baldwin, and one or two more, when we saw a jeep driving furiously towards us. A couple of American airmen jumped out and confronted us with an air photograph, still wet from the developing tent. It was a picture of Piccadilly landing ground, taken two hours previously. It showed almost the whole level space, on which the gliders were to land that night, obstructed by great tree-trunks. It would be impossible to put down even one glider safely. To avoid suspicion no aircraft had reconnoitred the landing grounds for some days before the fly-in, so this photo was a complete shock to us. We looked at one another in dismay.

Wingate, though obviously feeling the mounting strain, had been quiet and controlled. Now, not unnaturally perhaps, he became very moved. His immediate reaction was to declare emphatically to me that the whole plan had been betrayed—probably by the Chinese— and that it would be dangerous to go on with it. I asked if Broadway and Chowringhee, the other proposed landing places, had been photographed at the same time. I was told they had been and that both appeared vacant and unobstructed.

Wingate was now in a very emotional state, and to avoid discussion with him before an audience, I drew him on one side. I said I did not think the Chinese had betrayed him as they certainly had no knowledge of the actual landing grounds, or, so far as I knew, of the operation at all; but he reiterated that someone had betrayed the plan and that the fly-in should be cancelled. I pointed out that only one of the three landing grounds had been obstructed, and that it was the one which he had used in 1943 and of which a picture with a Dakota on it had appeared in an American magazine. We knew the Japanese were nervous of air landing and were blocking many possible landing sites in North and Central Burma; what more likely than that they should include a known one we had already used, like Piccadilly? He replied that, even if Broadway and Chowringhee were not physically obstructed, it was most probable that Japanese troops were concealed in the surrounding jungle ready to destroy our gliders as they landed. With great feeling he said it would be 'murder'. I told him I doubted if these places were ambushed. Had the Japanese known of the plan I was sure they would have either ambushed or obstructed all three landing grounds. Wingate was by now calmer and much more in control of himself. After thinking for a moment, he said there would be great risk. I agreed. He paused, then looked straight at me: 'The responsibility is yours,' he said.

I knew it was. Not for the first time I felt the weight of decision crushing in on me with an almost physical pressure. The gliders, if they were to take off that night, must do so within the hour. There was no time for prolonged inquiry or discussion. On my answer would depend not only the possibility of disaster with wide implications on the whole Burma campaign and beyond, but the lives of these splendid men, tense and waiting in and around their aircraft. At that moment I would have given a great deal if Wingate or anybody else could have relieved me of the duty of decision. But that is a burden the commander himself must bear.

I knew that if I cancelled the fly-in or even postponed it, when the men were keyed up to the highest pitch, there would be a terrible reaction; we would never get their morale to the same peak again. The whole plan of campaign, too, would be thrown out. I had promised Stilwell we would cut the communications of the enemy opposing him, and he was relying on our doing it. I had to consider also that one Chindit brigade had already marched into the area; we could hardly desert it. I was, in addition, very nervous that if we kept the aircraft crowded on the airfields as they were, the Japanese would discover them, with disastrous consequences. I knew at this time that a major Japanese offensive was about to break on the Assam front, and I calculated on Wingate's operation to confuse and hamper it. Above all, somehow I did not believe that the Japanese knew of our plan or that the obstruction of Piccadilly was evidence that they did. There was a risk, a grave risk, but not a certainty of disaster. 'The operation will go on,' I said.

Field-Marshal LORD SLIM

Unfortunately Wingate's force was prevented from achieving its primary purpose for two reasons. At an early stage in the operations a plane carrying Wingate crashed into a Burmese mountainside, Wingate was killed, and the hub round which the whole enterprise revolved disappeared. More importantly, during the second week of March the Japanese began their march on Delhi. The Penetration Force set up its strongholds and harried the Japanese, but the loss, at this time, of its remarkable leader and the

great drama now to be enacted dissipated its efforts. Bitter fighting followed,
in which once again both sides were hammered. One of Wingate's column
commanders describes a characteristic episode.

THE DEEP

The second crisis came when the close-quarter fighting at the Deep
reached the limit of human tolerance. I decided I must force the
Japanese farther away, at any cost. First, we removed the secondary
charges from the three-inch mortars and fired them with primaries
only. The bombs, fired from the middle of the block, arched high
and fell five or ten yards from our forward positions. Next, I called
for a heavy air strike, and told the air force to use 250-pound bombs.
I expected to kill twenty of my own men if they bombed accurately,
forty if they didn't.

Six fighter-bombers came. Chesty, standing with a radio in a
trench above the Deep, brought them down on successive east–west
runs across the foot of the sector, their target being the outer limit
of our wire. They raced down from the sky, one behind the other,
the great bombs slipped loose and whistled, shining, down. All my
mortars opened rapid fire, all the machine-guns opened rapid fire.
The hill quaked and heaved, the noise beat in huge waves against
my eardrums, steel splinters whined and droned over the hill and far
out across the valley, trees crashed and fell, raw white wounds
gaping, all the leaves vanished and hung in the boiling smoke and
dust. The aircraft dived lower, firing their multiple .50-calibre
machine-guns. For long moments one monstrous tearing roar filled
earth and sky and being.

When they flew away, no one moved for a long time, and no one
fired. We went down to remove and replace our casualties. There
were none.

One enemy sniper lived, and fired a few shots during the rest of
the day, and the usual attack followed that night, but the following
day no Japanese were within two hundred yards of our wire. I
bombed them again, this time with B-25s.

The enemy began to use his heavy mortar. Its shell weighed sixty
pounds (the shell of our heaviest, the three-inch, weighed ten
pounds), and when it landed on a weapon pit it saved the need for

burying parties. Every day Tommy and his padre moved about across the Deep sector, under sniping, speaking to the men in the trenches, pausing here and there to pick up a handful of yellow-stained earth and sprinkle it over the torn 'grave', and say a short prayer.

The rain now fell steadily. The Deep sector looked like Passchendaele—blasted trees, feet and twisted hands sticking up out of the earth, bloody shirts, ammunition clips, holes half full of water, each containing two pale, huge-eyed men, trying to keep their rifles out of the mud, and over all the heavy, sweet stench of death, from our own bodies and entrails lying unknown in the shattered ground, from Japanese corpses on the wire, or fastened, dead and rotting, in the trees. At night the rain hissed down in total darkness, the trees ran with water and, beyond the devastation, the jungle dripped and crackled.

A Japanese light machine-gun chatters hysterically, and bullets clack and clap overhead. Two Very lights float up, burst in brilliant whiteness. Click, click, click—boom, crash, boom, three mortar bombs burst in red-yellow flashes on the wire.

The third crisis came on May 17. On that day our Lightnings (P-38s) patrolled the valley for several hours, searching for the guns which had done us so much damage. They did not find them. Towards evening the P-38s left and I went down to the water point, as I usually did, to wash, shave, and brush up for the night's battle. While I was shaving, the enemy began to shell the block with 105s and 155s. Twelve guns or more were firing. Soap all over my face, I looked across at the ridge to the west, where the enemy had once put a mortar, and saw movement there. Mortar bombs from the ridge whistled into the block. The shelling grew more urgent and I walked quickly up to my command post—I tried never to run.

The shelling concentrated on the Deep and became a violent, continuous drumfire. My stomach felt empty and I was ready to vomit. I should have relieved the King's Own. This was more than human flesh could stand. Nothing to do now though. The attack would come in immediately after the bombardment.

The shelling increased again. For ten minutes an absolute fury fell on the Deep.

Major Heap, the second-in-command of the King's Own,

tumbled in, his face streaked and bloody and working with extreme strain. 'We've had it, sir,' he said. 'They're destroying all the posts, direct hits all the time . . . all machine-guns knocked out, crews killed . . . I don't think we can hold them if . . . the men are . . .'

I didn't wait to hear what the men were. I knew. They were dead, wounded, or stunned.

I took the telephone and called Tim Brennan, commanding 26 Column of the Cameronians, and told him to bring his whole column to the ridge crest at once, with all weapons and ammunition, manhandled, ready to take over the Deep. 'Yes, sir,' he said pleasantly. I had time to call Henning and order him to spread out to occupy Brennan's positions as well as his own, before going quickly, my breath short, to the hill crest.

The shelling stopped as I reached it. Tim arrived. Johnny Boden, the mortar officer, arrived. Now, now, the Japanese must come. I told Boden to stand by with smoke and HE to cover the Cameronians; 26 Column arrived, at the double. Still no assault. Tim ran down the forward slope, his men behind him. I waited crouched on the ridge top. Ordered Boden to open up with his mortars. The enemy must have this blasted slope covered by machine-guns. I knew they had. They didn't fire. It was twilight, but down the slope in the smoke I could clearly see Cameronians jumping into the waterlogged trenches, King's Own struggling out and up towards me. The Cameronian machine-guns arrived, men bent double under the ninety-pound loads of barrel and tripod. Bombs burst, smoke rose in dense white clouds. I told the officer to move the machine-guns again, after full dark, if he could. 'Of course, sir,' he said impatiently.

The men of the King's Own passed by, very slowly, to be gathered by Heap into reserve. They staggered, many were wounded, others carried wounded men, their eyes wandered, their mouths drooped open. I wanted to cry, but dared not, could only mutter, 'Well done, well done,' as they passed.

The minutes crawled, each one a gift more precious than the first rain. I sent wire down, and ammunition, and took two machine-guns from Henning's 90 Column, and put them in trenches on the crest, ready to sweep the whole slope. Full darkness came, with rain. An hour had passed, a whole hour since the enemy bombardment ended. In our own attacks we reckoned a thirty-second delay as fatal.

With a crash of machine-guns and mortars the battle began. All
night the Cameronians and the Japanese 53rd Division fought it out.
Our machine-guns ripped them from the new positions. Twice the
Japanese forced into the barbed wire with Bangalore torpedoes, and
the blasting rain of the mortars wiped them out. At four am, when
they launched their final assault to recover their bodies, we had
defeated them.

JOHN MASTERS

*

*The Japanese plan for the invasion of India in 1944 aimed at breaking
through to the great Imphal plain, an extensive British base area of dumps
and airfields and hospitals and headquarters whose capture would have been
disastrous, and the seizure of Dimapur, 130 miles further north, the main
railhead for supplies which was linked with Imphal by a single road on
which the little village of Kohima, sitting on its ridge, was a key point.
Slim decided to hold Kohima as a road-block, and to withdraw his main
army to Imphal where, fed again by air supply, it would stand a siege till
the Japanese effort was exhausted. So the battle went: and the defence of
Kohima, the Thermopylae of the Far East, by a scratch force of 'odds and
sods' placed the name of this obscure hamlet in the annals of the British
Army beside that of Lucknow. One of the many heroes of Kohima was
Lance-Corporal Harman of the Royal West Kent Regiment.*

As soon as they crossed the ridge and started down the far slope the
enemy opened a blaze of fire. They were well armed with automatics and, as the attacking troops drew nearer, they showered
grenades on them from the buildings. Men fell wounded and dead
and the attackers went to ground, taking cover in every little fold and
dip they could find. Donald called on his number twelve platoon to
increase their fire and they did this and slowly mastered the enemy in
the bashas. But off to a flank were two machine guns raking the
whole of the little valley with fire and it was these that were now
pinning down the attack. They were hidden in a small building in
the trees, away off to the left, so that twelve platoon could not bring
fire to bear on them.

When Lance-Corporal Harman saw the threat from these two
guns, he told Mathews to move his Bren a little over to the left to

give him covering fire while he assaulted the position. Mathews brought his gun to bear and saw Harman climb calmly out of his slit trench and walk towards the machine guns. The Japanese soon saw him coming and brought fire to bear and Mathews saw the bullets clipping up the ground at Harman's feet. But he went on, quite casually, and as he walked he took two grenades from his belt and pulled out the firing pins with his teeth. When he was only thirty yards from the building he put his rifle on the ground and lobbed the two grenades inside. The machine guns were silent for a moment and Mathews saw Harman pick up his rifle and run forward quickly until he was under the shelter of the wall. Then he disappeared round a corner and an agonising screaming came from the building, and two single shots. Then Harman walked out, carrying one of the two machine guns across his shoulders.

All the attacking troops were watching this action, and when they saw Harman come out with the machine gun, they broke into a great cheer and surged forward again. In a moment Lieutenant Wright's Indian sappers were up against the buildings, blasting in the walls. The men streamed in after them, shooting and bayoneting as they went. Then all was confusion, with cursing, sweating, struggling men killing each other in the narrow confines, among the piles of stores and crates and in among the ovens. Donald, who had led the attack into the first building, soon cleared it of the enemy and climbed up on the crates so that he could see what was going on around him. One by one he saw the buildings empty as his men came out, smeared with blood, with clothing scorched and torn, all exhausted after the nervous strain of the attack, the horror of the bayoneting, and the exertion of hand-to-hand combat. Because the buildings were now catching fire, and the ammunition in them exploding, he made them go back across the little valley, away from the confusion and the flames. Donald looked to his right and saw that in that direction the battle had been won. Then he looked to his left; on that side things had not gone so well. There was one basha, a little larger than the others, in which the enemy were still holding out. The sappers had not been able to blow the walls down, but even as he looked, Lance-Corporal Harman, who had come forward into the attack without orders, disappeared into the doorway.

Harman had seen at once, with extraordinary insight, that this

building was not going to fall to the main attack, so he decided that
it would fall to him. He went into the building and saw that it was
part of the bakery, with ten ovens inside. They were large brick
ovens, each large enough to hold a man, with heavy iron covers. As
he walked in he was at once shot at from two of the ovens, but the
bullets flashed past. He ran out of the door and back across the valley
to his own section position where grenades were stored. He seized a
box and, dragging it behind him, ran back into the building, taking
shelter behind the nearest oven. He smashed the box open and
pulled out a grenade. He put his hand on one of the steel covers and
let go the safety lever. There was a four-second delay on the fuse, so
he waited for three, then, lifting the lid, dropped the grenade into
the oven. As he let the lid fall back the grenade exploded. He crept
round all the other nine ovens and dropped a grenade into each.

The Japs did not seem to know what he was doing, or at least if
they did, they knew no way of stopping him. He had trapped them
in the ovens because, if they showed their faces for a moment, he
would shoot them. When he had finished Harman removed all the
lids to make sure that the men inside were dead. There were dead
men in five, but in two others the Japs were still alive, though badly
wounded. He pulled them out and, taking one under each arm,
carried them back across the valley to his section position. As the
men saw him return, they went wild with cheering. The cheering
became almost hysterical after the excitement of the battle and
Donald was unable to stop it.

ARTHUR CAMPBELL

*In a similar single-handed attack on a Japanese machine-gun post John
Harman was later killed at Kohima. He was awarded a posthumous VC.*

*At Imphal six routes converged on the plain like spokes on the centre of
a wheel. The Japanese were driven off these routes one by one, hunted into
the hills between them, and steadily destroyed. 'Our heaviest losses,' says
Slim, 'were among the officers, not only in the infantry who in this close
fighting could not fail to be conspicuous, but among the artillery observation
officers who to give accurate support pushed on with the leading troops, and
among the young tank commanders who, regardless of safety, kept their
turrets open or moved on foot so that they could guide their tanks through
the jungle.' This typical action by Lieutenant Weir explains why:*

Our barrage had begun. I raced back to the tank, mounted, and in about three minutes we were off on to Red Hill without mishap, where the Gurkhas were bobbing up and down throwing grenades while others worked their way round to the south flank. From the top of the hill I found that the guns could not be depressed on to either Pimple, so I had to advance over the hill and down the reverse slope. Three Japs ran out as I went over, but the Gurkhas were grand and killed them before they reached the tank. We were able to hold the tank on the slope with the engine, both sticks pulled right back, and the operator tugging on the parking brake with both hands.

Immediately we opened fire at about fifteen Nips who ran away over the top of First Pimple as we came over Red Hill. We then set about dealing with each foxhole and bunker in turn. These could be easily distinguished at the range of about 150 yards. The foxholes looked like what they are called, just a small black hole with a hint of disturbed earth about it.

Weir's tank was now hit, the gun jammed, and when he tried to reverse over the brow of the hill to safety he found that the soft ground and the steepness of the slope made this impossible. He continues:

We then discovered to our horror that immediately the steering sticks were let loose, the tank started slipping down hill. There was only one thing for it. I ordered 'Abandon tank'. The guns and wireless were made useless, and then I took over from the driver, and the crew left via the escape hatch.

I viewed tremulously the aspect in front of me. I could either let go of the sticks and try to jump out or else try and steer it to the bottom. The engine could not be started, as the moment the clutch was dipped, the tank again moved forward. I decided to steer the tank to the bottom. By this time I had quite forgotten my guardian angel, but he had not forgotten me, for I had not gone ten yards when the tank stopped on a not quite so steep place and against a small ridge on the ground. Thankfully I dropped through the escape hatch and, running faster than I thought I was capable of, I reached safety behind Red Hill where the rest of the crew were waiting for me.

                                           Lieutenant A. WEIR

On 22nd June the Supreme Commander, Admiral Mountbatten, was able to signal to Churchill that relieving forces had broken through to beleaguered Imphal. 'The road to the plain was open. On the same day the convoys began to roll in.' And now the pursuit of the retreating Japanese began.

I wandered with Henchy and my orderly Mohd Shafi through acres of jungle by this former Japanese headquarters to find smashed enemy lorries painted brown, sleek staff cars of which many had been captured from our own army, and scores of shelters built of branches and tarpaulins. Scattered over the ground, or half concealed beneath bushes and scrub-oak trees, appeared petrol tins and oil drums; Japanese cookhouses were indicated by blackened grass and the ashes of a hundred fires, sodden clothing and pots and pans; we stepped among steel helmets, and tiny camouflage nets, sodden boots and damp postcards. Terry's particular quest when he visited the place was tools for our trucks, and every lorry we found was ransacked for these rusty but invaluable additions to our deficient supply. In the back of one such lorry we came across a complete kit which appeared to have belonged to a second-class private in the Emperor's Army; white duck pyjamas, khaki suits, handkerchiefs and underpants, white socks without a shaped heel; all these items we unpacked from his packs and bags. Among a bundle of pamphlets and notebooks I drew out a parcel from Japan, as yet unopened from its brown paper wrapping; inside lay a reddy-brown woollen cardigan which I later wore in the mountains of Kashmir and Sikkim. Nearby was something that none of us had ever seen before, a lucky-charm body-belt of white silk about three feet in length, embroidered in one thousand red stitches with a realistic tiger, while on the front side were sewn Japanese hole-in-the-centre coins and wooden charms inscribed with red characters. We thought this an intriguing find, more original than the many photographs of enemy soldiers in training or in operations, of comely girl friends and numerous families from distant Japan; and preferable in its comparative rarity to the host of coloured postcards which littered every enemy camping-ground with extraordinary profusion. These postcards were to be found wrapped in tissue paper, in series of six, depicting many aspects of the home life of our squat and yellow foes; scenes of Japan, the blue mountains and pink fruit blossom, sheep grazing in green fields, horses and ploughing scenes, and the red-brown soil. Some cards showed two little sisters looking up at a cherry tree in full blossom, and others pictured women milking black and white cows while their children watched from the background. Whereas one favourite card portrayed a family scene, in which father smoked his pipe and read aloud a newspaper to his wife, to the cook and a row of chubby-cheeked, close-cropped boys, one of the most artistic showed two attractive young ladies reading a letter by the light of a paper lantern. In other series we found humorous cartoons or bird paintings and allegorical pictures, and in every case the colouring was pure and true to life, possessing considerable artistry. It seemed so incongruous that these fanatical, boasting and often barbaric enemies should scrawl home to their families on such peaceful and civilised postcards, a contrast of ugliness and beauty, of mass brutality and tender thoughts.

ANTONY BRETT-JAMES

*

During all these months of battle in Italy and the East the planning and preparations in England for the invasion of Europe had been steadily proceeding. Some were optimistic about the possible speed of its success, as is shown by the entries Montgomery recorded in his

BETTING BOOK

Admiral Ramsay, when shown some of the past bets, said he would certainly enter the lists. On the 26th January 1944 he bet me an even £5 that: 'the war with Germany will be over by January 1st, 1945'.

Not to be outdone by his C-in-C, Admiral Creasy bet me in April 1944, two months before D-Day, that: 'organised German resistance will have ceased by 1200 hrs on the 1st December 1944'.

General Crerar, Canadian Army, was the next victim. I was not able to place the First Canadian Army in command of the left flank of the British front in Normandy till the 23rd July, over six weeks after we had landed in Normandy and just before the break-out from the bridgehead began. Crerar was fearful lest the war should end before he could command the Canadian Army in battle, and he used to press me to let him assume command. On the 24th June he laid me a bet that: 'the war with Germany will be over by 1-9-44, ie that Germany will have asked for an armistice by that date'.

I had some interesting bets with General Patton, of the Third American Army. On the 1st June 1944, he laid me two bets which I quote in full:

'General Patton bets General Montgomery a level £100 that the armed forces of Great Britain will be involved in another war in Europe within ten years of the cessation of the present hostilities.

'General Patton bets General Montgomery that the first Grand National run after the present war will be won by an American-owned horse—an even £10.'

Field-Marshal LORD MONTGOMERY

*

The scene when Eisenhower made the decision which he alone could make, to launch the invasion armadas in the hope that the prevailing bad weather would improve, has often been described. One eyewitness was his Chief of Intelligence.

WE WILL GO

Eisenhower said he was quite positive that the order to 'go' must be given but in reply to a request he agreed that it should depend on a later confirmation of the weather position. The problem as he saw it was 'just how long can you keep this operation hanging on the end of a limb'. Arrangements were made for the group to reassemble at 4.15 am on 5 June, and at this meeting I was conscious of witnessing an historic decision, that had to be made by one man alone, who would carry the full responsibility for the result. Having listened to the comments of his commanders, Eisenhower got up from his chair and walked slowly up and down the room. It was an old habit; I had seen him do it many times before. His head was slightly sunk on his chest, his hands clasped behind his back. From time to time he stopped in his stride, turned his head quickly and jerkily in the direction of one of those present, and fired a rapid question at him. When he got the answer he thought for a moment and then resumed his walk. Montgomery showed some signs of impatience, as if to say that had he had to make the decision it would have been made long ago. Leigh-Mallory looked gloomy; we knew that we were watching a brave man called upon to face what he thought was an unnecessary sacrifice of other men's lives.

Suddenly Eisenhower stopped his walking. After a short pause he turned and faced us. 'OK, boys', he said. 'We will go.' With that he left the room. . . .

There are two sequels to this story. Two days later Leigh-Mallory wrote to Eisenhower to say he had been wrong about the airborne operation. He said that it was sometimes difficult in life to admit that one was wrong, but he had never had greater pleasure in doing so than on this occasion. He congratulated Eisenhower on the wisdom of his decision. This was the sort of gesture that gave great pleasure to Eisenhower and tremendously increased his respect and affection for the British. The second sequel came some weeks after, when Eisenhower produced from his wallet a small piece of paper with the following words scribbled on it in his own handwriting: 'Our landings in the Cherbourg-Havre area have failed to gain a satisfactory foothold and I have withdrawn the troops. My decision to attack at this time and place was based upon the best information available. The troops, the air and the navy did all that bravery and devotion to duty could do. If any blame or fault attaches to the attempt it is mine alone. June 5th.'

Major-General SIR KENNETH STRONG

*

Action followed decision. In the evening the spearheads of the invasion, the British and American airborne troops, emplaned for Normandy. The first of the aircraft carrying the pathfinders who were to guide the British 6th Airborne Division to its landing zones on the east of the Allied front contained, Chester Wilmot noted, 'a Berkshire hod-carrier and a toolmaker from Kent, a bricklayer from Edinburgh, a Worcestershire kennelman and a lorry driver from Dumfries, two "regulars", a deserter from the "army" of the Irish Free Staet and a refugee from Austria, led by a young lieutenant who, when war began, had been in the chorus of a West End musical comedy'. The division's commander followed them shortly afterwards.

'During the few days I had been on the station I had got to know the station commander and his staff very well. I remember I had once said that I liked treacle very much indeed. It was a thoughtful, friendly, and very charming gesture, therefore, when Group Captain Surplice handed me a tin of treacle to take to France just as I was emplaning.'

★

Thousands of gliders were leaving their base,
   Bound for a foreign shore,
Heavily laden with my pals and me,
   Going by air 'cause we daren't go by sea.
So we're saying good-bye to them all
   As into our gliders we crawl;
We are lucky fellers, we've got no propellers,
   So cheer up, my lads! Bless 'em all!

★

CAST-OFF

I was woken by a considerable bumping. We had run into a small local storm in the Channel. Griffiths was having a ticklish time and the glider was all over the place.

Between glider and tug there is an intercommunication line, so that the two pilots can talk to one another. In this bumping we received, the intercommunication line broke; the only means of contact for speech from the tug to the glider or vice versa was lost. The problem of cast-off would have to be solved by judgement. Griffiths merely said, 'The intercom has bust'.

It was only a few minutes after that that he said, 'We will be crossing the French coast shortly.' We were flying at about five thousand feet and we soon knew the coast was under us, for we were met by a stream of flak. It was weird to see this roaring up in great golden chains past the windows of the glider, some of it being apparently between us and the tug aircraft. Looking out I could see the canal and the river through the clouds; for the moon was by now fairly well over-cast and the clear crisp moonlight we had hoped for was not there. Nevertheless here we were.

In a few moments Griffiths said, 'We are over the landing zone now and will be cast off at any moment.' Almost as soon as he had said this we were. The whistling sound and the roar of engines suddenly died down: no longer were we bumping about, but gliding along on a gloriously steady course. Away went the tug aircraft with Crawford in it back to England. Round we turned, circling lower and lower; soon the pilot turned round to tell us to link up as we were just about to land. We all linked up by putting our arms round the man next to us. We were also strapped in. In case of a crash this procedure would help us to take the shock.

I shall never forget the sound as we rushed down in our final steep dive, then we suddenly flattened out, and soon with a bump, bump, bump we landed on an extremely rough stubble field. Over the field we sped and then with a bang we hit a low embankment. The forward under-carriage wheel stove up through the floor, the glider spun round on its nose in a small circle and, as one wing hit one of those infernal stakes, we drew up to a standstill.

We opened the door. Outside all was quiet.

General SIR RICHARD GALE, GCB, KBE, DSO, MC
(who commanded 6th Airborne Division)

ASHORE

The sergeant-major had gone below to bring up the rum but many of the men were too sick to draw their ration. I drank mine and the hot liquor shooting out its many tentacles quickly overcame my fear. We were watching all the time we sipped the rum for the first sign of land but the darker line at the foot of the sky seemed to be just cloud, until its consistent irregularity proved that it was solid. The order was given to prepare to land, and when I came up on deck again in my equipment the ridge ahead was sharply defined. I looked fixedly for those landmarks which I remembered so well from the aerial photographs and at last I saw, almost forcing the shore to appear by my effort to distinguish it, the row of houses immediately off the beach. I had no sooner made them out than I noticed a pale strip at their feet and as it quickly widened into a beach I saw that it was planted with black branched explosions. Two destroyed amphibious tanks were abandoned half-way up the sand, two landing-craft, one burning like a tar barrel, were stranded at its edge, and a handful of men appeared to be crawling along the barbed-wire entanglement. The order was given to stand by to land and as the men crouched down on the mess-deck and I stood on the gangway so that I could see the shore, a shell plunged over us and struck the craft on our port bow which heeled over and burst into flame. The branched explosions on the beach were not the engineers destroying the minefield as we had thought but the enemy systematically shelling it. The first troops to disembark scuttled past, their bodies hunched up to take the slight advantage of cover offered by the superstructure, and I followed on the heels of the last man. I observed, as I ran down the gang-plank, that the wire had been blown about three hundred yards to the right and knew that I must make that our goal. At the foot of the plank a man, kept up by the air in his equipment, floated on his back in the water, but though he was dying he did not ask us to stop, unless his moving lips were uttering a prayer which we could not hear through the staccato rattle of small arms and the bullying explosion of shells. I ran straight across the beach to get what cover I could from the sea-wall, and to avoid the destroyed tank whose exploding ammunition was fountaining up like fireworks. I found a disorganised group of engineers crouching in a deserted pill-box and, as I paused to see if I could not break though the wire at that point, an enemy sniper put a bullet clean through the skull of a man lying at length, and, as he imagined, at safety, on the sand. We began to run towards the gap I had seen on the right. The men floundered in the loose sand under their top-heavy loads of ammunition and I ran up and down the line yelling them on with every curse I could remember. My voice came up automatically in a rout of words, but the noise was so great that I could hardly hear what it said. Other troops, with the stupidity of sheep, were digging in along the length of the wire; they had not sense enough to realise that the enemy would blast it as conscientiously as a drill routine. One man, sitting upright as if he was alone on the sands, clutched his knee and wept over the bloody mess. We ran on without a stop, our hearts straining to match our wills, until we reached the gap and, turning through it, crouched down on the other side of a road under a garden wall.

It was like an abrupt change from a hot to a cold bath.

DOUGLAS GRANT

*

The fighting in the beachhead was a true 'soldier's battle', for the Normandy bocage, *the small fields surrounded by high, solid, hedge-topped banks, continually broke larger units into small groups. This passage from the diary of the second-in-command of the 1st Gordons is characteristic of the way it was.*

I found Jim and B Company in a quarry half-way up the hill, with C Company in a row of houses just behind. Jim told me that they had been stopped by very heavy light automatic fire, that a subaltern named Donald had been killed and nearly half the company were casualties. Moreover, most of them were lying out somewhere in front, which meant that there was now no possibility of using artillery. I said I would get the tanks round to the right and on to the ridge, and that with their support C Company would advance. I sent the 10 back to bring up A Company, and my carrier with the wireless sets.

The next hour was spent in futile attempts by the tanks to get on the ridge. I got so angry that I jumped into the co-driver's seat in the tank belonging to the second-in-command, who was in charge in the absence of his squadron-commander, still down at the railway station, and ordered him to proceed. We went about twenty yards and then it broke down. (7th Armoured Division found no difficulty in getting up there when they arrived two hours later.) Soon afterwards Harry ordered us to stay put.

David Martin arrived, driving my carrier himself. He said that they had been shot-up on the way through. Both the driver and little red-haired Chamberlain, my 18-set operator, were hit, and also a DR following behind. (Chamberlain's wound is a graze in the neck, so luckily he is not bad.) Beardwell was bringing his platoon up the street at the same time and was hit in the stomach. Murray Reekie came to report where A Company was. I told him to take care going back; but, when only twenty yards from my HQ, he was hit in the shoulder. CSM Muir was in a bomb crater and shouted, 'Come down here, Sir', but poor Murray, distraught with pain, ran round in a circle instead. A burst of automatic fire caught him in the face and jaw and I fear he is pretty bad. One or two people were both gallant and aggressive in going for these snipers. David got two, and CSM Muir another though not until he had received a nick in the neck, a bullet through his battledress blouse and a third bullet had hit his rifle. Meanwhile the Hun got a light mortar into position and we had yet a few more casualties, bringing them to five officers and forty-six ORS for a most ineffective day's work.

Lieutenant-Colonel MARTIN LINDSAY, DSO

RELUCTANT DRAGON

15 June 1944 'We were told to clear the church steeple, but we couldn't get at it, so I took my piat into the upstairs bedroom of the house opposite, stuck it up on the window-sill, and let fly at the tower. The bursts knocked half the top off. And later we found twelve dead Jerries up there; some had been killed by our stens, and the piat got the rest.'

'Was the church badly damaged?' asked the colonel. 'Not inside it wasn't, sir,' said Galeen. 'We just knocked the top off; we wouldn't have touched it if the snipers hadn't been there. And when I went in, sir, I did take my hat off.'

Corporal TOM GALEEN, reported by CHESTER WILMOT

CAEN, 9th JULY

Those of us who were on the Livisy Ridge, which runs down into the city from the north, came under shellfire from the Germans who were retiring on the opposite bank of the Orne. We bolted for the uncertain cover of the outer suburbs, and came at once upon such a desolation that one could think only of the surface of the moon. Where three- and four-storey houses had been, there were now merely hollows in the ground. Row after row of immense craters. New hills and valleys wherever you looked. The very earth was reduced to its original dust. House after house had been dragged down into the ground and there disintegrated, so that there were no longer streets or footpaths or any decided evidence that human beings had once been here and lived. There was a kind of anarchy in this waste, a thing against which the mind rebelled; an unreasoning and futile violence. We hid in the grey dust and waited for the shelling to stop. There seemed no point in going on. This was the end of the world, the end of the war, the final expression of man's desire to destroy. There was nothing more to see, only more dust. Quite possibly one was in a slightly fevered condition to let these ideas run through the mind. One of my companions said: 'It's four o'clock. We've just got time to catch the last edition'. Catch it with what? With this dust? That was no story.

ALAN MOOREHEAD

★

East of Caen, on 18th July, Montgomery flung in an attack by three armoured divisions, Operation 'Goodwood'. The vanguard consisted of a battalion of tanks and G Company of the 8th Rifle Brigade. The Company Commander describes

A DAY AT 'GOODWOOD'

At first we saw little sign of the enemy, and the few Germans we did see seemed completely dazed as they came in and gave themselves up. A German armoured car appeared from some woods on our right and made a dash for it right through the middle of us, unfortunately getting away with it, as the only tanks which could fire with any degree of safety were those in front and on either flank.

All went very much according to plan for the first five miles till we got to Grentheville. Here a 'Moaning Minnie' opened up just in front of us, but before the last of its six barrels had been emptied the turrets of a dozen Shermans swung round and blew it and the crew to pieces— the best thing we had ever seen happen to this diabolical weapon.

It was at this time that the armoured groups were to emerge from the alley and fan out to their objectives. On we went to the outskirts of Hubert Folie, and found ourselves stuck out in front with no one upon either flank, and we were ordered to wait here until the opposition encountered on our left had been cleared up. Shelling became rather unpleasant owing to our being in full observation of the enemy, and there was very little we could do about it.

In the meantime we were ordered to find out whether Hubert Folie was held. The approaches were all very open, so after a study of the air photographs of the village I decided to work a carrier section as close to the village as possible and then make a dash for it down the main street and out the other end. Diversionary fire was put down by the tanks and the carriers set off. After a few minutes of anxious waiting, they emerged from the village. David Stileman, who commanded the party, reported seeing no enemy, but as it turned out next day, the village was in fact occupied. The enemy were presumably rather shaken by the sight of three carriers with all weapons blazing hurtling towards them at top speed, or else they did not wish to disclose their dispositions.

The Germans had by now obviously collected their wits together after the first colossal onslaught *(by a large bomber force: Ed.)* and things rapidly became very unpleasant for us. Armour-piercing shells began coming in from all directions and we were unable for a time to pinpoint where any of them were coming from and tanks of the 3rd RTR began 'brewing up'. Then, on our left, Panthers appeared and the fun really began. The tanks had pulled back to positions from where they could engage the enemy a little more safely, and I found that my half-track and a section of carriers were stuck out in front of them all. The best we could do was to move back to a hedge behind which we could at least get a little cover from view, although none from fire. Unfortunately, the carrier section suffered heavy casualties, and it was only a very small percentage of their strength which managed to join us at the hedge. Sergt Fruin had done some wonderful work in getting them back, and his cool courage during this very unpleasant time was an example and inspiration to all around him.

We seemed to lie behind that hedge for hours, imagining every moment to be our last. I made a great mistake in passing round a bottle of gin, the effect of which lowered everyone's spirits instead of, as I had hoped, bolstering them up. During this period the Northants Yeomanry, whom we had been awaiting, arrived, but they did not appear to be quite in the picture, and it was not long before they too were suffering disastrous losses.

Eventually we were able to pull back and rejoin the rest of the Company, who by this time were hard at work with their digging materials. Two German observation posts with a wireless set had been discovered lying up just near them, and on their capture the shelling died down considerably. Plans were then made for our night dispositions, and as a result we moved back behind a railway embankment, which must have saved many of our lives, as shortly after we had got into our new positions 88s opened up from the village of Bras and tanks began brewing up one after another. A very persistent 'Moaning Minnie' was also sending over its missiles, which were dropping too close to be pleasant. So after our great start, we had ended up the day a very depleted force, and it was clear that we would not be able to carry out our original intention.

Major NOEL BELL, MC

*

CAMOUFLAGE IN THE *BOCAGE*

We can always tell an allied camp from the air and even decide which nation it belongs to. You see, in a British camp the tracks go round the edges of a field: in an American one they run all over it.

A GERMAN PILOT

Normandy was not all bocage: *there were bare, bleak ridges to be exposed on which might lead to*

A LITTLE LOCAL DISTURBANCE

For ten days we lived in our tanks, cooking, eating, drinking and sleeping. We did almost everything without getting out. And I mean almost everything.

Under the blazing sun the mud quickly turned to dust; and under the impact of this dust we drank a fair amount of liquid. Since our natural functions didn't cease just because we were living inside a round, armour-plated wall with shells bursting around us from time to time, we found an unorthodox use for empty shell cases. They were just the right shape for emptying out of the turret hatch. When more solid relief was necessary there was nothing else for it but to wait for one of the occasional shell-free spells and get out and seek an unoccupied shell hole.

But whenever possible this operation was carried out under cover of darkness. Especially after the case of Jim Steward.

The afternoon was unusually quiet and I was leaning out of the top of the turret getting a much-needed breath of fresh air. Some of the crews had dismounted and were stretching their legs while the slave carrier charged their tank batteries.

I saw Jim climb out of his tank, calmly take a spade from the clips on the engine-hatch, and set off across the hill.

I knew he wasn't going gardening. In those days people sought solitude with a spade for one purpose only.

I breathed a sigh of relief that I wasn't feeling that way myself right then, because the air was deceptively quiet. And since certain functions should be carried out in private I turned my attention to other things.

The wireless crackled and spluttered at my elbow and I wondered if we were flogging our batteries too much. And then I heard Alan's voice on the air and for once he'd lost his air of unhurried calm.

He was sending an urgent and peremptory message for a scout car to take away a casualty, and when I popped my head out of the turret I saw a group of men helping Jim back to the security of his tank.

The short point was that while Jim had been communing with nature he had been shot by a German sniper. He had his back to the enemy lines at that moment and the bullet had penetrated the fleshy part of his buttock, missing all the vital spots and making a not-too-serious wound.

The only lesson to emerge from that incident was that, despite propagandists' edicts to the contrary, the Germans have a sense of humour.

JOHN FOLEY

OFF AND ON THE RECORD

I started recording and looked out across the broad flat stretch of Normandy cornfield between us and the scraggy wood around Maltot. By now that wood was enveloped in smoke—not the black smoke of hostile mortars but white smoke laid by our guns as a screen for our infantry who were now being forced to withdraw.

We could see them moving back through the waist-high corn, and out of the smoke behind them came angry flashes as the German tanks fired from Maltot. But even as the infantry were driven back another battalion was moving forward to relieve them, supported by Churchill tanks firing tracers over the heads of the advancing men. They moved right past our hedge and out across the corn.

The Germans evidently saw them coming, for away off on our right flank machine-guns opened up and then the nebelwerfers— those many-barrelled mortars that put down the rocket-propelled bombs with the high wailing sobbing note. From this they've gained their various nicknames—'The Sobbing Sisters', 'Moaning Minnie', and 'Wailing Winnie'. But at least they do announce their coming unmistakably.

I had just finished my second disk when I heard the wail of a coming salvo. With fingers none too steady I picked up another disk, put it on, and swung the cutting head into operation. But I'd spoken only a few words of commentary when the mortars began thumping down along another hedge about a hundred yards behind us.

There must have been several nebelwerfers firing, for three distinct salvoes came over in quick succession. I talked on through the first, though my voice was completely drowned, but when the second began bursting rather closer I left the midget running, clipped the mike to a branch and dived for the bottom of the ditch, shoving as much of myself as possible into an old German dug-out.

When the last salvo had finished bursting I got up and looked at the midget. The second salvo had blown it 'off the air'. The cutting head had jumped and the sapphire point which actually cuts the groove had gone so deeply into the disk that it had stopped. If the midget had been fully wound at the start of the disk it might have continued cutting, but I realised then—too late—that in my haste I had forgotten to re-wind it fully after the previous disk.

I just had time to wind the midget and fit a new sapphire and another disk before the next warning wail. I set the recorder going and sought early refuge in the bottom of the ditch. The midget recorded perfectly right through the bursting salvo, for the mortars landed a little further away; and so, for the first time, we had a recording of the German weapon which our troops most disliked.

CHESTER WILMOT

*

LIBERATION

Troarn itself was completely smashed. There was not a habitable house in the town. Most of the houses had been reduced to rubble and some of the walls that still stood, precariously lurching out of line, were brought crashing down by the vibration of our transport. The air seemed to be grey and desiccated like the air over the sour hardened effluvia from factories, and the smells were ripe and heady with death. There was pitiable evidence of flight and terror. A child's dress lay crumpled in the gutter, a buckled pram, piled high with bedding, had been abandoned in the middle of a street, and a pair of glasses was crushed on the pavement. The Germans, with their mania for mechanical tricks and murder, had laid booby-traps throughout the wreckage. The most obvious was a mandoline that had been posed in a shattered shop-front where everyone that passed could see the treacherous glitter of its mellow unscratched wood. We touched nothing, but the troops who occupied Troarn a day or two later, while rifling the wreckage for loot, picked up an electric iron and blew themselves to pieces. As we searched the ruins for hidden snipers, we suddenly saw a doll swinging from the iron support that had once held out a shop sign over the pavement. It was made in the form of a young girl. Her neck was in a noose and her head was realistically twisted over her left shoulder. Her draggled black hair trailed across her shut eyes, and the pallor of the waxen skin was made more livid by the dribble of crimson blood that was depicted flowing from the corners of her mouth. The body was dressed in a thin black silk dress, such as a street-walker might have worn, which, hanging in tatters down her bare legs, had been ripped and soiled. It was the image of a murdered girl, and, instinct with some diabolic power, it suggested all the muffled terror of a hunt, a capture, a rape, and a slow murder. It was impossible to imagine the mentality of those who had hung it up for public display. Was it intended as a warning to French girls not to associate with Germans? Or was it a German way of advertising the fate of treachery? The epitome of wickedness, it swung inscrutably to and fro by its neck, as we wondered what obscene and corrupted mind had made it with such care that its malevolence was unmistakable. Its swinging was the only movement in the town and like a curse it seemed to be potent with future evil.

DOUGLAS GRANT

ST AUBIN d'AUBIGNÉ: AUGUST 1944

It was only a small place and they cheered us too much,
A couple of allies, chance symbol of Freedom newfound.
They were eager to beckon, to back-slap, even to touch;
They put flowers in my helmet and corn-coloured wine in my
                                                            hand.
The boy from Dakota and I, we had suffered too little
To deserve all the flowers, the kisses, the wine and the thanks.
We both felt ashamed; till the kettledrum clangour of metal
On cobble and kerbstone proclaimed the arrival of tanks.

Who saw them first, the exiles returning, the fighters,
The Croix de Lorraine and the Tricolor flown from the hull?
Who saw us moving more fitly to join the spectators,
The crazy, the crying, the silent whose hearts were full?

It was only a small place, but a bugle was blowing.
I remember the Mayor performing an intricate dance
And the boy from Dakota most gravely, most quietly throwing
The flowers from his helmet towards the deserving of France.

PAUL DEHN

THE SUMMER WAS DONE

The soul of Normandy hovered in the cloud of flies over the intestines of two German corpses, off the high road near Beny Bocage. They had been shot into human tripe by a tank. It showed in a dirty old peasant in a broken-down cottage on the way to Estry, who bared his chest to me and revealed a Cross of Lorraine on a chain round his neck, and bade me drink to France with him out of a full bottle of Calvados. It was with you when marching out of the Scottish Corridor like a man who had been condemned to the tomb and reprieved. And with the summer goes a last glimpse: that of a particular officer who once belonged to our Mess, dwelling among us like a small gale. For he was cheery and penetrating of voice to an extent that maddened, and people turned up their collars when they saw him approach, and everyone liked him. And coming from the Scottish borderland he requested, when we made wills at Worthing, that if he died a clump of trees should be planted in his memory among his home hills.

When we sailed he went back to First Line Reinforcements, only in due course he was diverted to the 1st Battalion. We later heard that he was found in Caen without a mark on him, quite dead from blast. Aged a rather young twenty-four. . . . The summer was done.

ROBERT WOOLCOMBE

*

During these summer days of liberation in the north, Alexander's armies in Italy, gravely weakened by the removal of experienced divisions for the cross-Channel invasion and the Franco-American landings in southern France, were labouring over rivers and mountains towards the last great German barrier in front of the Po valley and the Alps—the Gothic Line: the Line which was to doom them to another winter's warfare.

But before the rains came and the snows fell many a soldier must, as once did this party, have snatched a few hours

AWAY FROM THE WAR

We had been asked for two o'clock, but time in Italy is elastic, and dinner was far from being ready. The *signora* was busy with pots and pans; Assunta, the eldest daughter, was cutting up the *pasta* into long strips like tapeworms. The other children sat with the *padrone* just inside the door. At the hearth sat an ancient woman whom we had not met before; grey-haired, dressed in drab, ragged clothes, she looked like a benevolent witch. Introduced to us as *la nonna*, she croaked an unintelligible greeting, in dialect, and went on with her task of stoking the fire with olive-wood. Leonardo, who had taken his first communion that morning, was the hero of the occasion; with his face scrubbed, and wearing a little suit of snow-white linen, he looked cherubic and very self-important. With immense pride he showed us his *Ricordo della prima comunione*—a three-colour print showing an epicene Christ surrounded by very bourgeois-looking children, all with blond hair.

With many nods, gestures, and whispered thanks (as though the entire Corps of Military Police lay in ambush round the house) the blanket, the bully and the underclothes were secreted in a back room. A two-litre flask of wine appeared as though by magic: this was not good wine, the *padrone* explained; later we would drink good wine, *del vino tanto buono*.

It was good enough for us. We had had no dinner, and must have drunk nearly a litre apiece on the way. We distributed cigarettes to the *padrone* and Umberto, and chocolate to the children. Leonardo received six bars all to himself, and Giovanni, who resented his brother's hour of glory, burst into tears. He was consoled with half-a-glass of wine.

'Wish I'd been brought up like that,' said Charles.

'It's all for a cock, these bloody Catholic *festas*,' said Kurt, who, being both Jew and Communist, objected to Easter on religious and political grounds.

'Ah, you miserable old bugger,' exclaimed Charles, and, lifting Giovanni on to his knee, consoled him further with an extra piece of chocolate.

Presently the meal began: the steaming, fragrant tomato-juice was poured over the two enormous bowls of *pasta* and we sat down round the table.

'*Ancora, ancora,*' the *padrone* insisted, before we had finished our first platefuls. '*Oggi festa — mangiamo molto per Pasqua.*'

After the *pasta* there was chicken cooked with tomato and *peperoni*. This was followed by *salami* fried with eggs. Then came a dish of pork with young peas. Roast sparrows followed, and afterwards a salad. At about the *salami* stage, after several false alarms, the 'good' wine was produced: two bottles the size of magnums.

It was a Homeric meal. Kurt, who had been a student in Vienna before the war, quoted Homer very appropriately, but in German, which nobody understood. Charlie was trying to sing *Lilli Marlene* in Italian to Graziella, who sat on his knee. Umberto produced an ancient concertina and began to play it. Kurt, forgetting Homer, started to sing a very sad Austrian folksong. The *padrone*, for my benefit, kept up a running commentary on the proceedings, comparing the occasion unfavourably with Easters before the war.

'*Prima della guerra era bella, bellissima,*' he insisted. Today everyone was poor. '*E sempre la miseria.*' The Germans had taken everything. It could hardly be called a *festa* at all. He was ashamed: ashamed to offer such an Easter meal to his guests, and mortified, moreover, that Leonardo's first communion should be celebrated so wretchedly. '*Siamo poveri, poveri — noi contadini. Eh, la guerra — quando finirà?*'

I was not only extremely drunk by this time, but I had never eaten so much in my life. So far as I was concerned, Leonardo's first-communion party had been more than adequate.

Presently Umberto struck up a *tarantella*, and the whole family, as though at a given signal, took the floor. We all paired off, indifferent as to sex, and jigged in time to the music. Charlie insisted on taking *la nonna* for partner; I danced with the *signora*. I found to my surprise that I was perfectly steady on my feet. Moreover, it seemed that I had been dancing the *tarantella* all my life. Gravely, wearing her calm Demeter-like smile, the *signora* advanced and retreated, hands on hips, bobbed and circled and bowed, all with a goddess-like dignity. Her brown face, beneath her coloured kerchief, was as calm as though she were at Mass; only a beatific happiness irradiated it, as though Christ indeed were risen. She seemed immensely aware, too, of her own personal fulfilment: she had given pleasure to her man, borne him healthy children and (more recently) cooked a dinner fit for those Gods whose Olympian peer she seemed.

The music became faster, the dancing less restrained. The *padrone* whirled about like a ballet-dancer; Giovanni, still taking a rather disgruntled view of the occasion, did a little dance by himself in the corner. Leonardo didn't dance at all: he stood in the doorway and watched the proceedings with the distant air of one who has, that very morning, eaten the body of Christ for the first time. The two girls, Assunta and Graziella, danced a little apart: separated, it seemed, from the rest of us by a mysterious barrier, a mutual under-standing; it was as though they were priestesses, gravely celebrating the godhead of their mother. Umberto sat in a corner, with his concertina; an archaic, sculptured faun, younger and older than anyone else in the room.

At last we could bear it no longer, and staggered out into the late afternoon sun, to cool off. Charlie's face was scarlet, his battledress and shirt gaped open, showing a pink, damp expanse of skin. Kurt's hair had fallen over his square, heavy-browed face: he looked like Beethoven would have looked if he had ever got seriously drunk. I told him so.

'Ach, I could write great symphonies in moment,' he declared. 'I am great *Musiker*. Too bloody true I am, you old sod.'

'You're a fat Austrian c——,' Charlie remarked happily.

'It is a pity for you I am not, my friend,' Kurt replied.

Umberto came out, his concertina still slung over his shoulder.

He took my hand.

'*Sei felice?*' he asked, his teeth flashing white in his brown face.

'*Sono felice,*' I said.

Beyond the twin cypresses the country lay flooded in the warm, slanting light. Away on the horizon, hill upon hill lay revealed in the evening radiance, each topped with its fairytale village or castle. In the oak-copse nearby, where the Monkey Orchid grew, a chorus of nightingales shouted. Graziella had run into the field, and was gathering a bunch of white narcissi.

'*Eh, la guerra. Quando finirà?*'

JOCELYN BROOKE

★

*The further north the Allies advanced up Italy, the more possible it
became for escaped prisoners of war, shot-down airmen and other refugees
who had been hiding from the Germans in the hills to get back to their own
people. Stuart Hood had been fighting with the partisans. He was ordered
by them 'to go into Siena and act as liaison officer when the town fell to the
Allies'.*

I wandered on through the city. From a window in the Communist
Party headquarters Feruccio grinned and beckoned me over. I must
stop the disarming of the partisans. I contrived to escape. On the
public buildings they were busy with paint and chisel defacing the
symbols of tyranny. A South African said there was a truck going
back to base, wherever that might be. Half a dozen of us collected,
climbed over the tailboard and drove off. We were out of place in a
world of uniforms. We had stood still in time and did not know it.

The first staging point was a French prisoner-of-war camp. They
put us in beside the Germans. I sat on the grass and was dumb with
fury and reaction. That evening an American truck picked us up.
We drove all night over mountain passes and through ruined towns.
The dust of the bombardments swirled up over the tailboard. It was
bitterly cold. In the morning there was Civitavecchia, crumbling and
destroyed, American rations, ice-cream, white bread, strange, sloppy
troops. Before sunset we boarded a tank-landing craft. I was not to
leave the ship, I was told; must consider myself more or less under
arrest. There were two berths in my cabin. Someone woke up in the
lower one and switched on the light. A priest. I greeted him. He
smiled and did not immediately answer. Haltingly he explained that
he was German. I answered in his own tongue and he relaxed. The
vessel cast off. Soon we could feel the slap of her flat bows on the
waves. He told me his story. Called to attend the execution of a
young deserter he had comforted the boy, saying: *Du stirbst für die
gute Sache.* You are dying in a good cause. Then he had himself
deserted, found shelter in the Vatican, and now was on his way, a
volunteer, to serve in the prison camps of the Middle East.

A sailor looked in and said food was ready. The priest shook his
head and took up his prayer book. I went off after the sailor. In the
little wardroom I found the captain—a small, emphatic, bearded
Greek. He would have no Germans at his table, he said. Had I been

in uniform I would, I suppose, have agreed mutely, drunk my tot of gin and sat down. But I had been too long on my own, forming my own judgements. In that case, I said, I would prefer to wait and eat after the others, along with the priest.

From that moment the two of us were together. In a grey dawn we watched Ischia and Capri go past. There was a smirr of rain over the water. We had talked far into the night, discussing guilt and how one lived with it, debating whether original sin were the same as the dark forces we repress within us, whether punishment was absolute or whether judgement should be conditional on understanding of motive. I remembered the flaccid pietism of my boyhood Sundays and contrasted it with this man's arguments in which Freud and Jung reinforced theology. I told him of the deaths I had on my conscience and the difficulty of decision when all points of reference are gone. I explained the candid naive illusions of my youth, the absolute trust in human decency with which I had gone to war, the difficulty of preserving some balance between cynicism and despair on the one hand, hope on the other. You must not, he said, despair of men— your Italian peasants speak against it—but you must be prepared for disappointment, not expect too much, and accept goodness, when you meet it, as a manifestation of grace. By evening we had skirted along the Costa Amalfitana and were near Salerno. There were trucks waiting on the quay. We shook hands under the eye of the Greek captain and parted. He came from the abbey of Fulda. A man of medium height, round headed, dark haired, a Rhinelander. I owe him a great debt.

STUART HOOD

*

As the 7th Armoured Division made its dramatic dash from the Seine to Brussels, a dash which 'was to carry them past many a roadside signpost bearing names that would have stirred the memories of the earlier generation —Arras, Vimy, Lens, La Bassée, Menin and Ypres', the armoured cars of the 11th Hussars, 'The Cherrypickers', scouted ahead in the van as they had done all the way from Alamein. They experienced some strange incidents.

None, perhaps, was stranger than that of Trooper Bamford, the motor-cyclist despatch rider of 'C' Squadron Headquarters. When on his way to Oudenarde and still about eight miles behind the front, he ran into a German patrol in the small village of Eyne and was taken prisoner. Very soon afterwards, however, some Belgian Resistance men overwhelmed the patrol and captured them in turn. But presently more Germans began pouring into Eyne—at the height of celebrations for the liberation of the village by British troops the day before—and the Resistance men were forced to go underground. They took Bamford along, too, hiding his motor-bicycle and dressing him in civilian clothes, and he lived with them for the next two days.

His first day led him to witness a shocking incident, when a German column with Tiger tanks reoccupied Eyne in the course of a last desperate attempt to hold open the escape route. The villagers were caught while still in the process of their celebrations, whereupon the German tank crews raked the crowd with machine-gun fire, killing or severely wounding more than sixty men, women and children. Twenty-four hours later the operations of the 7th Armoured Division in clearing the area brought the County of London Yeomanry to the village. Their arrival not only liberated Eyne for once and all, but it cornered inside the entire German garrison. The Tiger tanks had gone; but Bamford had the satisfaction of seeing the Yeomanry wipe out some two hundred Germans and every one of the thirty vehicles in which they attempted to escape. He then reported himself to the nearest British officer, retrieved his uniform and motor-bicycle; and returned for duty at 'C' Squadron Headquarters.

Brigadier DUDLEY CLARKE

*

The Canadians also took their revenge. On 1st September they re-entered Dieppe.

I wandered around the place all day like a man in a dream. First, with a French guide, I went down to the harbour. The enemy had carried out some demolition there and sown some sea mines but had not had time to destroy the installations completely. The Army and Navy were able to get Dieppe operating, as a matter of fact, within a few weeks of its capture.

I walked past the ruined tobacco factory on the Esplanade. The factory had been set on fire during the raid and it was only a skeleton. All the buildings along the front were fortified and my guide and I went through a concrete pillbox out on to the Esplanade where the fiercest fire had raged during the Canadian attack. The Esplanade was covered with thick barbed wire and was mined from one end to the other. The pier jutting out on the west side of the harbour was mined and criss-crossed with wire. The main beach was piled with obstacles and wire and every foot of it was mined. The Casino, which the 'Rileys' had fought for and captured at the western end of the Esplanade, had been demolished to give a clear field of fire for the coast guns in the cliff face of the west headland. . . . Major Bult-Francis was down near the Esplanade, too. And it was there that he found the French girl who had bound his wounds in 1942 when he fell near the houses by the beach. She remembered him, and no woman of France was as surprised as she was when he walked up to greet her.

All the civilians in the town seemed to have been there two years before. All they would talk about was the raid. . . . The mayor pointed out a plot of grass near the church where he, then an air-raid warden, had talked with some of the Canadians during the heat of the battle and they had given him cigarettes. 'One of your men was hit right there,' he said. 'He lay on the grass and we could not reach him and he died there. We buried him with the other Canadians up on the hill behind the town.'

The French people of Dieppe had buried the Canadian dead. They took their bodies from the beaches and from the Esplanade and the streets of the town, and made a cemetery for them on the hill behind the town. Over each grave they placed a plain unpainted wooden cross and they gave their record of the names to the Division when it came back.

ROSS MUNRO

*

ARNHEM

The setting for this military failure and triumph of courage is put succinctly by Chester Wilmot. 'Sunday, September 17th, was fine but overcast. There was little wind and the clouds were high, ideal weather for an airborne drop. By noon more than a thousand troop-carriers and nearly five hundred gliders were heading for Holland, for the greatest airborne operation ever undertaken. This aerial armada carried the best part of three divisions which were to be dropped along the line Eindhoven–Nijmegen–Arnhem with the task of capturing the road bridges over the Maas, the Waal and the Neder Rijn and over five other waterways, thus clearing a corridor for the armoured and motorised columns that were to drive north from the Meuse-Escaut Canal to the Zuider Zee. With this one sabre-stroke Montgomery intended to cut Holland in two, outflank the Siegfried Line and establish Second Army beyond the Rhine on the northern threshold of the Ruhr. If all were to go well, the armour would reach the Zuider Zee on the fourth or fifth day, but the hazards were great—especially for the airborne forces.'

All did go well, except for the men at Arnhem, where the British 1st Airborne Division paid the full price for a hazardous enterprise. Dropped the far side of the Rhine to capture the Arnhem road-bridge over the river, they were never reached by the relieving columns, and until daybreak on the 26th, when the last of the survivors got back across the Rhine, they were surrounded by superior German forces, including tanks; their perimeter and their strength shrank daily until the end.

AT THE BRIDGE

Monday

We still had six hours to go till dawn. I made a hurried reconnaissance of the school. It had a basement, two floors and an attic, and I decided to fight the battle from the first-floor, merely holding the basement and ground-floor, and to observe from the attic. I had fifty men (seven wounded), one other lieutenant, six Bren guns, plenty of ammunition and grenades, and a certain amount of explosive; no anti-tank weapons, very little food, and only the water in our water-bottles; no medical supplies except morphia and field dressings.

There was a breathing-space of an hour before the next attacks were made: two were driven off before dawn. During lulls we went out and collected one or two wounded paratroops from the area.

Dawn was heralded by a hail of fire from the house we had been driven out of a few hours previously. As it was only 20 yards away, our positions on the northern face of the school became untenable for anything but observation. As soon as it was fully light, we could see the exact positions held by the enemy next door. They very foolishly remained in them, and it was easy to form a plan to eliminate them. One machine-gun was fired by remote control from one end of our northern face. It drew all the fire, while from the other end we opened up with two Bren guns, and killed all the machine-gun crews. More of the enemy attempted to recover the guns, and were immediately eliminated. The time was now 8 am.

Meanwhile a battle seemed to be developing round our southern face. The Germans were putting in a strong attack on the house 60 yards south of us, and against a small force holding the other corner of the cross-roads on the opposite side of the street. A great deal of firing was going on and tracers were flashing all around. Someone was firing a light ack-ack gun straight down the street. It was all very confusing. No one seemed to know who was who. We joined in with our southern machine-guns as best we could. The battle seemed to be reaching a climax about 9.30 when a cry came from one of the west rooms to say an armoured car had just gone past the window.

I rushed over and was in time to see a second go by. The ramp was on a level with our first-floor, with its edge about 12 yards away. We could do nothing against these armoured cars, having no anti-tank weapons. However, after five had gone by, some armoured half-tracks tried to sneak through. These have no roof on them and so were dead meat. The first went by with a rush, but we managed to land a grenade in it. The second came on with its machine-guns blazing, and a man beside me was killed before we could stop it by killing the driver and co-driver. The crew of six tried to get out and were shot one by one, lying round the half-track as it stood there in the middle of the road.

This caused the remaining half-tracks to stop just out of view, and gave me a breathing-space to organise a system for their elimination. Ten minutes later two came on together, firing everything they had, in an attempt to force the passage. As they passed the one that was already knocked out, we shot the driver and co-driver of the leading half-truck. The driver must have been only wounded, as he promptly put it in reverse, and collided with the one behind. They got inextricably entangled, and we poured a hail of fire into the milling mass, whereupon one went on fire.

As the crew tried to get out of both, they were promptly killed. The score was beginning to mount. Another tried to take advantage of the billowing smoke to get through. It was similarly dealt with and there were no survivors. There appeared to be a lull, when suddenly I heard a clanking just below me. It was about 5 feet away and I looked straight into its commander's face. I don't know who was the more surprised. It must have climbed down the side of the ramp and was moving down a little path, 9 feet wide, between it and the school.

His reaction was quicker than mine; for with a dirty big grin he loosed off three shots with his luger. The only shot that hit me smashed my binoculars, which were hanging round my neck. The boys immediately rallied round, and he and his men were all dead meat in a few seconds. The half-track crashed into the northern wing of the school.

There was a further lull of about half an hour, when another half-track came down the ramp at full speed. The driver was promptly killed. The vehicle swung right, rushed down the side of the ramp, crashed head-on into the southern wing, just below us, where the rest of the crew were dispatched. While this was going on, another nosed out from behind the burning trio on the road. The same system was employed, and another eight Germans joined the growing pile. We were doing well, and our casualties were comparatively light.

It was nearing mid-day, and although there was a certain amount of clanking in the distance, no further attempt was made to force a crossing from the south. In any case the bridge was now blocked by burning vehicles. This lull was too good to last. Ten minutes later, with a sighing sound, fifteen mortar bombs landed on and around us. I could hear fire orders being given in English from the other side of the ramp, and realised we were being mortared by our own side. Leaning out of the nearest window, I gave vent to some fruity language at the top of my voice, the authenticity of which could not be doubted. The mortaring stopped.

To clinch matters, we let loose our old African war-cry of 'Whoa Mahomet.' This had an immediate effect, and was taken up by all the scattered points and houses round the bridge. The firing died down, and soon the air was ringing with the sound. Morale leapt up. Throughout the succeeding days this was the only means of telling which buildings were being held. It was one thing the Germans, with all their cleverness, could not imitate. . . .

Tuesday

. . . Suddenly there was an appalling explosion in the south-west corner room. I rushed over with my batman. It seemed to be full of debris and someone was groaning in a corner. There was a blinding flash, and the next thing I remember was someone shaking me and slapping my face. I had been blown across the room, and was half buried under a pile of fallen brickwork. The whole south-west corner of the school, plus part of the roof, had been blown away. Everyone had become a casualty, and, by the time I was brought round, had been carried below, including my batman, who was blinded.

I found out later that the weapon that wrought this havoc was an anti-tank projector, which threw a twenty-pound bomb. The enemy failed to follow up his advantage, many of the boys being dazed by the explosions. We were given a breathing-space, but not for long.

Twenty minutes later, on looking out of a window, I was amazed to see a dozen Germans below me, calmly setting up a machine-gun and a mortar. They were talking and were evidently under the impression that all resistance in the house had ceased. A hurried reconnaissance revealed that we were entirely surrounded by about sixty Germans, at the range of some 10 feet, who were unaware of our existence.

It seemed too good to be true. All the boys were tee'd up at their windows, grenades ready with the pins out. On a signal, grenades were dropped on the heads below. This was followed up instantly by all our machine-guns and sub-machine-guns (six Brens and fourteen Stens) firing at maximum rate. The boys, disdaining cover, stood up on the windowsills, firing machine-guns from the hip. The night dissolved in sound, the din was hideous, the heavy crash of the Brens mixed with the high-pitched rattle of the Stens, the cries of wounded men, punctuated by the sharp explosions of grenades, and swelling above it all the triumphant war-cry, 'Whoa Mahomet'.

It was all over in a matter of minutes, leaving a carpet of field-grey round the house, together with a few machine-guns and mortars. . . .

Wednesday

By morning I had to issue more Bensedrine to face the dawn attack. No one had now had any sleep for seventy-two hours. The water had given out twelve hours ago and the food twenty-four hours ago. As expected, with dawn the tanks came rolling up from the water-front, with infantry supporting. We were now alone on the east of the bridge. Every house was burnt down, with the exception of the one on the opposite corner of the cross-roads, which was in German hands.

We drove off three attacks in two hours. The school was now like a sieve. Wherever you looked you could see daylight. The walls were no longer bullet-proof, rubble was piled high on the floors, laths hung down from the ceilings, a fine white dust of plaster covered everything. Splattered everywhere was blood: it lay in pools in the rooms, it covered the smocks of the defenders, and ran in small rivulets down the stairs. The men themselves were the grimmest sight of all: eyes red-rimmed for want of sleep, their faces, blackened by fire-fighting, wore three days' growth of beard. Many of them had minor wounds, and their clothes were cut away to expose a roughly fixed, blood-soaked field-dressing. They were huddled in twos and threes, each little group manning positions that required twice their number. The only clean things in the school were the weapons. These shone brightly in the morning sun, with their gleaming clips of ammunition beside them. Looking at these men I realised I should never have to give the order 'These positions will be held to the last round and the last man.' They were conscious of their superiority. Around them lay four times their number of enemy dead.

By ten o'clock the enemy gave up their attempts to take the school by storm. They concentrated on the force now under the arches of the bridge, about eighty men, nearly all that remained of the original four hundred. These were eliminated by about two o'clock, when our last cry of 'Whoa Mahomet' was answered by silence. We were now the last organised position holding out near the bridge. It was a matter of time before we succumbed. . . .

Lieutenant E. M. MACKAY

HQ: THE HARTENSTEIN HOTEL

In the hotel we now moved the operations room into the cellars. It was a tight squeeze. Down the aisle running through the main wine cellar, an arched dungeon from which coal was moved to make room for us, we had the ops table laid out with maps. A duty officer sat close up against it in order to make room for others to move between his chair and a roof support. My place was in the right-hand corner of the cellar between one of the blocked-up ground-level window grilles and a wine rack. Next to me was an officer of the Phantom Reconnaissance Unit, who had a direct wireless link to the War Office; then the chief clerk. On the far side of the cellar in a four-feet-deep recess leading to the other grille, which overlooked the gravel path outside, were several strangers, including two RAF officers who had been shot down during the re-supply operations.

By now, the over-populated hotel and its grounds were taking on the more objectionable aspects of such confined fighting. Everyone had been living and sleeping in the same clothes since we landed, and as the Germans had long since cut off our water supplies, the lack of washing facilities meant a good deal of body odour. There were only two lavatories in the hotel, both of which were blocked. As they could not be flushed either, we were forced to use the grounds where proper latrines were out of the question. It was more than slightly disturbing to be caught in the open on such occasions by the odd shell and mortar bomb.

Major-General R. E. URQUHART, CB, DSO
(who commanded 1st Airborne)

IN THE PARK

We spread out and moved into the wood rapidly but carefully, with weapons cocked. We had not gone more than twenty yards when things happened. Someone fired on us from a few yards' range with a Schmeisser machine carbine, then leapt up and ran. His burst missed all of us, and instinctively I fired a long burst at the green figure in peaked hat before he dived into a large patch of rhododendron. My shot hit him; the man gasped but plunged on, making rasping noises between his teeth. My blood was up, and without further thought I gave chase. I imagined that the German was a lone sniper hiding up in the wood. I knew that I had winged him, but he still had a Schmeisser slung round his neck and we could not go in safety with him at large. Chepstowe and I ran to the right of the rhododendron clump, while I shouted to the others to go round the left.

Of course it happened in a flash. The German and I fired almost simultaneously, and then I was sprinting round the clump to catch him as he reappeared. I ran on for about a hundred yards, across a road and into a clearing, then dropped down on one knee to see where he had gone. I saw him lying behind a tree and two other men bending over him. These two were wearing mottled camouflaged smocks and scrimmed helmets and looked not unlike British paratroopers. I peered for a second undecided, but then one raised his rifle and fired in our direction. He was wearing black leather equipment, and as he turned his head I saw the shape of his helmet. I shouted, '*Hände hoch!*' but when he swung his rifle towards me I gave them a couple of eight-round bursts. They rolled over without making a sound and lay huddled together.

I have only a vague impression of what followed. I saw the whole wood running with figures in green and mottled clothing, men jumping from half-dug trenches and throwing away picks and shovels, men scrambling for rifles propped against trees: the place was alive with Germans dodging and scurrying for the shelter of solid trunks. There was no time nor need to aim: they were in a semi-circle from twenty to thirty yards away. Two men with a machine-gun, a Spandau, tried to swing it round at me but died over their gun before they ever fired a burst. Two others fell as they dived for trees, another looked out from behind his cover and then crumpled up. I saw the dust fly up in the faces of two others peering over a bank twenty yards to my right, and they disappeared backwards: a single boot came up to the top and stayed there.

I kept thinking to myself, 'Why haven't I been killed yet? Another second perhaps . . . why on earth am I still alive?'

PETER STAINFORTH

CASUALTY STATION

During the night our house has taken on a totally different appearance. The long corridor is filled with wounded, they lie side by side on their linen stretchers and there is just room between them to put down one foot. I get through to the kitchen, where I find great activity. On the granite floor there are six or seven wounded men. . . . Trained orderlies give them morphia injections and in copying-pencil write on the patient's forehead the time and dose he has had. . . .

I go through the rooms. . . . Wounded everywhere, in the dining-room, in the study and garden-room, in the side corridor and even under the stairs. And in the lavatory. There is not a single corner free of them.

Of the planes of glass which yesterday were smashed and partly gone, not a trace to be seen, except of course the splinters which lie like sugar over the wounded. Our rooms are unrecognisable, for the furniture has been thrown out of the windows to make room for the wounded. . . . Then I go on to the padre, a captain, a kind little man with curly hair and spectacles; he is on the job the whole day and only yesterday I saw him cleaning out the indescribably dirty lavatory, while the privates stood round him, watching. A captain and even a chaplain doing such work! You should have had five years of German discipline! . . . A hurricane of explosions falls around us, the very walls shake round us. I hear the crackling of fire. The house on the other side of the road is ablaze . . . 'Phosphorus'! The thought flies through my brain. . . .

I read something to the children, some recollections of their infant years, at which they always laugh. . . . 'You are very brave children, it won't last much longer and then we shall be free.' And before the nightlight goes out everybody gets a cherry from the preserve bottle, to keep them from being too thirsty.

MEVROUW TER HORST

TANKS

The tanks and self-propelled guns had then to be stopped by Piats. Major Cain lobbed bombs over the roof of a house behind which a gun lay concealed, while an artillery officer, Ian Meikle, directed his fire from behind a chimney stack.

'I fired about 50 bombs from this weapon, which blew my left ear drum in *(says Major Cain)*. Meikle was shouting at me, giving me instructions, when the chimney pot from his house fell into the trench I was in. Meikle was killed. The other man in my trench got out screaming and scrambling. I told him to come back but he wouldn't and I never saw him again. Just after this a tank came up the road. The chaps told me about it. I crept to the corner and there it was coming up the road. I put the bomb into the Piat and fired at the tank. The range was about 100 yards. I think it must have struck the track. The tank fired immediately in my direction and this raised a huge cloud of dust and smoke. As soon as I could see the outline of the tank again, I let it have another. This also raised a lot of dust again. The tank gun fired back, straight down the road. Then I looked again and watched, and through the dust I saw the crew of the tank baling out. They opened up with Schmeissers, but I got a couple of Brens on to the road and told my men to keep up a continuous fire and the Germans were killed.'

Cain then fired at another tank, but the 'bomb went off in the Piat', he said. 'I got bits of stuff in my face and two black eyes. It blew me over backwards and I was blind. I was shouting like a hooligan. I shouted to someone to get on to the Piat because there was another tank behind. I blubbered and yelled and swore. They dragged me off to the Regimental Aid Post.'

Within half an hour, however, this courageous man had regained control of himself and was back in his trench again.

CHRISTOPHER HIBBERT

THE LAST PIGEON

1. Have to release birds owing to shortage of food and water.
2. About eight tanks lying about in sub-unit areas, very untidy but not otherwise causing us any trouble.
3. Now using as many German weapons as we have British. MGS most effective when aiming towards Germany.
4. Dutch people grand but Dutch tobacco rather stringy.
5. Great beard-growing competition on in our unit, but no time to check up on the winner.

A message sent from Airborne Div HQ in the Hartenstein Hotel
by a signals officer, Lieutenant J. HARDY

*

BATTLE OF THE BULGE

Saturday, 16th December 1944, the day of the German offensive, was bitterly cold in Versailles. It threatened later to become overcast in all areas near Paris; over much of the enemy-held area the ground was covered in snow and ice, and the fog and low cloud of the previous few days still persisted. Because of the continuing bad weather we had been without air reconnaissance of the enemy's front line and rear areas for several days. Just before breakfast I received reports of an enemy attack during the night and early morning in the area of the Ardennes. Several enemy divisions had already been identified in action, perhaps more than one would normally expect on such an occasion.

I had to attend a meeting called by General Eisenhower at 2 pm in his Map Room at Versailles and for the moment dismissed from my mind the Ardennes news, though the latest information was discussed very briefly. The meeting, at which were present Generals Bradley, Bedell Smith and Bull, together with Air Marshal Tedder and General Spaatz, was being held primarily to discuss the shortage of reinforcements, for the Arnhem affair and the broad front strategy had drawn much of the available reserve manpower. As soon as reserves arrived in France they were being absorbed into the battle so that Supreme Headquarters was not only hard put to keep up the strength of the divisions taking part in the offensive operations but was finding it difficult to create further reserves. I also knew that Bedell Smith looked on the occasion as an opportunity for infusing new direction into the Allied effort and it was in connection with this that I had been asked to attend. The six of us took our places informally round a table while Eisenhower explained that he had no intention of remaining inactive while the enemy perfected his defences and trained new divisions, but that he proposed to maintain his offensives to the limit of his ability. Bedell Smith had just started to ask Bradley what chances he thought the northern offensive had of capturing the dams on the Roer river, when I was called urgently away.

My deputy, Brigadier-General Betts, was at the door. Betts was normally a calm, phlegmatic man, but on this occasion he appeared to be rather shaken. His news concerned the Ardennes, where the situation had become serious.

Major-General SIR KENNETH STRONG

STYMIED

On the morning of the 16th December I felt in need of relaxation. So I decided to fly up to Eindhoven in my Miles light aircraft, land on one of the fairways of the golf course, and play a few holes of golf. The HQ of the Air Force Group supporting Second Army was in the Club House, and Dai Rees the well-known golf professional was there as driver of the AOC's car. I knew Rees very well and we were great friends; we had been through the desert together. . . . I asked if Rees could meet me when I landed with a club or two. All was arranged satisfactorily and we began to play. But our game was soon interrupted by a message to say that the Germans had launched a heavy attack that morning on the front of the First American Army, and the situation was obscure. I said good-bye to Rees and flew straight back to my Tac Headquarters at Zonhoven.

Field-Marshal LORD MONTGOMERY

*

Thus the Allied principals heard of the German assault of which Field-Marshal von Rundstedt later said: 'I strongly object to the fact that this stupid operation in the Ardennes is sometimes called the "Rundstedt offensive". That is a complete misnomer. I had nothing to do with it. It came to me as an order complete to the last detail. . . . It was a nonsensical operation, and the most stupid part of it was the setting of Antwerp as the target. If we had reached the Meuse we should have got down on our knees and thanked God—let alone try to reach Antwerp!' Still, though the plan was of Hitler's devising, it looked at first, as Montgomery would have said, as though it had 'knocked the Americans for six', falling as the stroke did on a wide sector of their front which was thinly held. The British contribution to its final repulse was the provision of troops as a close reserve in case the Germans got to or over the Meuse crossings, and of Montgomery to supervise all Allied operations on the northern flank of the German thrust.

DINANT

The Company had by now arrived and the platoons settled down to make strong-points of their positions. Order was beginning to appear out of chaos and I did at least know that, as far as operations were concerned, I was in command of all forces at Dinant.

The bridge over the Meuse had been prepared for demolition and all that was necessary to do was to press a button and up it would go. This was the most appalling responsibility of all. If the bridge went up, all sorts of people would be stranded the other side and I wondered what on earth I should do if the Germans ever broke through and tried to rush the defences.

Evening came and we heard with great relief the distant rumble of tanks, which signalled the approach of the first squadrons of the 3rd Royal Tank Regiment. We now felt we were fairly secure, and although an enormous amount of sorting out remained to be done, the Dinant crossing would now present a very reasonable obstacle to the German advance. . . .

Reports of the enemy came flooding in from all quarters, some of them entirely false and most of them grossly inaccurate. My headquarters was packed all day with people either volunteering or seeking information, and by midday we were almost exhausted and our replies were sometimes curt to say the least of it. We had eventually to put up a notice on the door restricting visits to a maximum duration of five minutes, and even this did not seem to ease our burden. The 'star' caller of the day was an American full Colonel who had been sent from SHAEF, to quote his own words, 'to make absolutely sure that the various commanders in Dinant know who is responsible for the bridge and for the blowing of the bridge'. This he must have repeated to me a dozen times, adding 'I want you to understand that you are Field-Marshal Montgomery's personal representative on the bridge'. He was the most delightful fellow, but got hopelessly tied up as to who was in command of who, writing masses of names down in his notebook, none of which can have conveyed anything to him. Still, he went away delighted with everything, ending up by telling us that he was wearing every stitch of clothing with which he had ever been issued, and I certainly have never seen anyone with so many clothes on.

Major NOEL BELL

COUP DE GRÂCE

Captured German orders for this offensive had stressed the importance of night fighting, so after the first night, when the defence had been concentrated round the bridge, a squadron moved across the river and one tank was put out to cover each approach road. If the Germans attacked in strength, the bridge would be blown and the tanks on the wrong side were to hold the enemy as long as possible and then to place themselves in such a position as to form a road block when they were knocked out. None was to come back.

This was wryly called a 'death or glory' operation but as is so often the case when the worst is expected, nothing happened during the whole of that first night of waiting. Orders were unchanged for the night of December 23/24 but lack of sleep began to tell—so that when the point of the leading German armoured column, probing forward to test resistance, did advance up a road towards a hull-down Sherman, its exhausted crew was fast asleep. They were awakened by the noise of straining engines and clanking tracks, and in the confusion the startled sergeant tank commander shouted the order to fire. The equally confused gunner hastily aimed at the lead vehicle, but neglected to bring down the range of his sight, so his high-

explosive shell hit a truck further down the German column—
which was evidently a truck full of ammunition: the resulting
explosion set fire to another truck full of fuel—and successfully
stopped the advance.

The Sherman's crew, now a little better organised, then methodically worked down the line, destroying a Mark IV, a half-track, and
a scout car before a German self-propelled gun, determinedly
pushing past the blazing wreckage, opened fire and forced the
Sherman back.

Radio crackled busily on both sides. 'Heavy armoured resistance',
the Germans reported; 'We tore him apart!' was the modest British
claim, and it was all a great boost for morale, in addition to putting
the rest of the tank crews on their toes. Quarter of an hour later,
another Mark IV was destroyed on a different approach, followed by
the destruction of two Panthers moving along yet another back
road. The Germans were now fired at whenever they moved, and
British artillery west of the Meuse, firing their mediums at maximum
range, did such great damage that the II Panzer Division stopped
where they were. They had advanced further than anyone else in
Army Group B—some 60 miles in eight days and to within sight of
the Meuse (just as they had got within sight of Dunkirk in 1940 *and*
of the towers of the Kremlin in 1914)—but once again they were to
be disappointed.

Had II Panzer not been held for two critical days at the very outset
of the offensive by the US 28th Infantry Division, and then further
delayed by the illogical refusal of the defenders of Bastogne to
surrender, they would have reached Dinant earlier and would most
certainly have formed a bridgehead through which the rest of
XLVII Panzer Corps would have poured. . . . As it was, the delays
used up their ration of fuel and they found none to capture; the
steam thus went out of their advance, and when they were met by
the fire of a few British tanks and guns they most uncharacteristically
hesitated for a fatal day: fatal because during that day there moved
swiftly down from the north the US 2nd Armoured Division of
14,000 men, 3,000 vehicles, and 390 tanks—about a third as many
tanks as the Germans were able to commit in all three armies that
launched their offensive.

This mighty force swept from north to south between the thin line of British and the weary Germans, and very soon afterwards cab ranks of Lightnings came over and strafed everything that moved— including C Squadron, Third Royal Tank Regiment, who luckily only incurred one casualty.

The British from the Rifle Brigade and the Tanks had a grand-stand view of this attack. After the aircraft had reduced almost everything to rubble at least 50 American tanks moved slowly forward as though on parade, their machine guns blazing contin-uously against absolutely no opposition. 'There's no doubt', said one of the British tank commanders wistfully, 'that if you've got the ammunition, that's the way to use it.'

The battered II Panzer Division was ordered to escape and, abandoning its vehicles—many were found undamaged but without a drop of petrol in their tanks—made its way back on foot. But not all, for in the area where the point of the German advance was broken it lost 1,1000 prisoners and left behind 900 dead. After the battle was over and the fighting had moved on, the indefatigable Captain de Villefagne 'went carefully over the battlefield. It was a great cemetery of destroyed vehicles and abandoned equipment half-buried in the snow. I counted 840 vehicles including 40 tanks.' It was a humiliating end to an advance that was to change the whole war on the Western Front.

                                              PETER ELSTOB

1945

Year of Victory

'I tink it must be Kingdom Coming
And de year ob Jubilo!'
                    Negro song during
                 the American Civil War

*After the Germans had turned and shown their teeth in the Ardennes in
December the front solidified again. The enemy was defending his own soil,
from the fortifications of the Siegfried Line.*

FLAMING

On the way back, Barber told Wilson about the operation they
were going to do. The enemy was holding a big cutting in the
ground, marked on the map as 'unfinished autobahn'. The infantry
battalion and a squadron of Shermans were going to assault it. When
it was taken, some AVRES[1] would lay fascines, and the Crocodiles[2]
would go across and flame the next enemy position in a village about
half a mile beyond.

Wilson briefed the crews, and in the afternoon they drove out to
the place where they were to wait with the AVRES while the infantry
and Shermans carried out Phase One. The AVRES were already there.
It was a vast meadow, and the enemy was mortaring it methodically,
yard by yard.

The attack began at sixteen hundred; but it was soon clear from
the calls which flew across the wireless that it was going badly. The
enemy had expected it. The Shermans had run into eighty-eights,
and the infantry were pinned down by Spandaus. Back in the
Crocodiles' waiting area, the mortaring never ceased. A bomb had
hit one of the AVRE's fascines. It started to burn like a giant bonfire,
angry and red against the cloud-darkened sky.

Just before nightfall the Crocodiles were ordered to pressure up
and come forward to help. Then, just as they were running on to the
battlefield, the action was suddenly stopped. They were ordered into
a little copse, covering the infantry's flank, while Brigade made a
new plan of attack.

In the darkness, Barber brought the new plan from brigade headquarters. There was going to be a night attack with Kangaroos.

Kangaroos were old tanks with their turrets removed to make
space for carrying infantry. They advanced under fire with the
infantry crouched inside; then, when they neared the objective, the
infantry jumped out and attacked on foot.

[1] AVRE—tank chassis fitted with engineer equipment for ditching, bull-dozing, etc.
[2] Crocodile—tank equipped with flame-thrower.

Zero was at twenty-one hundred. At half-past eight he heard the Kangaroos down the road behind him, where they were taking a couple of companies aboard. He lit a cigarette and waited. The artillery opened up, the hand of his watch reached zero. Behind the barrage the Kangaroos must be jerking forward into no-man's-land with their big noisy engines. Lifting one of the headphones from his ear he tried to catch the sounds outside. A minute or two passed, and machine-guns started up.

A Sherman troop came on the air and said the Kangaroos were almost at the autobahn.

The operator leaned over from his hatch. 'It looks as if they'll make it,' he said.

Next moment there was an outburst of noise and a sudden confusion of messages. Every station was shouting 'Bazookas'. Kangaroos were being hit one after another. A Sherman was alight. From out in the darkness came a clash of Brens and Brownings and Spandaus. When the noise at last died down, and situation reports came through, it appeared that the infantry had got one side of the autobahn with the Germans still clinging to the other. Phase Two was to wait until morning.

All through the night the Crocodiles stayed on guard because of the danger of a counter-attack. Inside the turret, with the hum of the wireless and the lamps gleaming dully on the steel of the breech-block, Wilson tried hard to keep awake. Outside there was utter silence and darkness. Shadows, which might have been trees or men, seemed sometimes to be advancing, sometimes retreating. From time to time he got out and walked round the tanks.

Then at first light Barber came on the air, telling them to come back for more bottles.

The air blew cold and damp as they rolled down the road to the rendezvous. Gun crews stood in their pits drinking tea. The cold air, the effect of all the delays, the weariness from lost sleep, made everything seem unreal.

At the rendezvous the other troops were drawn up; they'd come over the river during the night.

'What's going on?' said Sherrif. 'Have you flamed yet?'

Wilson shook his head.

Dunkley came over.

'Hear that, Peter?' said Sherrif. 'They haven't flamed.'

Jest then Barber drove up in his scout car. 'Hurry up,' he shouted. 'The infantry are attacking the village.'

While the crews were putting in the bottles, the water-truck driver thrust mail into their hands. Wilson had two letters which he pushed unread into the pocket of his map-case.

The way back to the battle seemed very short. They followed the path which the Kangaroos had taken. Then they climbed a bank of excavated earth from the autobahn, and all at once the landscape was littered with dead and burnt-out vehicles. A few feet in front of a knocked-out Kangaroo lay a dead German, still gripping the discharger rod of a Panzerfaust.

They rolled down a slope towards a ruined farmhouse, where a company was already moving off to the attack with trailed rifles. He ran his troop between some outbuildings and jumped down. German dead lay everywhere, some of them crushed by his own tank tracks.

There was a moment's vision of the CO—a tall rosy-cheeked man who might have been a farmer.

'Crocodiles, sir!'

He looked round. 'Where have you been?'

'Getting new bottles.'

The CO gave his orders. There was some open ground, a thousand yards long by about three hundred across. On the left was a long wood; on the right a kind of smallholding ending in an orchard. The village lay at the far end. The infantry were going up on the flanks, using the cover of the trees. The Crocodiles were to keep level with them. Then a hundred yards from the village they were to go in and flame. There was a troop of Shermans in the orchard to shoot them in.

Wilson ran back to the troop, and told the sergeant and corporal what was happening.

The tanks were already pressured up.

In the turrets the gunners and operators were in their places. The shells in the racks had their clips off. The red light glowed on the seventy-five firing circuit. The driver let out the clutch and 'Supreme' surged forward into the open.

As the troop broke cover Wilson had a clear view of the village.

It seemed far away. The run was going to take four or five minutes.

'Item Four Able, Item Four Baker. . . . Line abreast.'

The sergeant and corporal swung out from behind and took up their stations on either side of him. They still had their hatches open and he could see their heads bent over the microphones.

They crossed a ditch and the mortaring started. Out on the left, Wilson watched the infantry advancing, dodging the bursting shells. A little ahead in the orchard he could see the olive-khaki Shermans, the tracer of their guns leaping towards the village like red darts. Time to get his own guns going.

'Co-ax seven hundred. . . .' The Besa roared into life. Through the smoke and noise of the gun Wilson watched the village come towards him, gaining depth and detail.

The ground rolled out before him, green and flat and clear. Then, without warning, the ridiculous happened. Suddenly the soil wasn't firm any longer. The driver slammed down into first gear. But it was no good. The tank began sinking, clawing at the bog. It tilted a little, sucked and surged, and stopped.

The sergeant's tank bogged as well. Only Corporal Milner escaped. They were six hundred yards from the objective. He called Milner on the wireless and told him to exchange tanks.

As Wilson ran across to 'Superb', the ground squelched under his feet. The air was full of explosions. Milner, passing him, grinned and gave a thumbs-up sign.

Putting on Milner's still warm headset, Wilson thought: 'There's only one way now.' He pulled down the turret flaps and ordered: 'Advance Full Speed.'

Beyond the orchard the ground spread wide and flat. He had a sense of nakedness. Suddenly the front of the village crackled with fire. Something slammed into the ground beside the Crocodile. He felt a curious sense of detachment.

A seventy-five fired from behind; the rushing shell skimmed his turret and exploded with a flash on a small red building on the left. He remembered that it was Milner's brother driving this tank, and he thought: Milner's going to devastate this village.

Other shots slammed past. The Crocodile was moving fast—twelve or thirteen miles per hour. All the time he kept searching the ground in front for the watery greenness of bog or the tell-tale circles of yellowing grass, which meant mines.

They crossed a road—a gravel track which went from the orchard to the left edge of the village. He'd been sure there'd be mines there, but there weren't. The ground beyond was firmer. Three hundred yards to go. He picked up the microphone. 'Prepare to flame.' He hadn't done this since 'sHertogenbosch.

He came in on the left. Suddenly the enemy had stopped firing. There was nothing to show where he was any longer. He set the Crocodile at a building like a barn. The distance closed, and he waited for the *panzerfausts*.

Something exploded immediately in front of him.

'Flame gun, fire!'

The yellow rod, the slapping fuel. The flame leapt out, roaring and rolling towards the barn. Were there enemy behind it? He didn't know. But the enemy was somewhere. The Crocodile closed in. 'Up!' he shouted. The flame lifted for a moment, cascading on the roof.

Another explosion. Fifteen yards from the barn the Crocodile swung round, flinging great clods of earth from its tracks. Walls, gardens, fences rolled past the periscope. The tank straightened up. A cottage stood ahead with shuttered windows.

'Flame!'

Again the slapping of the gun, the roar and spread of burning fuel.

One after another, buildings swept into the path of the flame as the Crocodile ran down the face of the village. There was no time to stop and no time to choose targets.

Down in the driving compartment, Milner kept wrenching his steering-bar, trying to throw the *panzerfausts* off aim. At the end of the village they had to turn. Suddenly there was a clatter from the bogies. Wilson felt a sudden helplessness. 'Not now,' he prayed: 'not a track off now!'—as if God, in his impartial love of armies, could care also for flame-throwers. A few seconds later the track slipped into place again.

They started on a second run. Some buildings were not on fire yet and he looked for places where the enemy might still be hiding. There was a wooden shed. As the flame hit it, the wood blew away in a burning mass, and there in the wreckage was the body of a Spandau.

He looked for more. Suddenly he was seized by the same unfeeling madness which he had experienced long ago at Rosmalen.

As the tank turned for the third run, the Besa jammed. The gunner reached for the cocking-handle, trying vainly to clear it. He stood there steadying himself against the lurching of the tank, sweating over the opened mechanism.

'Leave it,' shouted Wilson. 'Go on seventy-five HE.'

The gunner gripped his trigger. Swinging the turret down the front of the burning village, he began firing off the seventy-five at point-blank range.

He came up for the fourth run. Where, oh where, were the infantry? As always in action, he had lost all count of time. Wherever he swung the cupola, he saw fire and smoke and the track of destruction. But the flame was beginning to fall short and the rack of seventy-five rounds was almost empty.

Then all at once it was over. By the barn a little group of grey-clad Germans appeared, without helmets or weapons, waving a sheet on a pole.

He gave the order to stop firing and opened the hatches. The air was full of smuts and the sickly sweet smell of fuel. He made a sign for the Germans to come out into the open. They moved slowly. At first there were ten; then there were thirty or forty. Wilson circled round them, making a sign towards the rear.

In the hush of the moment he felt a great elation: if ordered, he could have driven through the smoking village and right on to the enemy's divisional headquarters. Nothing could have stopped him; he couldn't be harmed.

Then the infantry came swarming into the village, dodging the mortar shells which the enemy had started dropping now. In the confusion, the Germans began to bring out their wounded, blinded and burned, roughly bandaged beneath their charred uniforms. Some of them looked at the Crocodile. What were they thinking?

ANDREW WILSON (who was a captain in the 141st Regiment,
Royal Armoured Corps)

*

To consummate Germany's defeat the Rhine must be crossed and the Ruhr subjugated. Before this could be done all German forces between the Meuse

and the Rhine's west bank must be eliminated. Horrocks, on 8th February,
drove southwards in great strength to meet in due course the northward
advance of Simpson's 9th American Army and catch the Germans between
the jaws of a powerful vice. This was the battle of

THE REICHSWALD

The front line was held by two Canadian divisions and as I studied
the country from one of their observation posts I saw in front a
gentle valley with small farms rising up on the other side and
merging into the sinister blackness of the Reichswald (German
forest), intersected by rides but with only one metalled road running
through it. North of the forest ran the main road from Nijmegen to
Cleve—that is from Holland into Germany. North of this again was
the low-lying polder land which had been flooded by the Germans
and looked like a large lake with the villages—built on slightly
higher ground—standing out above the water. To the north flowed
the broad expanse of the Rhine. The Germans were holding the far
bank. South of the Reichswald was more low-lying ground which
ran down to the River Meuse. This was completely dominated by
the southern edge of the forest. The British 2nd Army held the other
side of the river. We were therefore faced with a bottle-neck
between the forest and the polder land and this had been heavily
fortified in depth by the Germans. Moreover the whole area was
lousy with mines.

We had to get through this bottle-neck before we could break out
into the German plain beyond and the key to the bottle-neck was
the high ground at Nutterden. This was the hinge of the door which
led to the open country. The front was held by one German division,
the 84th, supported by about 100 guns, but we estimated that there
were approximately three infantry and two panzer divisions in
reserve which could be brought into the battle pretty quickly.

The first essential was to smash through the 84th as quickly as
possible and get the high ground, the hinge, before the Germans
could bring up their reserves. It was a race for Nutterden, but at the
same time I had to clear the Reichswald itself, otherwise the Germans
could have concentrated troops there and struck at my communications. Moreover, I wanted the road running through it because I

knew how difficult it would be to supply a large modern army with
all its complicated needs along one road. To smash through quickly
I determined to use the maximum force possible from the outset and
support it with a large amount of artillery.

The success of this plan depended on two things. First, obtaining
complete surprise, and secondly on the weather. . . .

This was the biggest operation I had ever handled in war. Thirty
Corps was 200,000 strong that day, and we were attacking with five
divisions in line supported by 1,400 guns. It soon became clear that
the enemy was completely bemused as a result of our colossal bombardment; their resistance was slight. The main trouble was mines—
and mud, particularly mud. I am certain that this must be the chief
memory of everyone who fought in the Reichswald battle. Mud and
still more mud. It was so bad that after the first hour every tank
going across country was bogged down, and the infantry had to
struggle forward on their own. The chief enemy resistance came
from the cellars in the villages.

It has been said that no two attacks are ever alike, and that was
exemplified in this battle.

Lieutenant-General SIR BRIAN HORROCKS

*As mud delayed men and vehicles, the 'slight' resistance of the Germans
inevitably stiffened. Horrocks continues:*

From now on the battle developed into a slogging match as we
inched our way forward through the mud and rain. It became a
soldier's battle fought by the regimental officers and men under the
most ghastly conditions imaginable. It was a slog in which only two
things mattered, training and guts, with the key men as always the
battalion commanders. The Germans rushed up more and more
divisions. Eventually we were opposed by more than 1,000 guns,
700 mortars and some ten divisions; they were certainly fighting
desperately to prevent our getting to their famous Rhine.

*One of the divisions inching through the Reichswald was 51st Highland.
The way that a battalion commander could be a key man is shown in this
account by the second-in-command of the 1st Gordons, then acting Battalion
Commander:*

CLEARING THE ROAD

I didn't like it at all. But the position simply had to be taken. I remembered the message I had received an hour before. I knew that both the Divisional and Corps Commanders were waiting for the news that the 1st Gordons had opened up the road. Failure was unthinkable. Although D Company had already made three attacks that day, I decided to use them, with the dismounted carrier platoon in reserve. It seemed to me that the responsibility for this attack was altogether too great for a company commander—even Danny—so I decided to take personal command of it. . . .

Danny Reid and I talked it over and decided to take a start-line running northwards from a German command post which had already been cleared. So we marched round towards it in single file, along a narrow path at the foot of the very steep ridge, with trees on either side of us: Macpherson's platoon in the lead, then Danny and I, then the remainder of the company, followed by Moir and his carrier platoon. Just as we got there we were ambushed. There was a burst of schmeisser in front, and the sharp explosions of one or two German grenades. Immediately five or six Germans came to life in trenches on either side of the path. They must have been asleep, for one-third of us had already passed them. There was an instantaneous crash of automatic fire from the column and every one of them fell, riddled with bullets. It was all over in about two seconds, and our only casualty was Macpherson, slightly wounded in the leg. Actually it was a most efficient performance on our part, but all I thought at the time was: 'God, how bloody! Ambushed before we've even started, this is going to be the bloodiest show that's ever been.'

We climbed up the face of this steep ridge and the four platoons deployed, two in front with two behind them, facing west and behind the imaginary start-line. But the wood was jungle, so many branches and trees having been felled by our shelling. We might as well have been in darkest Africa. Every hundred yards took us about fifteen minutes, and the confusion was indescribable. I found myself scrambling along with Porter, at the head of his platoon, he in front with an automatic very much at the ready, and me close up, keeping direction with a compass. I knew that Sergeant Matthew's platoon was just behind us; but as to where Danny and Macpherson and the rest of the company was, I hadn't a clue. All we could do was to push on slowly, climbing over tree trunks and branches or crawling under them. 'What an awful balls-up of this I've made,' I thought to myself, having lost all control. 'It's all going to be a ghastly failure.'

Then we heard some shooting in front, and soon came upon Danny and Macpherson in a clearing. They had taken the first position and had some prisoners. Danny said that the enemy were dug-in round the houses a hundred yards ahead of us. We went forward a little to see the form. Several spandaus were firing vaguely in our direction and a light mortar was crashing its stuff down on the main road fifty yards to our left. It was fearfully dark among the trees in spite of many flares behind the Canadian lines. Much red tracer was also going up beyond and a fine display of fireworks and distant explosions told me that an air-raid on Mook was taking place. It was a lovely sight, a real Brock's benefit, and for an instant I thought of the Fourth of June and the Eton Boating Song and wished I could forget all about the job in hand.

They pressed on right through the German position, taking many prisoners.

It was obvious that there were no more enemy, and soon there was no attempt at military formations or precautions: just a score of men scrambling over the obstacles, in high spirits that the job had been done and a little elated, as everybody always is, by bright moonlight on a perfect night. Danny and Porter were in the lead, walking side by side, and I was perhaps ten yards behind them. We heard the pipers of the Camerons of Canada and knew that we had not far to go. Then there was a loud bang and Danny fell down with a groan.

'Everybody stand still exactly where you are,' I shouted, for it was obviously a schu-mine. 'Danny, how bad is it?'

I knew it was either a broken ankle or the whole foot blown off— what the doctors call traumatic amputation. Danny's language and Porter, who at great personal risk stepped two or three paces over to him and applied a field-dressing, told me that it was not too bad.

We shouted at the tops of our voices to the Canadians for pioneers with mine-prodders and stretcher-bearers. I looked around and realised now that we were in a narrow no-man's-land, only fifty yards wide, between the German and Canadian positions. Danny, Porter and I were in the middle of a minefield, but fortunately those behind us were still in the old German diggings so I told them to go back.

A Canadian company commander came forward to a wire fence in front and said that the stretcher-bearers would not be long. He told us how pleased he was to see us as they had had seven men killed by snipers during the last week, from the position which we had just cleaned up. Danny was getting restive lying there on the ground, and his language progressively worse.

'Never mind, Danny,' I shouted. 'The moonlight's lovely and I'll get you a bar to your MC for this day's work, you mark my words.'

But I, too, was becoming impatient for all this time I was standing on one leg—literally, and for about three-quarters of an hour—not daring to put the other to the ground. I don't think I've ever felt quite so foolish in my life. Then the Canadians came bustling up with two or three officers and four or five stretcher-bearers. I thought there was altogether too much bustle. 'For God's sake . . .' I shouted, and there was another loud bang and one of them fell down, badly injured. It now took a long time to get out the two wounded men, with every footstep being prodded first. Danny had ceased to be talkative, and I learned that he had received a lot of wood splinters in the back of the head, as Porter had in the face. When the stretcher party had left, the Canadian pioneer sergeant prodded his way up to me and led me safely out of the minefield by my planting my feet precisely in his footsteps.

By this time Macpherson, who had carried on in spite of his leg wound, had been evacuated, so D had lost all its four officers in the course of the day. I formed up the company and marched them back. I was dead-tired, and felt none of the elation to which I was entitled when I reported to Brigade that the road was now clear.

Lieutenant-Colonel MARTIN LINDSAY

*

The Burma front was now also well ablaze, for Slim's Fourteenth Army had started out on that great drive which was to carry it irresistibly southwards from the Indian frontier right through the heart of Burma. Operations in the East were, however, not all large scale. Along the sea coast, on the great rivers and among the multitudinous waterways, a number of specialised units were at work. There was the Combined Operations Pilotage Patrol; the Swimming Reconnaissance Unit who probed where even canoes could not reach; No. 2 Commando Special Boat Section; D-Force, whose job was with a few men to pretend to be a large force making an attack while the real attack went in elsewhere. The following are excerpts from the diary of one Special Boat Section reconnaissance.

Teknaf. 14.1.45

The boats were all loaded last night, and we sailed from Teknaf at 0800, with nine teams in two MLs (one team being two men in a folboat). Passing the black and white lighthouse on Oyster reef, we were well out in Combermere Bay by dusk, the land only a pale mountainous outline in the fading light. A chain of pale blue blobs on the horizon ahead marked the line of islands which shelter Kyaukpyu on the north. This time, we had chosen the cove under Catherine Bluff as our slipping point, and the MLs lay rocking on the smooth swell with their engines humming as the boats were slung over the side, meeting the water in a surge of phosphorescence, and we climbed down into them as they bobbed alongside. Torch, binoculars, R/T set, weapons, rations, water-bottles were passed down and stowed away, and last of all the long paddles. One by one the boats pushed off and took up their stations, the crews raising their paddles as soon as they were ready to go.

We got away at midnight, following the narrow channel between Tankharo Island and Sinbaikchaing, slipping along between the steep, wooded heights with a strong tide under us. After a couple of miles we saw a fire blazing among the trees on the Tankharo side, casting a red glare across the channel. Remembering Harry's report about Jap watchfires and Burmese lookouts, we stopped paddling and let ourselves drift slowly past on the tide. There were several men—Burmese—round the fire, but they did not see us.

At last we emerged into the open water of the harbour, and saw the shadowy hill of Laws Island 4 miles away in front. A tedious

spell of paddling brought us to it, and we felt our way in under the
black shadow of the land to a sandy cove fringed with bushes.
Having made sure that no one was about and posted sentries on the
approaches, we got the boats into cover and settled down to doze
for an hour before dawn.

Laws Island, Kyaukpyu. 15.1.45
As soon as it was light, we reconnoitred the whole area and arranged
a defence plan, though the country people say the Japs seldom visit
the islands. Corporals did sentry, while officers and sergeants maintained a watch on Kyaukpyu with binoculars. Though we had
found the town itself ruined and overgrown when we visited it last
week, from this distance it seemed intact, with the red-roofed
houses rising out of the trees, the monastery on a hillock in the
middle, and the low wooded hills behind. There seemed to be some
wire on the beach, and what looked like bunkers here and there.
Canoes were drawn up in front of Pyinpyumaw, where we bumped
into a Japanese post on our last visit, and Burmese in brightly
coloured clothes were walking about. The most significant thing
was that from dawn to 0800, a constant stream of people could be
seen crossing Ngalapwe creek by the ferry from Zaingehaung, all
going into Kyaukpyu. This suggested market day—if any—or, more
likely, forced labour. In either case, there must be people in Zaingehaung who knew what was going on in Kyaukpyu. I sat down with
maps and tables to plan a visit there during the night.

In the afternoon, a sentry reported a local approaching: he was
gathering shell-fish, it being low tide. When he got near enough, we
gathered him in, pale and shivering with funk, and Sergeant Bra-
ganze (Burma Intelligence Corps, interpreter) set to work to calm
him down. We gave him biscuits and cigarettes, but it took over an
hour to get him coherent. He confirmed that the Japs seldom come
to the islands, that there were none in Kyaukpyu itself (which we
knew) and none in Zaingehaung, which was good news, if true.
There were about 200 in Gonschwein, on the sea-side of Kyaukpyu,
where they were digging defences (probably a company: say 150, as
we know Jap units are under strength). . . .

And so the patrol continued its researches successfully until

Akyab. 18.1.45

The tide would not serve before midnight, so we sat smoking and drinking tea. The stars sparkled among the wind-tossed tree-tops, and the lamplight flickered on faces brown and pale. At last, it was time to go. In single file, we picked our way along the narrow path, and climbed down among the rocks to the little cove where Stan had the boats already ranged along the water's edge. San Hla Baw was tucked into Sergeant Smith's boat, and we started on the four hours' paddle to the rendezvous. The wide spaces of the harbour, the low land of Kyaukpyu in the distance, and the high wooded hills all lay dark and silent as we passed through Tankharo Channel on the ebb tide, and emerged near Catherine Bluff. The ML was hard to see in the shadow of that high crag, but we steered inshore and soon picked her up against the clear horizon. She called up her partner from the alternative rendezvous at Pagoda Rocks, and soon we had got the boats on board, and were heading out past Satellite Island as dawn came up over the mountains.

In the event, the information provided by this reconnaissance enabled 15th Corps to recast its plans for the attack, and when 26th Indian Division landed at Kyaukpyu on January 21, the Japanese defences were smothered by an accurate bombardment from sea and air. The place was occupied at a cost of only 14 casualties.

Captain RICHARD LIVINGSTONE

*

To readers of the recollections quoted in this volume it may well come as a sobering thought to be reminded that the troops who fought in South East Asia so hard, so long, and in the end so victoriously took as their title, with some bitterness and much justification, that of the

FORGOTTEN ARMY

After the heavy heat, the wind came
Fast and hard out of the South,
Destroying sun-drugged moods like flame
Scalding a lotus-oozing mouth.

Wind's lust is strong and male, not hooded
Like the evil of the calm—
A satyr leaping down the wooded slopes,
Raping the naked palm.

Tired bodies stirred then, sensing life,
And raised up languid heads to hear
The long whine like a flying knife
That hits with power, that calls for fear.

Raw violence swept, a cosmic purge
Scouring through decay and rust,
Made blood-mad by deadly surging,
Followed by its jackal—dust.

Hot in the valley curled red smoke,
Choking, blinding, toothed with grit,
While shapeless, mindless sand awoke
And, rabid, tore and clawed and bit.
After the brassy heat, the wind came,
But in the wind the unclean dust,
Until the dust was beaten tame
By rain that swamped the months-old crust.

Beyond the rain, the mud, a vile
Slow worm that fouled the earth
And crushed with hungry, sightless guile
The life that wind had ripped to birth.

The heat—the wind—the dust—the mud
Each grasps its hour, is cut away,
Savaged and slashed within its bud.
But we—we still await our day.

                              JAMES K. CASSELS

(James Cassels served in South East Asia in the West African Signals. His poem, incidentally, is taken from an anthology of British poetry of the Second World War, The Terrible Rain. Of the 119 poets included, about one-sixth died between 1939 and 1945.)

★

The day of Fourteenth Army had now arrived. It advanced remorselessly through heat, wind, dust and mud. Mud, for example, on

THE CHOCOLATE STAIRCASE

The name given to the Tiddim road where in seven miles it climbed three thousand feet with thirty-eight hairpin bends and an average gradient of one in twelve. The road surface was earth, and marching men, animals, and vehicles soon churned it into ankle-deep mud. The hill-side, and with it the road itself, often disappeared in thunderous landslides; then every available man had to turn to with pick and shovel to shape the track again. No soldier who marched up the Chocolate Staircase is ever likely to forget the name or the place.

Field-Marshal LORD SLIM

In re-conquering Burma, Slim's problem was analogous to that of Mont-gomery's as he invaded Germany. It was a matter of securing crossings over the great waterways which faced them. By the end of 1944 Slim's army had secured bridgeheads to the east of the Chindwin, the first major obstacle, and built over it what was then the longest Bailey bridge in the world, 1,154 feet in length, pre-fabricated and assembled in twenty-eight hours. Now there remained the broad Irrawaddy—the Rhine, one might say, of Burma. By February, Slim's divisions were breasting up to its banks. The plan was to pretend that Mandalay was their objective, but to make the real thrust further south, crossing the river at Pakokku and striking for the enormous Japanese base and airfields around Meiktila. It was essential that the real thrust via Pakokku should remain secret.

CLANGER, FIRST CLASS

One morning, when these plans were boiling up, I had to go into Calcutta on some piece of business directly after breakfast. I had arranged that someone else should draft the communiqué. I did not get back to Barrackpore until dinner-time, when I asked if everything had gone all right. It had. The communiqué had been written and had been passed by all concerned and sent off. Next morning I was rather late going to breakfast and I came into the mess in the middle of the All India Radio news broadcast. As I was sitting down

I heard these words: 'Troops of the 14th Army are pressing forward in the direction of Pakokku.'

In moments of frightful stress one's heart is supposed to miss a beat and one's blood is supposed to run cold. One can also be rooted to the ground. I suspect that all these things happened to me simultaneously. After a few stunned seconds I uprooted myself, dashed out of the mess, and began running in the direction of my office. I found the previous day's communiqué on the file. As sure as fate it contained the frightful sentence. . . .

I hoped that the Commander and his Chief of Staff, to say nothing of the Commander, 14th Army, would take this gaffe as calmly. *(As Arnold's subordinate did: Ed.)* The telephone rang. Would I go at once to the Chief of Staff? He was not taking it calmly at all; and the Army Commander had already been through to him on the telephone. I spent a nightmare morning, in the course of which I visited Lady Canning's tomb. In moments of stress at Barrackpore I always went there. Lady Canning was the wife of India's first Viceroy.

RALPH ARNOLD

But all was well, and by 3rd March, after a desperate battle, Meiktila had fallen. Slim watched one attack.

The southern shore of the lake, for nearly a mile, ran roughly parallel to the northern edge of the town. Between them was a strip about half a mile wide, of rough, undulating country, cut up by ditches and banks, with here and there clumps of trees and bushes. Three hundred yards from us, scattered along water cuts, peering round mounds, and lying behind bushes, were twenty or thirty Gurkhas, all very close to the ground and evidently, from the spurts around them, under fairly heavy fire. Well to the left of these Gurkhas and a little farther forward, there was a small spinney. From its edge more Gurkhas were firing Bren-gun bursts. A single Sherman tank, in a scrub-topped hollow, lay between us and the spinney, concealed from the enemy but visible to us. In the intervals of firing, we could hear its engine muttering and grumbling. The dispositions of our forces, two platoons and one tank, were plain enough to us, but I could see no enemy.

Then the tank revved up its engine to a stuttering roar, edged forward a few yards, fired a couple of shots in quick succession, and discreetly withdrew into cover again. I watched the strike of shot. Through my glasses I could see, about five hundred yards away, three low grassy hummocks. Innocent enough they looked, and little different from half a dozen others. Yet straining my eyes I spotted a dark loophole in one, around which hung the misty smoke of a hot machine-gun; I could hear the *knock-knock-knock*, slower than our own, of its firing. Searching carefully, I picked up loopholes in the other mounds. Here were three typically Japanese bunkers, impervious to any but the heaviest shells, sited for all-round defence, and bristling with automatics—tough nuts indeed. The tank intervened again. Without shifting position it lobbed two or three grenades and a white screen of smoke drifted across the front of the bunkers. One of the Gurkhas below us sprang to his feet, waved an arm, and the whole party, crouching as they went, ran forward. When the smoke blew clear a moment or two later, they were all down under cover again, but a hundred yards nearer those bunkers. A few small shells burst in the water at the lake's edge. Whether they were meant for the tank or the Gurkhas, they got neither, and the enemy gunners made no further contribution.

When I looked for it again, the tank had disappeared, but a smoke-screen, this time, I think, from infantry mortars, blinded the bunkers again. The Gurkhas scrambled forward, dodging and twisting over the rough ground, until some of them must have been hardly thirty yards from the enemy. Somewhere behind the spinney, the tank was slowly and methodically firing solid shot at the loopholes. Spurts of dust and debris leapt up at every impact.

As the fight drew to its climax, we moved out of the pagoda enclosure to a spot a little forward and to the right where, from behind a thick cactus hedge, we had a clearer view. The tank reappeared round the spinney's flank and advanced still shooting. Gradually it worked its way round to the rear of the bunkers, and suddenly we were in its line of fire with overs ricochetting and plunging straight at us.

One army commander, one corps commander, an American general, and several less distinguished individuals adopted the prone position with remarkable unanimity. The only casualty was an unfortunate American airman of our crew, who had hitch-hiked with us to see the fun. As the metal whistled over his head he flung himself for cover into the cactus hedge. He was already stripped to the waist and he emerged a blood-stained pin-cushion. However, he took his misfortune very well and submitted to what must have been a painful plucking with fortitude.

After this little excitement, the tank having, to our relief, moved again to a flank, we watched the final stages of the action. The fire of the Brens and rifles swelled in volume; the tank's gun thudded away. Suddenly three Gurkhas sprang up simultaneously and dashed forward. One fell, but the other two covered the few yards to the bunkers and thrust Tommy guns through loopholes. Behind them surged an uneven line of their comrades; another broke from the spinney, bayonets glinting. They swarmed around the bunkers and for a moment all firing ceased. Then from behind one of the hummocks appeared a ragged group of half a dozen khaki-clad figures, running for safety. They were led, I noticed, by a man exceptionally tall for a Japanese. Twenty Gurkha rifles came up and crashed a volley. Alas for Gurkha marksmanship! Not a Japanese fell; zigzagging, they ran on. But in a few seconds, as the Gurkhas fired again, they were all down, the last to fall being the tall man. The tank lumbered up, dipped its gun and, with perhaps unnecessary emphasis, finished him off. Within ten minutes, having made sure no Japanese remained alive in the bunkers, the two platoons of Gurkhas and their Indian-manned tank moved on to their next assignment which would not be far away. A rear party appeared, attended to their own casualties, and dragged out the enemy bodies to search them for papers and identifications. It was all very businesslike.

If I have given more space to this one incident, that was being repeated in twenty places in the battle, than I have to much more important actions, I plead some indulgence. It was the closest I had been to real fighting since I had been an army commander, and it was one of the neatest, most workmanlike bits of infantry and armoured minor tactics I had ever seen. There is a third reason. The men who carried it out were from a Gurkha regiment of which I have the honour to be Colonel.

Field-Marshal LORD SLIM

*

*Next to fall, in mid-March, to the 19th Indian, the 'Dagger', Division,
under its remarkable General, 'Pete' Rees, was*

MANDALAY

We stood, so to speak, on top of Mandalay. We also stood, at much
closer range, on top of a good many Japanese. The temples, cellars
and mysterious chambers covering Mandalay Hill were made of
reinforced concrete. The 4th Gurkhas had taken the summit, and no
Japanese was alive and visible; but scores of them were alive,
invisible, in the subterranean chambers.

A gruesome campaign of extermination began, among the temples
of one of the most sacred places of the Buddhist faith. Sikh machine-
gunners sat all day on the flat roofs, their guns aimed down the hill
on either side of the covered stairway. Every now and then a Japanese put out his head and fired a quick upward shot. A Sikh got a
bullet through his brain five yards from me. Our engineers brought
up beehive charges, blew holes through the concrete, poured in
petrol, and fired a Very light down the holes. Sullen explosions
rocked the buildings and the Japanese rolled out into the open, but
firing. Our machine-gunners pressed their thumb-pieces. The
Japanese fell, burning. We blew in huge steel doors with Piats,
rolled in kegs of petrol or oil, and set them on fire with tracer
bullets. Our infantry fought into the tunnels behind a hail of
grenades, and licking sheets of fire from flame-throwers. Grimly,
under the stench of burning bodies and the growing pall of decay,
past the equally repellent Buddhist statuary (showing famine,
pestilence, men eaten by vultures) the battalions fought their way
down the ridge to the southern foot—to face the moat and the
thirty-foot-thick walls of Fort Dufferin.

Pete brought up the medium artillery, and the 5·5s hurled their
60-pound shells at the wall, over open sights, from four hundred
yards. The shells made no impression. He called in the air force.
P-47s tried skip bombing, B-24s dropped some 1,000-pound bombs,
some inside the fort and some outside—among our troops.

We found a municipal employee who knew where the sewers led
out of the fort, and prepared an assault party. All the while the
infantry fought in the brick and stone rubble of the burning city,

among corpses of children and dead dogs and the universal sheets of
corrugated-iron. The night the sewer assault was to go in the
Japanese withdrew from Mandalay. Next morning coal-black
Madrassi sappers blew in the main gate, and Pete walked in,
surrounded by a cheering, yelling mob of a dozen races. Just as Pete
—but not his superiors—had planned, the Dagger Division had
taken Mandalay.

JOHN MASTERS

Through all this noise and the clatter of men clearing a battlefield,
came a strange sound—singing. I followed it. There was General
Rees, his uniform sweat-soaked and dirty, his distinguishing red
scarf rumpled round his neck, his bush hat at a jaunty angle, his arm
beating time, surrounded by a group of Assamese soldiers whom he
was vigorously leading in the singing of Welsh missionary hymns.
The fact that he sang in Welsh and they in Khasi only added to the
harmony. I looked on admiringly. My generals had character.

Field-Marshal LORD SLIM

*

Prime Minister to Marshal Stalin   23 Mar 45
I am with Field-Marshal Montgomery at his HQ. He has just
ordered the launching of the main battle to force the Rhine on a
broad front with Wesel at the centre. The operation will be supported
by about two thousand guns and by the landing of an airborne
corps. . . .

In his 'Memoirs' Churchill continues:

In the morning Montgomery had arranged for me to witness from
a hill-top amid rolling downland the great fly-in. It was full daylight
before the subdued but intense roar and rumbling of swarms of
aircraft stole upon us. After that in the course of half an hour over
2,000 aircraft streamed overhead in their formations. My view-point
had been well chosen. The light was clear enough to enable one to
see where the descent on the enemy took place. The aircraft faded
from sight, and then almost immediately afterwards returned to us

at a different level. The parachutists were invisible even to the best field-glasses. But now there was a double murmur and roar of reinforcements arriving and of those who had delivered their attacks returning. Soon one saw with a sense of tragedy aircraft in twos and threes coming back askew, asmoke, or even in flames. Also at this time tiny specks came floating to earth. Imagination built on a good deal of experience told a hard and painful tale. It seemed however that nineteen out of every twenty of the aircraft that had started came back in good order, having discharged their mission. This was confirmed by what we heard an hour later when we got back to headquarters.

The assault was now in progress along the whole front, and I was conducted by motor on a long tour from one point to another, and to the various corps headquarters. It was late in the evening when I returned. My private secretary, Jock Colville, had work to do for me, and could not come with me in the car. He had however made a plan of his own, and actually crossed the Rhine in one of the boats during the morning. There was no opposition to the passage, but the lodgments on the other side were under artillery fire. A shell burst near him and an officer with whom he was talking. A soldier of our airborne division standing beside them was severely wounded, and Jock was drenched in his blood. He naturally would have said nothing about this incident but for the fact that he arrived back at headquarters at precisely the same time as Montgomery and I. His blood-stained tunic caught the Field-Marshal's eye, and he asked what had happened. He then complained that a civil servant should have crossed the river without his personal permission having been obtained. I protected Jock from his wrath, and promised to rebuke him myself, which I did in suitable terms after learning what had passed, and pointing out how much inconvenience he would have caused to the work of my Private Office if he had been killed. Who would have decoded and presented to me the secret telegrams that came in every few hours? He expressed his contrition, and I advised him to keep as far away from the Field-Marshal as possible during mess. This he did by dining elsewhere, and all passed off quietly. He is now forgiven. . . .

At 8 pm we repaired to the map wagon, and I now had an excellent opportunity of seeing Montgomery's methods of conducting a battle on this gigantic scale. For nearly two hours a succession of young officers, of about the rank of major, presented themselves. Each had come back from a different sector of the front. They were the direct personal representatives of the Commander-in-Chief, and could go anywhere and see anything and ask any questions they liked of any commander, whether at the divisional headquarters or with the forward troops. As in turn they made their reports and were searchingly questioned by their chief the whole story of the day's battle was unfolded.

WINSTON CHURCHILL

*

It was a success story. British and American armies were starting to move eastwards from the Rhine along a great stretch of its course: the Ruhr, the Elbe, the Baltic and Berlin were beckoning, and the Allies galloped. As the Germans retreated to their last ditches, they dragged their human booty back with them.

IT ALL DEPENDS ON THE SPEED
OF YOUR TANKS

Early in March '45 about a hundred of us were herded to one side after roll call and marched down to Fallingbostel Station and loaded into cattle trucks. We had no idea why this was done and where we were going, and this terrible uncertainty every day of a prisoner's life is something he has to adapt himself to or go mad. As it happened we were being taken just a few miles down the line to a small wayside station. British rocket-firing Typhoons had caught a train there which was a mixture of civilian wagons and petrol tankers. The train had been completely destroyed and the Germans were using a Tiger tank to pull the engine off the line. On a nearby ditch lay the charred remains of about 100 people piled on top of one another. We were forced to clear the bent and twisted track in order that German railwaymen could lay some new. It was raw, cold, wet weather and our only meal was half a pint of swede soup daily at noon. We had to walk down the line to get it and eat it walking back in order that we didn't waste any time getting the line cleared.

The guards for this job, which lasted about a week, gave us a hard time. They were old, sick and fed up both with the war and us. Some of them had lost sons on the Russian front and whole families in air raids and one day a chance remark by a Belgian prisoner sent one old guard berserk. He beat the Belgian unmercifully until restrained by one of the German NCOs. I was beaten up myself on this job by a Pole, one of the many who joined the German Army. I had tried to shelter for a minute or two from the rain and cold to eat my 'skilly'.

No sooner was this job completed than the Germans formed a larger working party of 300 men, they called these slave labour details *Kommandos*. Despite still open wounds and being by now down to 7 stone through a bad attack of dysentery, I was picked as one of the 'fit' ones to go. Many of us were not sorry to see the back of Stalag XIb for it was a truly terrible place. A former concentration camp with, so rumour had it, 30,000 dead buried in mass graves.

The *Kommando* offered fresh sights and sounds and perhaps the chance of escape. We were searched by ss men in the camp theatre before leaving and then marched out to Fallingbostel Station.

On the way we passed a party of British prisoners just captured and they gave us the heartening news that the Allies were across the Rhine.

This was about the first definite news we had received since capture and we cheered and even sang. Once again we climbed into cattle trucks and after an uneventful journey arrived at a fairly large station at dead of night. It was interesting to see the almost familiar activity but we were soon marched out of the goods yard and through the town. We shouted 'Wakey-Wakey' at intervals to annoy the townsfolk. We were billeted in a very large building which was a sort of barn. We slept on straw on either side of a cobbled road which led through the middle of it, and it wasn't long before we discovered that the straw was lousy. There was one cold-water tap for washing between 300 men and one latrine which was a large wooden box with carrying handles. This was situated in a small windowless room at the end of a passage and it was lit by one faint bulb. I never dream of Arnhem but I sometimes dream of that terrible toilet and the smell and general weird atmosphere, it was a real nightmare.

We discovered the town was Uelzen, a large market town and

also an important rail junction. From 7 am to 7 pm we slogged to work in all weathers, shifting wreckage on a cup of acorn coffee for breakfast, half a pint of swede soup for lunch and one slice of black bread and a cup of rose-leaf tea every evening. Despite the work, the brutality and lack of food, it was better than the Stalag because there was so much to see. The activity of a large German town during wartime, the constant arrivals and departures of trains, the many strange uniforms, the German civilians, some friendly, some fearful and some who showed their hate by throwing stones at us.

One or two attempts to escape were made but these were very dicey affairs and the chances of success were practically nil. All the men who made such attempts were recaptured and rigorously dealt with and lucky not to be shot. There was no chance to hoard even a small food supply necessary for an attempt and most of us were so emaciated we found it all we could do to get through the day.

Every day the USAAF droned over in blocks of thirty or more Fortresses. Never was the complete supremacy of the Allies in the air so apparent.

There was ample evidence that Uelzen had already been bombed quite heavily especially near the station area and there was the fuselage of a B-17 lying on one of the goods platforms. Whilst actually at work, although constantly under German Army guards, we were directed by civilian foremen and we found them quite decent, also the engine-drivers who would give us hot water if we wanted it.

The civilian in charge was only interested in keeping his beloved railway running and his son was glad to be back helping him, having been invalided out of the Luftwaffe. He had been shot down near Leningrad and his empty sleeve was a mute testament to the accuracy of Russian AA fire.

Within two weeks all the main lines through Uelzen were clear and one particular day there were no less than four military trains in all at the same time. Two were bound for the Eastern front, one carrying tanks and the other Dutch and Belgian ss volunteers. The ss jeered us and as the train moved off we pelted them with bricks.

Going west were two other trains, one composed of youths being hurried from the training camps to the front line. The other train was full of wounded from the Russian front. From my observations it would appear that Uelzen was some sort of clearing area for badly wounded, as one saw many soldiers and sailors who had amputations. What a target and not a bomber in sight, only late in the day a lone Mosquito circling three times before making off home.

Another dreary day started and we had a quick sluice, gulped down our acorn coffee and marched to the station where we drew our picks or shovels and were spread out along various sections of the track to work. At 9 am a lone Fortress appeared from the west which was very unusual and we dived for cover as it suddenly dropped a bomb. At least we thought it was a bomb because of the familiar whistle but when it hit the ground there was only a muffled report.

Its path was a trail of white smoke which hung like a beckoning finger over Uelzen Station. From the west came a dull drone of many aircraft engines and when we looked our hearts stood still, for the sun glinted on block upon block of Flying Fortresses. As if a signal had been given we all started to put as much distance between us and the station as we could. ss, German Army guards, old people, prisoners, women and children, all heading for the open country as fast as possible. Some of us, because of old wounds and general poor health, found it difficult to maintain the pace and the guards were nearly frantic. We finally reached the shelter of some woods as the first bombs came down. Beside me an ss officer cringed in fear as a stick of bombs fell near and a German mother tried to soothe a frightened child. The ground shook as explosion after explosion rocked the whole junction and a huge pall of yellow dust arose and blotted out the sun. One B-17 was hit by AA fire and the pilot put it on automatic control so that it circled lower and lower. At each revolution a crew member 'hit the silk' and all the crew escaped, before it finally plunged to earth and exploded.

The raid continued all morning and we got no 'skilly' that day at all and over 100 prisoners were killed in the bombing, for at 15,000 feet one cannot distinguish friend from foe. We had to pick our way through a lunar landscape when the raid was over. . . .

After the devastation of the town the Germans moved a Flak-train in and it was commanded by a stocky, good-natured German warrant officer. Red-faced, with a chest full of decorations and a cigar always in his mouth, he was a complete realist.

When we asked him how long the war would last he replied, 'It all depends on the speed of your tanks.' He was not upset about the idea of losing in 1945 and said something I, for one, have never forgotten. 'Ten years from now you'll be paying me to help you keep out the Russians'—prophetic words.

JAMES SIMS

*

THE ARMOUR ARRIVES

The whole of Hamburg is deserted except for this square, where a number of pompous German officers dressed in their finest boots, spurs and breeches, are drawn up under their Commanding General, all ready to make a melodramatic handover to the British.

A water-bug belonging to the 7th Queen's flashes through the square, obviously miles off its route. The group of German officers stiffly ignore it.

Several minutes later the silence is broken by the familiar note of a Daimler Dingo approaching the scene. Obviously the General Officer Commanding the 7th Armoured Division is arriving to receive the official surrender of Hamburg. The group of officers spring to attention and one of them, armed with quite a nice camera, rushes forward to photograph the vehicle. The Dingo comes to a halt, and out steps a figure dressed in an American combat jacket, a pair of corduroy trousers and an 11th Hussars cap. This figure then walks round to the ration box of his Dingo, pausing only to remove the camera from the German officer, and produces a packet of Army biscuits, with which he starts to feed a number of pigeons which are walking sedately around the centre of the square.

Brigadier DUDLEY CLARKE

*

GERMAN FINALE

It was now nearly 6 pm. I gave orders for the ceremony to take place at once in a tent pitched for the purpose, which had been wired for the recording instruments. The German delegation went across to the tent, watched by groups of soldiers, war correspondents, photographers, and others—all very excited. They knew it was the end of the war.

I had the surrender document all ready. The arrangements in the tent were very simple—a trestle table covered with an army blanket, an inkpot, an ordinary army pen that you could buy in a shop for twopence. There were two BBC microphones on the table. The Germans stood up as I entered; then we all sat down round the table. The Germans were clearly nervous and one of them took out a cigarette; he wanted to smoke to calm his nerves. I looked at him, and he put the cigarette away.

In that tent on Luneberg Heath, publicly in the presence of the Press and other spectators, I read out in English the Instrument of Surrender. I said that unless the German delegation signed this document immediately, and without argument on what would follow their capitulation, I would order the fighting to continue. I then called on each member of the German delegation by name to sign the document, which they did without any discussion. I then signed, on behalf of General Eisenhower.

Field-Marshal LORD MONTGOMERY

The instrument of total, unconditional surrender was signed by Lieut.-General Bedell Smith and General Jodl, with French and Russian officers as witnesses, at 2.41 am on May 7. Thereby all hostilities ceased at midnight on May 8.

WINSTON CHURCHILL

MIDNIGHT: 7th MAY 1945

Thunder gathers all the sky,
Tomorrow night a war will end,
Men their natural deaths may die
And Cain shall be his brother's friend.

From the lethal clouds of lead
Thickening hatred shall descend
In fruitful rain upon the head:
Tomorrow night a war will end.

Thunder, mock not Abel's cry:
Let this symbolic storm expend
The sum of man's malignity!
—And Cain shall be his brother's friend.

There are no words to be said:
Let the future recommend
The living to the luckless dead.
Tomorrow night a war will end.
                                              PATRIC DICKINSON

*

Popski, who had led his Private Army through to the end, found even there
a suitable method of celebration.

PRIVATE TRIUMPH

I felt that the war in Italy would end in a few days and that the time
had now come to carry out the plan I had told Cameron about when
we were on our way from Taranto to Bari a year and a half earlier—
a purposeless piece of swagger, indeed, but a flourish can be an end in
itself. We loaded five jeeps in three RCLs and, young Thomas leading
recklessly among the German mines, we sailed from Chioggia to
Venice up the lagoon, entered the Canal San Marco and moored our
craft on the quay. I started my jeep and, trembling with excitement
for the one and only time during the war, drove into the Piazzetta,
passed between the columns, turned left into Piazza San Marco, and,
followed by the others, drove seven times round the square. This
was my hour of triumph.
                          Lieutenant-Colonel VLADIMIR PENIAKOFF

*

In his Victory Broadcast Churchill reminded the nation that 'We must
never forget that beyond all lurks Japan, harassed and failing, but still a
people of a hundred millions, for whose warriors death has few terrors. I
cannot tell you tonight how much time or what exertions will be required to
compel the Japanese to make amends for their odious treachery and cruelty.'

*The time was not long. The first atomic bomb blasted Hiroshima on 6th
August and the second Nagasaki on 9th August. Attlee, now Prime
Minister, announced the Japanese capitulation in a broadcast at midnight
on 14th August. Slim had the place he had earned at the formal ceremony
of surrender.*

THE WAR WAS OVER

In Singapore on the 12th September 1945 I sat on the left of the
Supreme Commander, Admiral Mountbatten, in the line of his
Commanders-in-Chief and principal staff officers, while the formal
unconditional surrender of all Japanese forces, land, sea and air, in
South-East Asia was made to him. I looked at the dull impassive
masks that were the faces of the Japanese generals and admirals seated
opposite. Their plight moved me not at all. For them, I had none of
the sympathy of soldier for soldier, that I had felt for the Germans,
Turks, Italians, or Frenchmen that by the fortune of war I had seen
surrender. I knew too well what these men and those under their
orders had done to *their* prisoners. They sat there apart from the rest
of humanity. If I had no feeling for them, they, it seemed, had no
feeling of any sort, until Itagaki, who had replaced Field-Marshal
Tarauchi, laid low by a stroke, leant forward to affix his seal to the
surrender document. As he pressed heavily on the paper, a spasm of
rage and despair twisted his face. Then it was gone and his mask was
as expressionless as the rest. Outside, the same Union Jack that had
been hauled down in surrender in 1942 flew again at the masthead.

The war was over.

Field-Marshal LORD SLIM

★

*Something was certainly over. But one of the prisoners to whom Slim
refers had other thoughts.*

NO ONE AT HOME WOULD BELIEVE IT

Three days later even the Japanese themselves admitted that we need
no longer work. But the war had not been won: nor lost. It had

simply, for the moment, stopped. They ceased to bellow *'Currah'* and instead bowed politely when we passed. The food which they had recently declared to be non-existent, they now produced in vast quantities so that we might eat our fill. Likewise drugs appeared from everywhere and in profusion.

Then we all assembled, thousands upon thousands of men, until there were 17,000 there, in Changi gaol. British paratroopers arrived and were greeted politely by the Japanese. Then Mountbatten arrived and (though we were ordered not to by our Administration) a few of us walked the seventeen miles into Singapore to see him accept Itagaki's surrender. At that brief ceremony, when Mountbatten drove fearlessly down through hundreds of thousands of hysterical Malays and Chinese, standing upright in an open car: when Itagaki met him on the steps of the civic hall and handed over his sword—for that brief moment I felt that the war really was over. But it didn't last.

I walked down to the harbour and on board the *Sussex*—where I was fed and washed and given clean clothes by the ever-hospitable matelots of the Royal Navy. I stayed there, smuggled away, for two days: then returned to the gaol in a jeep with eighteen other 'sight-seeing' POWS. . . .

We said all our good-byes.

Mario left, waving an excited Latin farewell, for Italy. Ron Searle and Chris departed for Britain—the one for fame, the other for medicine. Hap Kelly flew ostentatiously and swiftly back to Texas in a Skymaster, sent promptly by an ever-attentive government. David Griffin flew to Sydney and the Bar: Downer to Adelaide and the Federal Australian Parliament. Hugh went home on one ship, Piddington on another, I on a third.

The careful fabric of one's personal life, built up over four years, disintegrated at a single blow. One felt curiously alone as the ship sailed out of Singapore Harbour—except for the moment when old Harry Smith was spotted leaning, as melancholy as ever, against the rail of a ship we passed. As one man, our vessel roared: 'You'll never get off the Island', at which Harry waved miserably and we laughed.

Then the sense of loneliness returned. All those blokes, Pommies and Australian: all those ties—gone. And then I realised, as I looked back and in the distance saw Changi's tower with its radar screen

that didn't work, and above it the flagmast from which the poached
egg had now vanished and the Union Jack flew, what was the
trouble. This disintegration wouldn't matter if it had been caused by
the *end* of the war. *That* was the trouble. For us, and for the un-
defeated Japanese soldiers all over South-East Asia, the war hadn't
ended. It had just, momentarily, stopped. The tower slid out of view;
the symbol of our captivity was gone—but now I could think only
of the words of a thousand guards, of Saito himself, of Terai the
intellectual who spoke English and wrote plays: 'War finish one
hundred years.'

So, for those of us who had suffered under them, and for the
Nipponese themselves, this was just an interlude—the Hiroshima
Incident, probably, they would call it. But the war itself, that of Asia
against the white man, that—under one guise or another: in one
place or another—still had ninety-five years to go. The trouble was,
of course, that no one at home would believe it.

RUSSELL BRADDON

*

ONE WAY OUT . . .

In the early summer of 1945 I climbed into a Dakota on an airfield
in East Germany with all my worldly possessions—a pistol and ten
rounds, and a few cigarettes. There were a dozen other men on the
plane, all very dirty and most of them asleep. Nobody talked much,
and at three in the afternoon we came down on a runway in a field
full of buttercups in Oxfordshire. I had been away four years. It was
England all right: there was that special kind of early summer light
calming down the romantic distances and making the hedgerows
into dark blue mists. Sweet reason was the prevailing atmosphere on
the air-strip. Soothing girls gave us tea, rock cakes and cigarettes and
asked soothing, ridiculous questions. They took down our names
and units and addresses, doctors plied their stethoscopes, beat on our
knees with little rubber hammers, and took blood samples. Quarter-
masters of a new kind to me, young and deploying a winsome charm,
issued new underclothes and shoes. Orderlies showed us into bed-
rooms with beautiful white sheets and bathrooms attached. The first

bath for three years was such a revelation for me that I made it last nearly two hours. Then I hacked off my beard and shaved.

They're softening you up, I said to myself from time to time. It's a trap. My neighbour in the next room, a bald major, put his head round the door with another version of events. 'I can only suppose,' he said, 'that the man who runs this place wants to get into Parliament.'

'I'm not stopping here,' I told him, 'no matter what they say or do. If I have to bust out I'm taking off tonight.'

'Oh, I don't know,' the major murmured, 'might give the bed a trial.' At this innocent speech such a fury rose in me that I had to move away at a run in case I fell upon him tooth and claw. So I went into the assembly hall where there was to be an announcement.

'Won't waste your time with speeches,' the commandant was saying, 'The sergeants sitting at tables down both sides of this room are experts in cutting red tape. They're here to see you get your advances on pay, temporary identity card, ration books, coupons, and all the bumf you need nowadays in the quickest possible time. Only one snag. Nobody leaves here until he is past the psychiatrist. The examination will take some time. There are 25 of you and three psychiatrists, so some of you will be staying the night. Any volunteers?' To my amazement and contempt he got 12.

The psychiatrist was Viennese and cat-like. 'I am not at all sure that you're fit to take your place in the civilian world. I ask you to stay. Will you stay?'

'No,' I said. 'I'll break out.'

'That would be very foolish, but also of some inconvenience to me,' the psych said. 'Have you a permanent address, a telephone number, somebody to look after you during your first three or four weeks?'

'My wife has taken a flat in South London,' I said, 'and she is expecting me.'

Quite suddenly I had to put on an absolutely blank face over one of those appalling rages which had been invading me ever since I got free from the prisoner-of-war camp. Deceit was the only thing. Bluff your way out. 'Oh, I think I'll be all right,' I said easily.

'Very well, you get three months' leave,' and he filled in a card. I hadn't taken him in, though: I saw the card later: 'Manic depressive

type. Educated. High IQ. Possibly disturbed. Marked aggression.'
Then two red asterisks.

'Have a drink,' said this abominable man, and I drank a large
whisky very slowly to deceive him.

Twelve of us left for London by the 9.30 train, and if I was
madder than most of them there wasn't much to choose between us.
By midnight seven wives had a drama on their hands once more for
better or for worse, and for the first time in history their dramas
were being produced by the War Office. When I first heard this I
was so furious I thought I was going to have a stroke. 'Do you mean
to say,' I yelled, 'that the bloody army gave you lessons in how to be
married to me?'

'Well, they told us what we might expect.'

'To hell with that,' I roared, and went off to the pub and stayed
away for three days.

When I got back I said: 'I took off because I will not have my life
interfered with.' 'Oh yes,' my wife said, 'they told us about that, too.'

RENÉ CUTFORTH

ANOTHER WAY OUT . . .

*In 1942 Laurens Van Der Post was captured by the Japanese when working
behind their lines in Java. In 1968 he was interviewed about his experiences
on BBC Television by Cliff Michelmore:*

How did you come to be condemned to death?

I was accused of the worst crime of which you could be capable
in the Japanese military mind at the time. I was accused of an offence
called the spirit of wilfulness, in that I had gone on trying to make
war against the Japanese after my commander-in-chief himself had
surrendered. Therefore my war was illegal, it was wilful.

*How did you feel when you went into the cell—when you really thought
you were going to be shot?*

Well, it didn't all happen at once, you know. There were rumours
and counter-rumours, and I was taken out and made to see other
people killed in all sorts of ways; and finally I can say that my life
was saved by St Francis Xavier who went to Japan in the sixteenth
century and converted some of the Japanese to Christianity. They

went underground, these Christians, and one of them came to me and said: 'You know I have never lied to you and I am sorry to tell you that I think they are going to kill you in the morning.' And at that moment I just had an enormous feeling of relief, because there was some certainty at last. I was very ill—I had malaria and dysentery. I had been badly beaten about. I was half starved—I had been living on this man's rice. And curiously enough, the only thing that worried me was *how* I was going to be killed. I found that one has a preference when faced with the issue of how one wants to be killed.

What was your preference?

I didn't want to be strangled, I didn't want to be hanged, I didn't want to be buried alive, I didn't want to be bayoneted—all forms of execution which I had seen. I wanted to be shot. And I thought: the great thing is to think of an argument, a way of putting it to them so that they shoot you in the morning. This seemed to me of vital importance. There was an immense storm going on at the time and listening to the thunder I remember being so relieved—it was the greatest music I'd ever heard, because I kept on saying to myself: there is something they don't control, there is something more powerful than all of us making this miserable little war. And then I went to sleep.

You weren't shot . . . ?

No. That's another story.

What scars did your imprisonment leave behind you? Would you say that it left a scar inside you?

I have looked for it and I don't think so. I went straight back to active service, weak and ill as I was, and I was the only one who stayed behind. All my chaps came back to England. They were taken to rehabilitation centres in England and they all wrote to me and said: 'It is a most extraordinary thing, they want to rehabilitate us, but we think it is the rehabilitation officers who need rehabilitating, not us.' I have met many people who have been in prison with me and I find no bitterness, and no resentment, and no scars. In fact, I think all of us have as a result of it a heightened perception of what life is about, and of how it should be lived.

Some people, when they are in prison, seem to lose their self-respect. . . .

I think you've put your finger there on something which is relevant to the time in which we live, because what is wrong with

us all at the moment, as a nation, is ultimately a matter of self-respect.
Most of the troops I found in prison, unlike my little guerrilla band,
had been surrendered without a fight, and this is a terribly humiliating experience for a man. I was horrified when I came out of my cell
to find that the first day the Japanese paraded the officers their own
men booed them. And I thought: well, something is wrong. We
started an educational system. We told people: 'Look, this imprisonment isn't really an interruption of your continuity as human beings.
This is a new challenge. You have what all human beings long for—
the chance now to rethink your lives, to rethink how you will live
when you come out of prison. Think about it and whichever way
you want to do it we will educate you for it.' And in between being
beaten up by the Japanese and having hates and having executions
and things, we went on as if our lives were going to last for ever.
This was a kind of school that we were in. Due to the quality of the
British people, who when challenged can respond in that way, we
came out without any scars.

LAURENS VAN DER POST

*

AFTERMATH

... But now as years pass and the war is done
I find myself of evenings often enchanted
And guessing what goes on within my brain,
Conceive myself as of being haunted
By corpses more alive than his own flesh:
They dog me with a brittle tenderness
That breaks upon a whim, but nothing breaks
Through my continual sense of loss and sense
Of being cut off by simple slight mistakes,
Everyday errors, from an innocence
That still is mine though it lives a life apart
Folded transparently in the transparent heart.

BURNS SINGER

*

It was February 1954, and I was sitting in the War Office watching the Whitehall rain beat down into the courtyard, and talking to a young subaltern just home from Kenya.

He was explaining how, in order to combat the Mau Mau terrorists, the Royal Engineers had built log roads through the jungle.

'Oh, yes; I know the idea,' I said. 'Same as they did in the Reichswald. You weren't in that battle, were you?'

He smiled faintly.

'No, sir,' he said. 'But we heard all about it at my prep school.'

'Then that just about makes it history, doesn't it?' I said pleasantly.

JOHN FOLEY

Envoi

REMEMBERING THE WAR

It isn't easy. I suppose for me
The war means wartime childhood. I suppose
I'd grant the fact my father died should be
One cause of tragic poetry in war's prose:

The sense of honour it asserts, the sense
Of having paid a price, seen something through
At such an early age helps the pretence
That war is strengthening, half-pleasant, too.

Yet war's first shock was trivial, too slight
For someone seven years old. It seemed like news
For older people who could feel its bite.
Not even my father dying changed these views.

War meant less chocolate, luminous badges bought
For walking in the blackout, one bleak night
Spent crouched downstairs behind the hall door, short
Of rugs to keep me warm, and feeling fright.

War was at worst the warlike games I played,
The shrapnel, and the *Flights* and *Aeroplanes*
I saved for, gas-masks, and half-crowns I paid
For savings-stamps, and soldiers on the trains.

Yes, soldiers on the trains. One understands
What one can see and feel, not what one's told.
War's closest tragedies were waving hands
On crowded platforms, shivering with cold.

GEORGE MACBETH

Glossary

AIF	Australian Imperial Force
ADS	Advanced Dressing Station (a forward First Aid Post)
BEF	British Expeditionary Force (France 1939–40)
BRA	Brigadier Royal Artillery (Staff Officer responsible for the artillery of a Corps)
CCS	Casualty Clearing Station (handling wounded sent back from an ADS)
CIGS	Chief of the Imperial General Staff
CLY	County of London Yeomanry
CO	Commanding Officer (normally a lieutenant-colonel commanding eg an infantry battalion, or an artillery or armoured regiment)
CRA	Commander Royal Artillery (responsible for the artillery of a division)
CRE	Commander Royal Engineers (responsible for the engineers of a division)
CSM	Company Sergeant Major
DR	Dispatch Rider
ESO	Embarkation Staff Officer
GPO	Gun Position Officer
GOC	General Officer Commanding (normally a divisional commander)
HE	High Explosive
IO	Intelligence Officer
LCT	Landing Craft (Tank)
MGGS	Major-General, General Staff
ML	Motor Launch
MM	Military Medal
MO	Medical Officer
MP	Military Police
NZEF	New Zealand Expeditionary Force
OP	Observation Post
OR	Other Rank
RAMC	Royal Army Medical Corps
RE	Royal Engineers
RHA	Royal Horse Artillery
RIASC	Royal Indian Army Service Corps
RTO	Railway Transport Officer
RTR	Royal Tank Regiment
SHAEF	Supreme Headquarters, Allied Expeditionary Force
SOE	Special Operations Executive
SP	Self-propelled (artillery)
Tac HQ	Tactical Headquarters (eg, an Army Commander's forward command post)

Authors and Sources

Unless otherwise stated, all quotations from each author come from a single source

Alanbrooke, Field-Marshal Lord, quoted in Arthur Bryant, *The Turn of the Tide*, Collins

Arnold, Ralph, *A Very Quiet War*, Rupert Hart-Davis

Ash, Bernard, *Norway 1940*, Cassell

Attiwill, Kenneth, *The Singapore Story*, Frederick Muller

Bain, Donald, 'War Poet', quoted in Brian Gardner, *The Terrible Rain*, Methuen

Banks, Capt. R. L. quoted in *The Royal Artillery Commemoration Book*, Bell

Barker, A. J., *Eritrea 1941*, Faber

Barnett, Corelli, *The Desert Generals*, Kimber

Bell, Major Noel, *From the Beaches to the Baltic*, Gale and Polden

Braddon, Russell, *The Naked Island*, Werner Laurie

Brett-James, Antony, *Report My Signals*, Harrap

Brooke, Jocelyn, *The Military Orchid*, The Bodley Head

Calvert, Michael, *Fighting Mad*, Jarrolds

Campbell, Arthur, *The Siege*, Allen and Unwin

Campbell, Roy, 'One Transport Lost', from *Talking Bronco*, Faber

Cassells, James K., 'Forgotten Army', from *Poems from India*, Oxford University Press, India

Catling, Skene, *Vanguard to Victory*, Methuen

Cave, Corporal A. H., quoted in W. B. Kennedy Shaw, *Long Range Desert Group*, Collins

Chaplin, Lieutenant-Colonel H. D., *The Queen's Royal West Kent Regiment 1920–1950*, Michael Joseph

Chapman, Lieutenant-Colonel Spencer, *The Jungle is Neutral*, Chatto and Windus

Churchill, Winston S., *The Second World War*, Cassell

Clarke, Brigadier Dudley, *The Eleventh at War*, Michael Joseph

Clay, Major Ewart W., *The Path of the 50th*, Gale and Polden

Clifton, Brigadier G., *The Happy Hunted*, Cassell

Crisp, Robert, *Brazen Chariots*, Frederick Muller

Cutforth, René, 'One Way Out . . .' quoted in *The Listener*, 19th December 1968

Dehn, Paul, 'St Aubin d'Aubigné', from *The Day's Alarm*, Hamish Hamilton

Dexter, David, *The New Guinea Offensive*, Australian War Memorial, Canberra

Dickinson, Patric, 'Midnight: 7th May 1945', from *A Stone in the Midst*, Methuen

Divine, A. D., *Dunkirk*, Faber

Dobree, Lieutenant-Colonel, quoted in *The Royal Artillery Commemoration Book, 1939–1945*, Bell

Douglas, Keith, 'Aristocrats', from *Collected Poems*, Faber
                'Alamein: the Aftermath', from *Alamein to Zem-Zem*, Faber

Durnford-Slater, Brig. John, *Commando*, Kimber

Elstob, Peter, quoted in *History of the Second World War*, Purnell Vol. 6, No. 4,

Evans, Lieut.-Gen. Sir Geoffrey, *The Desert and the Jungle*, Kimber

Evans, Major-General Roger, *The Fifth Inniskilling Dragoon Guards*, Gale and Polden

Fergusson, Brigadier Sir Bernard, *Beyond the Chindwin*, Collins

Foley, John, *Mailed Fist*, Granada Publishing Ltd.

Gale, General Sir Richard, *With the Sixth Airborne Division in Normandy*, Sampson Low

Graham, Brigadier W. D., quoted in *The Royal Artillery Commemoration Book, 1939–1945*, Bell

Grant, Douglas, *The Fuel of the Fire*, Cresset Press

'Gun Buster', *Return to Dunkirk*, Hodder and Stoughton

Gwynn-Browne, A., *F.S.P.*, Chatto and Windus

Harris, Captain Harold, private contribution

Harrison, Ada C., *Grey and Scarlet: Letters from the War Areas by Army Sisters on Active Service*, Hodder and Stoughton

Hastings, Major Robin, *The Rifle Brigade in the Second World War, 1939–1945*, Gale and Polden

Hibbert, Christopher, *The Battle of Arnhem*, Batsford

Hickman, Max, quoted in John Laffin, *Digger*, Cassell

Hodson, J. H., *Through the Dark Night*, Gollancz

Hood, Stuart, *Pebbles From My Skull*, Hutchinson

Horrocks, Lieutenant-General Sir Brian, *A Full Life*, Collins

Horst, Mevrouw ter, quoted in Christopher Hibbert, *The Battle of Arnhem*, Batsford

Howard-Vyse, Major-General R. G., quoted in B. H. Liddell Hart, *The Tanks*, Vol. I, Cassell

Joly, Cyril, *Take These Men*, Constable

Kippenberger, Major-General Sir Howard, *Infantry Brigadier*, Oxford University Press

Lewis, Alun, 'The Mahratta Ghats', from *Ha! Ha! among the Trumpets*, Allen and Unwin

Liddell Hart, Captain Sir Basil, *The Tanks*, Cassell

Lindsay, Jack, 'Squadding', from *New Lyrical Ballads*, Poetry London

Lindsay, Lieutenant-Colonel Martin, *So Few Got Through*, Collins

Livingstone, Captain Richard, quoted in *The History of the Second World War*, Purnell, Vol. 6, No. 5

Macbeth, George, 'Remembering the War', quoted in *The Listener*

Mackay, Lieutenant E. M., *Royal Engineers' Journal*, Vol. LXVIII, No. 4

Macksey, Major Kenneth, *Armoured Crusader*, Hutchinson

Macneice, Louis, 'Sentries', from *Collected Poems*, Faber

Majdalany, Fred, 'The Monastery', from *Cassino, Portrait of a Battle*, Longmans
          'The Kill', from *The Monastery*, The Bodley Head

Masters, John, *The Road Past Mandalay*, Michael Joseph

Montgomery, Field-Marshal Lord, *Memoirs*, Collins

Moorehead, Alan, all quotations from *African Trilogy*, Hamish Hamilton
  (except 'Caen' from *Eclipse*, Hamish Hamilton)

Morgan, Sir Frederick, *Overture to Overlord*, Hodder and Stoughton

Munro, Ross, *Gauntlet to Overlord*, Macmillan Company of Canada

Nash, Captain K. A. quoted in Capt. W. A. T. Synge, *The Story of the Green
  Howards, 1939–1945*, published by the Regiment

Needham, Fusilier D., quoted in Hugh Pond, *Salerno*, Kimber

Nicholls, Major A. W. D., quoted in Brigadier E. W. Underhill, *The Royal
  Leicestershire Regiment 17th Foot* (published by The Regiment, Glen Parva
  Barracks, South Wigston, Leics.)

Nicholson, General Sir Cameron, quoted in *The Royal Artillery Commemoration
  Book 1939–1945*, Bell

Norman, Philip, in *Alamein and the Desert War*, Sphere Books

Pakenham-Walsh, Maj.-Gen., *History of the Corps of Royal Engineers, Vol. 8
  1938–1948*, The Institution of Royal Engineers

Patterson, Hugh, quoted in John Laffin, *Digger*, Cassell

Peniakoff, Lieutenant-Colonel Vladimir, *Popski's Private Army*, Jonathan Cape

Phillips, Brigadier C. E. Lucas, *Alamein*, Heinemann

Reed, Henry, 'Naming of Parts', from *A Map of Verona*, Jonathan Cape

Reeves, Major F. C. M., quoted in *The Royal Artillery Commemoration Book*, Bell

Roberts, Major-General G. P., quoted in Liddell Hart, *The Tanks*, Cassell

Schuster, Lieutenant, quoted in Rudolf Bohmler, *Monte Cassino*, Cassell

Sing, Jemadar Dewan, quoted in Lieutenant-Colonel G. R. Stevens, *Fourth
  Indian Division*, McLaren and Son Ltd

Singer, Burns, 'The Transparent Prisoner', from *Still and All*, Secker and
  Warburg

Slim, Field-Marshal Lord, *Defeat into Victory*, Cassell

Smyth, Brigadier Sir John, *Before the Dawn*, Collins

Stainforth, Peter, *Wings of the Wind*, Falcon Press

Stephanides, Capt., quoted in I. McD. G. Stewart, *The Struggle for Crete*, O.U.P.

Strong, Major-General Sir Kenneth, *Intelligence at the Top*, Cassell/Giniger

Sweet-Escott, Bickham, *Baker Street Irregular*, Methuen

Sykes, Christopher, *Orde Wingate*, Collins

Trevelyan, Raleigh, *The Fortress: a Diary of Anzio and after*, Collins

Tuker, Lieutenant-General Sir Francis, *Approach to Battle*, Cassell

Urquhart, Major-General R. E., *Arnhem*, Cassell

Van Der Post, Laurens, 'Another Way Out', from interview by Cliff
  Michelmore quoted in *The Listener*, 19th December 1968

Vaux, Brigadier P. A. L., private communication

Verney, John, 'Summer Manœuvres', from *Going to the Wars*, Collins
          'Capture at Tertenia' and 'A dash for it', from *A Dinner of Herbs*,
          Collins
Waugh, Evelyn, 'To Norway' and 'Death in the Afternoon', from *Put Out
    More Flags*, Chapman and Hall
Weir, Lieut. A., quoted in Geoffrey Evans and Antony Brett-James, *Imphal*,
    Macmillan
Wheeler, Sir Mortimer, *Still Digging*, Michael Joseph
Wilmot, Chester, quoted in *War Report*, Oxford University Press
Wilson, Andrew, *Flame Thrower*, Kimber

Index

Contributors' names are italicised